CHARITIES
THE NEW LAW

THE CHARITIES ACT 1992

CHARITIES
THE NEW LAW

THE CHARITIES ACT 1992

Fiona Middleton LLM, Solicitor
Stephen Lloyd BA, ACII, Solicitor

With an introduction by Andrew Phillips BA, Solicitor

The authors are all partners in Bates, Wells & Braithwaite

JORDANS
1992

Published by
Jordan & Sons Ltd
21 St Thomas Street
Bristol BS1 6JS

British Library Cataloguing-in-Publication Data
A catalogue record for this book is available from the British Library.

ISBN 0-85308-140-9

Typeset by Rowland Phototypesetting Limited,
Bury St Edmunds, Suffolk
Printed by Henry Ling, The Dorchester Press, Dorchester

CONTENTS

TABLE OF STATUTES

References in the right-hand column are to paragraph numbers

ix

CHAPTER 1

INTRODUCTION

It intrigues 'foreigners' when they learn that our law of charity dates back to the Middle Ages, and is still based on a repealed preamble to a statute of 1601. The fact that the old Commonwealth countries (the United States of America included) have broadly kept to that foundation, sometimes incorporated into their statute law, adds piquancy to this legal oddity.

That successive governments here have largely been content to keep their hands off charity law and, in particular, the definition of what is charitable, has been a great blessing. As one of the Law Lords wryly observed in the debate on the 1960 Charities Bill, statutory redefinition would only be of assured benefit to one group, namely the lawyers of Lincoln's Inn!

Douglas Hurd's White Paper of May 1989, *Charities: A Framework for the Future* (Cm 694) (1989, HMSO), which was the launch pad for the Charities Act 1992, came to the same conclusion, concluding that 'there would appear to be few advantages in attempting a wholesale redefinition of charitable status – and many real dangers in doing so'.

Even in the two areas where the White Paper did leave open the possibility of statutory redefinition – namely, which religious organisations should be allowed charitable status, and which political activities should be permissible to charities – the Government decided to hold off. To have done otherwise would have led into a parliamentary minefield which would have blown up any prospect of a non-partisan approach to the Charities Bill.

That such a major piece of legislation as the Charities Act 1992 should have reached the statute book on the eve of a hard-fought general election also says much for the settled view which prevails in this country vis-à-vis charities. In achieving this, MPs and Lords undoubtedly mirrored public sentiment which warms to the sector's diversity, fierce independence and its deep roots. Like a well-known beer, charity 'reaches the parts that others do not reach'. Its absolute separateness from business and political interests sees to that.

As it was, those on the front benches on both sides of the Commons kept their dogmatists in check, and were content in the end to nod through the hard work and careful consideration which had been given to the Bill in the House of Lords. Their Lordships, it is generally thought, did pretty well. So, to be fair, did the Government. An outside observer would have been hard put to have detected much party political bias in debate, and should have been impressed by the breadth and depth of the contributions made by peers whose experience ranged from the greatest charities to the littlest parish ones, and from the most sophisticated legal understanding of the niceties of this arcane subject through to workaday involvement in front line activity. As a result, and given some deft and often liberal helmsmanship by the Government spokesman, Earl Ferrers, the Bill went through, much amended and much improved.

True to the tradition of measured reform in this field, the 1992 Act was preceded by a long series of consultative events of which, prior to the White Paper, the *Efficiency Scrutiny of the Supervision of Charities 1987*, under the Chairmanship of Sir Philip Woodfield, was undoubtedly the most influential.

It was therefore a surprise – and an unpleasant one – when the Bill went against the advice of Woodfield, the White Paper and almost everyone else right back to Goodman and Nathan, in criminalising failure to comply with the new and extensive statutory requirements. Although, as this book makes clear, prosecutions under Part 1 of the 1992 Act can only be instituted with the consent of the Director of Public Prosecutions, and although s 27 of the Act limits conviction for the more mundane offences to those who 'without reasonable excuse are persistently in default', the overall impact is likely to be severely negative. There are already signs of a rapid growth of anxiety on the part of those contemplating trusteeship (by whatever name it is called), and the 1992 Act would have aggravated that unease even without the criminalisation provisions.

Nor is it of much solace to be told that only a few people (possibly 100 or so per year) will be prosecuted as an example to the rest of us. Apart from being a capricious way of enforcing legislation, the 'in terrorem' effect may still be disproportionately damaging.

The other major caveat, of course, is the scope and scale of the legislation. Seventy-nine sections and seven Schedules, occupying 94 closely printed pages, will be supplemented by a welter of subsidiary legislation, which is likely to double that length.

At the time of going to press, the Charity Commission expects the relevant statutory instruments to be legislated in five batches, which may take until the autumn of 1993 to complete.

It is, at least, reassuring to know that the new Chief Commissioner, Richard Fries, is fully seised of the extraordinarily delicate task which confronts the Charity Commission in exercising its manifold powers under the new Act. Yet, however successful the Commissioners may be in that attempt (and we wish them well), the law is the law. Furthermore, lawyers are lawyers, and there can be little doubt but that the relative freedom from lawyer infestation, which the charity sector in this country has enjoyed hitherto, is not likely to last much longer.

It is not as if we only have the 1992 Act to contend with. Already, the European Community is intent on muscling in on the voluntary sector, and the draft statute of European Association is currently doing the rounds – 'doing the rounds', at least, among the handful of people who are aware of its existence, capable of understanding its grisly complications and ambiguities, and interested enough to try to do so. Soon, we may all have to.

Perhaps the 1992 Act is the price which has to be paid for continued public confidence in charities. If so, those with any influence in these matters should make a concerted effort to minimise the bureaucratisation and obfuscation which will otherwise ensue.

The assumption by some that 'professionalism' is necessarily and always a good thing, and that efficiency is as much the hallmark of the good charity as it is of the successful business, needs qualifying. There is a real danger that the voluntary sector, year by year, is losing touch with a crucial chunk of its constituency. It is a truism to say that the voluntary sector must remain voluntary. To do so it must also encourage those citizens who lack confidence, and those who may not by some be thought particularly 'capable', to be volunteers. Often those selfsame people possess more than their fair share of that goodwill, compassion and insight without which charity is not charity.

In an age marked by inhuman giantism and dehumanising systems, it would be a tragedy if voluntary sector 'professionalism' stifled the free, generous creativity and caring essence of voluntarism. If we want a thousand flowers to continue blooming, our society must go steady with the fertilisers and insecticides.

This book, then, is written in that spirit, and seeks to clarify and explain a difficult piece of legislation. How difficult it is was vividly (and comically) demonstrated by a series of contributions to the House of Lords debate in relation to the wording of s 21(1). Several times the Government resisted the formulation which is now in the Act, the parliamentary draftsman claiming that reference to 'gross income or total expenditure' would yield the wrong interpretation unless there was added to it the words 'or both'. The fact that, in the end, Earl Ferrers, with a weary sigh, gave in without abandoning that argument means that on this, as on many other points, the legislation is of uncertain effect.

It was a pity that the 1992 Act was not wedded (or 'keeled' as they say) into the 1960 Act. This has been overcome by including the text of the 1960 Act, as amended by the 1992 Act.

More material will undoubtedly be published when the statutory instruments are in place, and it will probably not be as long again before Parliament legislates further in relation to charity law. Meanwhile, it is hoped that this book will be of practical help.

CHAPTER 2

REGISTRATION AND DECLARATION OF REGISTERED CHARITY STATUS

Introduction: Registration under the Charities Act 1960: Exempt Charities under the Charities Act 1992: Registration of Small Charities: The Meaning Of 'Income': The Register – Contents, Access and Charges: Declaration of Registered Charity Status: Penalties for Non-compliance: Summary of Requirements (Fig 1)

2.1 Introduction

A public register of charities has been maintained by the Charity Commissioners since 1960. By the mid-1980s, this was regarded as defective in many ways. Reform was needed to the way in which the register was maintained (which the Commissioners have carried out by implementing a programme of computerisation). However, more fundamental statutory reform was needed both in respect of the charities required to register and in the system for updating the information on the register on a regular basis.

2.2 Registration under the Charities Act 1960

The Charities Act 1960 ('the 1960 Act') required all charities to be registered unless they fell within one of the categories set out in s 4(4) of that Act. These were as follows:

(a) exempt charities listed in the Second Schedule to the 1960 Act, for example universities and polytechnics, industrial and provident societies and national institutions such as the British Museum;
(b) charities excepted from the need to register by order or regulations, for example charities associated with the armed forces and scouts and guide associations;
(c) small charities without permanent endowment or the use or occupation of land, and with an income from property (including investments) of less than £15 a year; and
(d) charities registered under the Places of Worship Act 1855.

Section 4(2) of the 1960 Act permitted charities not subject to compulsory registration to apply to the Commissioners on a voluntary basis.

2.3 Exempt Charities under the Charities Act 1992

Section 4(4)(a) of the 1960 Act excluded 'exempt charities' from the duty to register but, relying on s 4(2) of that Act, a number were registered in the past on a voluntary basis. However, more recently, the Commissioners developed a policy of declining to register exempt charities, since they had no means of compelling an exempt charity to submit to their jurisdiction, for example to submit accounts.

The Charities Act 1992 ('the 1992 Act') effects two important changes:

(a) s 2(3) removes from exempt charities the possibility of registering on a voluntary basis; and
(b) s 2(8) goes further to terminate automatically the existing voluntary registrations of exempt charities from the date when s 2(3) comes into effect.

As a result, an exempt charity registered on a voluntary basis will no longer be able to claim that it is a registered charity or refer to a registered charity number. However, as evidence of its charitable status, it may state that it is an exempt charity under the Second Schedule of the 1960 Act, recognised as charitable by the Inland Revenue and able to quote its Inland Revenue reference number.

If a registered exempt charity wishes to continue as a registered charity, it will need to change its legal status, for example by converting an industrial and provident society to a charitable company limited by guarantee.

2.4 Registration of Small Charities

2.4.1 Section 4(4)(c) of the 1960 Act excluded from compulsory registration any charity which had no permanent endowment, no use or occupation of land and whose income from investments or other property did not exceed £15 a year. By 1992, a charity with a relatively small sum placed on deposit earning interest might easily have income in excess of £15 a year and require registration. On the other hand, a charity funded by substantial donations for immediate distribution which are not invested even on a short-term basis would have no 'income from property' and would not require registration. As a result, substantial charities with large turnovers were able to escape the scrutiny of the Commissioners.

2.4.2 Section 2(4) of the 1992 Act amends s 4(4)(c) of the 1960 Act. A small charity will require registration if:

(a) it has a permanent endowment; or
(b) it has the use or occupation of land; or
(c) its income from all sources in aggregate amounts to at least £1,000 a year.

The threshold of £15 has been increased to £1,000, but the source of the income is irrelevant. It may be investment income but equally it may be income from donations. (For the meaning of 'income' see **2.5**.) A small charity which was subject to compulsory registration, but no longer requires to be registered as a result of the change in the income qualifications, may continue its registration on a voluntary basis relying on s 4(2) of the 1960 Act. Alternatively, it may apply to the Commissioners to be removed from the register. The Commissioners are bound to comply with that request.

There is flexibility in the £1,000 threshold. Section 2(7) of the 1992 Act introduces two new subsections (8A) and (8B) into s 4 of the 1960 Act, enabling the Secretary of State to alter the figure of £1,000 by statutory instrument, either to keep pace with inflation or in order to extend the scope of the exception from compulsory registration in s 4(4)(c) (so that, for example, the Commissioners do not become overburdened).

2.5 The Meaning of 'Income'

2.5.1 Elsewhere in the 1992 Act, the terms 'gross income' and 'annual income' are used. For the meaning of 'annual income' see **4.6.1**. 'Gross income' is defined by s 1 to mean the gross recorded income of a charity from all sources, including special trusts (see **4.5.2**). Section 2 refers simply to 'income' in the phrase 'whose income from all sources does not in aggregate amount to £1,000', since it is amending s 4 of the 1960 Act and, therefore, uses the terminology of the 1960 Act. The 1960 Act refers merely to 'income'.

2.5.2 To avoid inconsistency, s 45(4) and (5) of the 1960 Act, which are the relevant definition sections, have been amended by s 47 of and Sch 3 to the 1992 Act. As a result, the term 'income' in s 2 of the 1992 Act (amending s 4 of the 1960 Act) is similar to the term 'gross income' elsewhere in the 1992 Act, but it is not identical. The key points are as follows.

(a) Income, in s 2, is assessed according to the 'gross revenues' of a charity as distinct from the 'gross recorded income'. It is not clear if there is any substantial difference between these terms, for example whether a legacy would fall within one but not the other.

(b) An institution established for the special purposes of a charity may be treated as forming part of the charity or as forming a separate charity as the Commissioners direct. If the Commissioners give an appropriate direction, the income of special trusts will be aggregated with income of the main charity, to determine whether it exceeds the £1,000 threshold, making registration compulsory. The meaning of 'income' in s 2, therefore, is not as certain as the definition of gross income under the 1992 Act, which automatically includes the income of special trusts. A charity may be uncertain whether it is subject to compulsory registration until the Commissioners have given a direction as to whether the income from the special trusts should be aggregated with the income from the main

---

charity. However, if a main charity is registered with subsidiary charities under the same charity registration number it would seem appropriate to aggregate their income.

2.6 The Register – Contents, Access and Charges

Contents

2.6.1 Section 2(4) of the 1992 Act introduces a new s 4(2)(A) into the 1960 Act, requiring the register to contain the name of every registered charity and such other information as the Commissioners think fit. The reference to the name of a registered charity is significant in relation to the provisions governing charity names, introduced by ss 4 and 5 of the 1992 Act (see **Chapter 3**). The phrase 'such other particulars of and such other information' is more extensive than the original provision in s 4(2), which referred only to 'such particulars'. It could, for example, enable the Commissioners to enter on the register general information about a charity, such as whether or not the statutory duties of trustees to file annual accounts, reports and returns have been discharged.

Access

2.6.2 As a partial result of computerisation, s 2(6) of the 1992 Act has introduced s 4(7A) and (7B) into the 1960 Act to follow s 4(7) which concerned public access to inspect the register and the public right to obtain copies of entries on the register. Section 4(7A) provides that, where information contained on the register is not in documentary form, it should be available for public inspection in legible form. Reading the information from a visual display unit would suffice. Section 4(7B) enables the Commissioners, at their discretion, to exclude certain information from public access.

Charges

2.6.3 Section 51(1) of the 1992 Act enables the Secretary of State to make regulations to set fees to be charged by the Commissioners in respect of some of their functions. The Government has indicated that it intends to set charges in three areas: for registering new charities, for access to the computerised register and for consent orders for the disposition of land (see **Chapter 6**). A flat fee of £50 is likely for new registrations – a figure comparable with the fee payable on the incorporation of a new company.

2.7 Declaration of Registered Charity Status

Under s 3 of the 1992 Act, a registered charity with a gross income[1] in the previous financial year in excess of £5,000, must state that it is a registered charity on certain documents specified in s 3(2). The Government's declared purpose in introducing this provision is to alert people dealing with a charity that it is subject to the supervisory regime of the Commissioners and to the legal constraints which bind charities.

The documents to which the provision relates are set out in s 3(2) and are:

(a) notices, advertisements and other documents issued by or on behalf of the charity for soliciting money or other property for the benefit of the charity;

(b) bills of exchange, promissory notes, endorsements, cheques and orders for money or goods, purporting to be signed on behalf of the charity; and

(c) bills, invoices, receipts and letters of credit.

The statement of registered charity status must be in English in legible characters. This is so even if the literature of the charity is normally published in another language. In that case the charity may wish to make the statement in both English and in the language which it would normally use.

Section 3 is similar, but not identical, to s 30C of the 1960 Act, which requires a charitable company, which does not include the word 'charity' or 'charitable' in its name, to state that it is a charity on certain documents (similar to those listed in s 3), but including business letters, which are not listed in s 3. However, s 30C is concerned with charitable status rather than registered charity status. It applies to all charitable companies, whether registered or not. Charitable companies will need to review the action taken to comply with s 30C to ensure that they also comply with s 3 of the 1992 Act. For example, the words 'a charity' on a cheque issued by a charitable company which is a registered charity will no longer suffice: they should be replaced by the words 'a registered charity' to comply with both statutory provisions.

Paragraph (a) (above) applies whether the solicitation is express or implied, and whether or not the money or other property is to be given for consideration. Therefore, it would apply to direct fund-raising material, but also to newsletters providing information about projects which have the indirect purpose of raising funds. It would apply to documents seeking outright donations, but also to documents inviting contributions in exchange for some benefit, for example admission to some fund-raising event. Since the provision relates to solicitations issued on behalf of a charity, it is also relevant to solicitations issued on behalf of a charity by professional fund-raisers and commercial participators (see **Chapters 11 and 12**).

---

1 'Gross income' is defined by s 1 to mean gross recorded income from all sources, including special trusts (see **4.5.2**).

2.8 Penalties for Non-compliance

2.8.1 The most controversial aspect of s 3 of the 1992 Act is the imposition of criminal penalties for failing to comply with its provisions. Under s 3(4), any person who issues or authorises the issue of any document which does not carry the necessary statement is guilty of an offence and liable on summary conviction to a fine. Section 3(5) imposes a similar penalty on any person who signs a document falling within s 3(2)(b) – a cheque being the most obvious example – without the necessary statement of registered charity status. Liability rests on the individual who issues, authorises or signs the document. He might be a trustee or an employee of the charity, or even, in the case of advertisements soliciting funds, a professional fund-raiser or a commercial participator.

2.8.2 These offences are ones of strict liability. The individual is guilty, whether or not he committed the default knowingly. Section 55 of the 1992 Act does, however, provide that no proceedings may be instituted except by or with the consent of the Director of Public Prosecutions. Proceedings would be instituted by the Crown Prosecution Service. During the passage of the Charities Bill through the House of Lords, it was suggested that proceedings would not be instituted except in the most extreme cases. No indication was given of what might constitute a 'most extreme case'.

2.9 Summary of Requirements

Fig 1 indicates, according to charity type, the need for a charity to be registered, to declare its status as a registered charity in accordance with s 3 of the 1992 Act and to declare its status as a charity in accordance with s 30C of the 1960 Act.

Fig 1

This table indicates, according to charity type, the need for a charity to register under s 4 of the 1960 Act, as amended, to declare its status as a registered charity under s 3 of the 1992 Act, if its income in the last financial year exceeded £5,000 and to declare its status as a charity under s 30C of the 1960 Act, if the name 'charity' or 'charitable' does not appear in the name of the charity.

KEY TO CHARITY TYPES

1 Exempt charity, including industrial and provident society.
2 Charity excepted from registration by order or regulation.
3 Charity with permanent endowment, not falling into categories 1 or 2.
4 Charity having use or occupation of land, not falling into categories 1 or 2.
5 Charity with gross income in excess of £1,000 a year, not falling into categories 1 or 2.
6 Charity with gross income not exceeding £1,000 a year, or falling into categories 1 or 4.

Charity type	Registration	Declaration of registered status*	Declaration of charitable status**
1	None possible	Not applicable	If a company
2	Voluntary	Compulsory	If a company
3	Compulsory	Compulsory	If a company
4	Compulsory	Compulsory	If a company
5	Compulsory	Compulsory	If a company
6	Voluntary	Not compulsory	If a company

*If income in the last financial year exceeded £5,000.
**If the word 'charity' or 'charitable' does not appear in the name.

CHAPTER 3

CHARITY NAMES

Introduction: Which Charities?: Reasons for Change: Time Limits: The Direction: The Resolution: Checklist

3.1 Introduction

Before the 1992 Act there was a lacuna in the Commissioners' powers. They could not refuse to register a charity with a name similar to that of another charity or with a name which was misleading in some way. For example, the name of a local charity might suggest that it was associated with some national charity, when in fact there was no connection. Sections 4 and 5 of the 1992 Act give the Commissioners power to require charity trustees to change the name of their charity.

3.2 Which Charities?

The powers of the Commissioners to require a change of name apply to all charities, whether registered or not, save for exempt charities which are excluded by s 4(9). However, the power in s 4(2)(a) (see below) is concerned specifically with changing the registered name of a registered charity.

3.3 Reasons for Change

3.3.1 There are five sets of circumstances when the Commissioners may require a change of name.

(a) If the registered name is the same or too like the name of another charity at the time the name is entered in the register. The key points of this new power are as follows.

  (i)   The registered name is the name entered in the charities register, not an acronym or popular name used as an alternative (see **2.6.1**).
  (ii) The other charity, whose name is protected by the Commissioners' action, need not be a registered charity.
  (iii) The similarity must exist when the name is entered in the charities register. This power cannot be used to protect the former name of an

existing charity which has been changed or the name of a charity which has ceased to exist.

(iv) The Commissioners may disregard minor differences in the names of the two charities in reaching a conclusion that the names are the same or too like (s 4(7)).

(b) If a charity's name is likely to mislead the public as to the true nature of the purposes or activities of the charity.

(c) If a charity's name includes a word or expression specified in regulations made by the Secretary of State and which will mislead the public as to the status of the charity. These regulations are likely to include words which suggest academic pre-eminence, for example 'institute' and 'institution' or words which suggest international pre-eminence, for example 'International' and 'European'.

(d) If a charity's name is likely to give a misleading impression that it is connected in some way with HM Government, a local authority or some other body or individual.

(e) If a charity's name is offensive. There is no statutory indication of what may be regarded as offensive.

3.4 Time Limits

The Commissioners must give the direction to require a charity to change its registered name under s 4(2)(a) within 12 months of the date when the name was entered in the register. However, the powers to require change under s 4(2)(b), (c), (d) and (e) are not subject to any time limit. These powers could be used by the Commissioners to require a charity to change a name which has been in use for some time.

3.5 The Direction

The Commissioners exercise their power to require a charity to change its name by giving a formal direction to the charity trustees under s 4(1). Under this direction the charity trustees are required to change the name of the charity. The new name is to be determined by the trustees, with the approval of the Commissioners. The direction will also specify the period within which the change must be effected.

Section 57 of the 1992 Act deals with directions of the Commissioners generally. The principal features of a direction are:

(a) a direction must be in writing but does not require any other formality – a letter will suffice;

(b) there is no right of appeal against a direction, but the Commissioners can vary or revoke a direction by a further direction; and

(c) a direction can be enforced by contempt proceedings in the High Court under s 41 of the 1960 Act.

3.6 The Resolution

3.6.1 The charity trustees must pass a resolution to change the name of the charity, regardless of any provisions in the trusts of the charity. They cannot refuse to comply on the grounds that they have no power to amend the trusts or that the power to amend rests with others or is subject to the consent of some other individual. In particular, ss 4(8) and 5 make it clear that in the case of a charitable company, the name is to be changed by resolution of the directors rather than by special resolution of the members, which would be the normal procedure under company law. A resolution to change the name of a charitable company must, however, be filed with the Registrar of Companies in the usual way and will not be completed until a certificate of incorporation on change of name has been issued. The Registrar of Companies retains the power to object to a new name and it is, therefore, essential that the Charity Commission and the Registrar of Companies adopt a co-ordinated approach.

3.6.2 Under s 4(5) the trustees must notify the Commissioners of the charity's new name and of the date on which the change occurred. If the charity is a registered charity, the Commissioners will then enter that new name in the register.

3.7 Checklist

Charity trustees should take the following steps if they receive a direction from the Commissioners to change the name of their charity.

(a) Consider whether there is evidence to justify the name and, if so, submit this to the Commissioners with a request that they revoke the direction.
(b) If the direction is to be complied with, select a new name and submit this to the Commissioners for approval.
(c) If the charity is a company, check that the new name is not the same or too like that of a registered company.
(d) Pass a resolution to change the name, following the trustees' normal rules of procedure.
(e) If the charity is a company, transmit a certified copy of the resolution to the Registrar of Companies with the statutory fee on change of name (currently £50.00) and await the certificate of incorporation on change of name.
(f) Transmit a certified copy of the resolution to the Commissioners (with a certified copy of the certificate of incorporation on change of name, if a

company). If the charity is a registered charity, ask for confirmation that the charity register has been amended.

(g) If it is not possible to complete the change of name within the time limit specified by the Commissioners in the direction, ask the Commissioners to vary the directions to permit more time.

CHAPTER 4

CHARITY ACCOUNTS: ACCOUNTING AND REPORTING PROCEDURES

Introduction: The 1960 Act Regime: Recommendations for Reform: Accounting Records: Statements of Account: Audit or Independent Examination: Commissioners' Power to Order Audit: Annual Reports: Annual Returns: Public Access to Accounts: Penalties for Non-compliance: Summary of Requirements (Figs 2 and 3)

4.1 Introduction

Radical changes to the accounting and reporting procedures of charities are introduced by the 1992 Act to improve the quality of charity accounts and the systems for supplying information to the Commissioners on a regular basis – necessities if the Commissioners are to monitor charities effectively. Charities which fall within the ambit of the new provisions are required to maintain accounting records and to send annual accounts, an annual report and an annual return to the Commissioners. For the first time, there is a general requirement that the accounts of a charity be audited or, alternatively, in some cases, that they are examined by a suitably qualified independent examiner.

4.2 The 1960 Act Regime

4.2.1 Section 32 of the 1960 Act required trustees of all charities, whether registered or not:

(a) to keep proper books of accounts; and
(b) to prepare consecutive statements of account consisting of an income and expenditure account for a period of not more than 15 months and a balance sheet relating to the end of that period.

A charity might also be subject to some other statutory regime, in which case that regime would prevail. For example, a charitable company would need to comply with the accounting requirements of the Companies Act 1985 and could not rely simply on having satisfied the requirements of s 32.

4.2.2 There was no general requirement for charity accounts to be audited. Trustees might be under an obligation to submit accounts for audit, either because of the requirements of some other statute governing the charity (for example the Companies Act 1985), or because of an express requirement in the trusts of the charity. In addition, the Commissioners were able, under s 8 of the 1960 Act, to order an audit of a charity's accounts (other than those of an exempt charity), but on condition that the Commissioners met the costs of the audit.

4.2.3 There was no general requirement for trustees to send their accounts to the Commissioners. However, trustees were required to submit statements of account, complying with the Charities (Statements of Account) Regulations 1960, SI 1960/2425, to the Commissioners on request and trustees of a permanently endowed charity were required to send a statement of account relating to the permanent endowment without any request (s 8 of the 1960 Act). In practice, the Commissioners requested all newly registered charities to send in accounts on an annual basis. However, without an annual reminder the request was soon forgotten. Accounts were not sent and many charities believed that they were under no obligation to do so.

4.3 Recommendations for Reform

Charities: A Framework for the Future (Cm 694) (1989, HMSO) ('the White Paper'), identified the regular provision of good quality financial information by charities as an essential element in their public accountability and an important means for their supervision. It proposed that:

(a) in future, all registered charities should submit statements of account to the Charity Commission annually;
(b) charities should model their accounts on the Statement of Recommended Practice on Accounting by Charities (SORP 2), published by the Accounting Standards Committee, involving the preparation of not only statements of account, but also a trustees' report and a statement of legal and administrative details;
(c) the requirements governing the contents and auditing of accounts be graduated, so as not to add unnecessarily to the burden of trustees of smaller charities; and
(d) charity trustees should make copies of their charity's accounts available to the public on request.

4.4 Accounting Records

4.4.1 Section 19 of the 1992 Act requires charity trustees to ensure that accounting records are kept, which record the financial transactions of the charity on a day-to-day basis.

The accounting records required by s 19 are more extensive than those required by s 32 of the 1960 Act. They must be sufficient:

(a) to show and explain all the charity's transactions;
(b) to disclose at any time and with reasonable accuracy the financial position of the charity at that time;
(c) to show entries on a day-to-day basis for all sums received and expended, identifying the matter in respect of which the transaction took place and to include a record of assets and liabilities; and
(d) to enable the trustees to ensure that any statements of account required by the 1992 Act comply with the statutory requirements.

The requirement that the records should disclose a charity's financial position at any time with reasonable accuracy does not mean the charity must update its accounting records daily. The records should be sufficiently detailed, showing transactions on a daily basis, to enable the accounts to be drawn up to reveal the financial position of the charity on any particular date in the past.

Section 19 does not apply to charitable companies. They are excluded by s 19(5), but they must maintain identical accounting records by virtue of s 221 of the Companies Act 1985, the wording of which is mirrored in s 19. Nor does s 19 apply to exempt charities. They are excluded by s 24(1), which makes clear that exempt charities must continue to comply with the general obligation to keep accounts laid down by s 32 of the 1960 Act. Section 32 is itself amended by Sch 3 to the 1992 Act, to apply only to exempt charities.

4.4.2 By s 19, accounting records must be preserved for at least six years from the end of the financial year to which they relate. The Commissioners may, however, agree to the destruction or disposal of records in some other way if a charity ceases to exist.

A similar rule is imposed on exempt charities. They are also required to preserve records for six years (s 32 of the 1960 Act as amended by Sch 3 to the 1992 Act). However, neither s 19 of the 1992 Act nor s 32 of the 1960 Act applies to charitable companies. Section 222 of the Companies Act 1985 deals with the preservation of their accounting records. A public company must preserve records for six years, but a private company need only preserve records for three years. Since charitable companies are established as private companies, it would appear that they need only preserve records for three years. This would seem to be an oversight and charitable companies would be well-advised to observe the six-year requirement.

4.5 Statements of Account

4.5.1 Section 20 of the 1992 Act introduces new provisions for the preparation of annual accounts. Two categories of charity are excluded from the requirements of s 20, although they may be subject to other obligations to prepare annual accounts. The excluded categories are as follows.

(a) Charitable companies are excluded by s 20(7), but they must comply with the requirements of the Companies Act 1985. It is likely that the Secretary of State will exercise the power conferred on him by s 257 of the Companies Act 1985 to prepare regulations setting out the accounting requirements of charitable companies in order to mirror the regulations which are to be made under s 20 for unincorporated charities and charities incorporated by Royal Charter.

(b) Exempt charities are excluded by s 24(1). However, they must keep proper accounts in accordance with s 32 of the 1960 Act and may have special requirements imposed on them by some other statutory regime (for example, industrial and provident societies are bound to comply with the Friendly and Industrial and Provident Societies Act 1968).

4.5.2 Under s 20, full accounts must be prepared for a charity with a gross income in excess of £25,000 in the relevant financial year. These consist of a statement of accounts complying with requirements which are to be prescribed by regulations made by the Secretary of State.

Simplified accounts may be prepared for a charity whose gross income in the relevant financial year does not exceed £25,000. These consist of a receipt and payments account and a statement of assets and liabilities. Confusingly, this combination is described in the 1992 Act as 'an account and statement' as distinct from a 'statement of accounts' required of larger charities.

The term 'gross income' is defined in s 1 of the 1992 Act to mean the gross recorded income of a charity from all sources, including special trusts. There may be some problems in identifying what should be treated as 'income'. For example, the Statement of Recommended Practice on Accounting by Charities ('SORP 2'), recommends that new permanent endowment funds (eg a bequest subject to a restriction against using the capital) should not be taken through the income and expenditure account. Should this, therefore, be treated as 'income' for the purposes of the definition of 'gross income'? This seems likely, given the wide definition 'gross recorded income *from all sources*'.

Section 20(6) empowers the Secretary of State to alter the sum of £25,000 by order, providing a mechanism for the threshold to at least keep pace with inflation.

4.5.3 The White Paper indicated that regulations specifying the form and contents of full accounts would reflect revised recommendations of SORP 2 requiring:

(a) an income and expenditure account;
(b) a balance sheet;
(c) notes to the accounts, providing explanatory information about the figures in the accounts, and the assets and commitments of the charity;
(d) details of the separately accountable funds of the charity, distinguishing permanent endowment and other restricted funds (for example, funds

which must be applied for a particular project of the charity) from unrestricted funds which can be applied freely for the purpose of the charity, and identifying designated funds within the unrestricted funds which have been earmarked by the trustees for a particular purpose; and

(e) an explanation of the accounting policies used, including an explanation of how administrative expenses have been apportioned between items such as accommodation, office expenses, salaries, fund-raising and publicity.

Given the greater emphasis on the accountability of charities and the effective use of charitable funds, the proposed regulations are likely to require the disclosure of information about the gross and net receipts of fund-raising efforts and the administrative costs of a charity, as distinct from direct expenditure on projects. The White Paper also indicated that the regulations would require statements of account to include details of grants made by charities out of their income and property, in particular disclosing the names of institutional beneficiaries (but not individual beneficiaries) together with the amount of grant paid.

4.5.4 There is an obligation to preserve any statement of account or account and statement for six years from the end of the financial year to which it relates. This is similar to the obligation to preserve accounting records (see **4.4.2**).

4.6 Audit or Independent Examination

4.6.1 Section 21 of the 1992 Act requires the annual accounts of a charity to be audited or examined by an independent examiner. The following three categories of charity are excluded from this requirement. These are:

(a) charitable companies (s 21(9)) (which must, however, comply with the audit requirements of the Companies Act 1985). Section 21(9) expressly preserves the power of the Commissioners, under ss 8(3) and (6) of the 1960 Act, to require the accounts of a charitable company to be audited, but at the cost of the Commissioners;

(b) exempt charities (s 24(1)); and

(c) charities with an annual income in the relevant year below £1,000 and which are not registered on a voluntary basis (s 24(2)). Section 24(2) uses the term 'annual income' unlike other provisions which refer to 'gross income' (see **4.5.2**). Unlike gross income, there is no statutory definition of 'annual income'. However, it is clear from the reference in s 24(2) to s 4(4)(c) of the 1960 Act (small charities exempt from compulsory registration) that 'annual income' means the 'income' arising in a financial year of a charity and that 'income' means income as defined in the 1960 Act (see **2.5.2**).

4.6.2 If the gross income[1] or total expenditure of a charity exceeds £100,000[2] in the year for which the accounts are being prepared or either of the two immediately preceding years, the accounts must be audited by a person who is eligible to act as a company auditor under s 25 of the Companies Act 1985 (ie a registered auditor) or under regulations to be made under the 1992 Act (s 21(2)).

If the gross income or total expenditure of a charity is below £100,000 in both the year for which the accounts are being prepared and the two immediately preceding years, s 21(3) permits the charity trustees to have the accounts examined by an independent examiner as an alternative to an audit.

An independent examiner is defined, in s 21(3), as an independent person who is reasonably believed by the trustees to have the requisite ability and practical experience to carry out a competent examination of the accounts. This does not necessarily mean a professional accountant, but would include a bank or building society manager, a retired accountant or a local authority treasurer.

---

1 'Gross income' is defined by s 1 of the 1992 Act (see **4.5.2**), but there is no statutory definition of 'total expenditure'.
2 Section 21(8) confers on the Secretary of State the power to alter the £100,000 threshold.

4.6.3 Under s 21(7) of the 1992 Act the Commissioners may give guidance to charity trustees – either generally or to charity trustees of a particular charity – about the selection of an independent examiner and may give directions relating to the carrying out of an examination.

Regulations will be made under s 22 dealing, among other things, with the duties of an auditor, the form of the report to be produced by the auditor or independent examiner and their rights of access to the books, documents and records of the charity. The regulations will also deal with the auditor's right to require information and explanations from past and present trustees (whether managing trustees, holding or custodian trustees), and past and present officers or employees of the charity. The regulations will specify in which circumstances the Commissioners may waive the need for audit or independent examination by a particular charity in a particular year.

4.7 Commissioners' Power to Order Audit

4.7.1 Section 21 of the 1992 Act places the obligation to submit accounts for audit or independent examination on the trustees. In those circumstances, the costs of the audit or independent examination will be an administrative expense, to be met from the charity's funds. Section 21(4), (5) and (6) does, however, confer power on the Commissioners to make an order requiring the audit of accounts. In certain circumstances, the costs of such an audit fall automatically on the trustees personally. This is a fundamental change from the arrangements in s 8 of the 1960 Act (see **4.2.3**).

Section 21(4) confers on the Commissioners a power to order the audit (or examination of accounts, if appropriate) if the statutory requirement for accounts to be audited or examined has not been complied with within 10 months of the end of the relevant financial year.

In these circumstances the appointment of the auditor or examiner is a matter for the Commissioners but the costs are the responsibility of the trustees. Section 21(6) provides that expenses, including the auditor's re-muneration, are to be met, in the first place, by the trustees, who are personally liable jointly and severally. The Commissioners, therefore, may seek to recover the expenses from one of several trustees. The expenses can only be met from the funds of the charity if the Commissioners are of the view that it is not practical to recover the expenses from the trustees. There is no discretion in the matter.

Section 21(4) also confers on the Commissioners a power to order the audit of accounts, which have already been subject to independent examination, if the Commissioners are of the view that an audit is desirable. In these circumstances, the auditor may be appointed by the trustees and, provided the trustees comply with the Commissioners' order, the costs of the audit will be met from the funds of the charity.

The Commissioners' power under s 21 to order an independent examina-tion or audit of accounts does not apply to the three categories of charity excluded from the scope of s 21: charitable companies, exempt charities and charities with an annual income in the relevant year below £1,000 and which are not registered (see **4.6.1**).

However, the Commissioners may require the accounts of such charities, other than exempt charities, to be audited under s 8 of the 1960 Act at the cost of the Commissioners.

4.7.2 Section 56 of the 1992 Act deals generally with the making of orders under that Act and applies the provisions of ss 40 and 41 of the 1960 Act. There is no right of appeal against an order made by the Commissioners under s 21 of the 1992 Act, although the Commissioners do have power, under s 40(3) of the 1960 Act, to discharge the order within 12 months of the making of an order if they are satisfied that it was made by mistake or as a result of misrepresentation.

4.8 Annual Reports

4.8.1 Under s 23 of the 1992 Act the trustees must prepare an annual report in respect of the financial year of a charity. This must be sent to the Commissioners within 10 months of the end of that financial year, with the accounts and with the report of the auditor or independent examiner as appropriate. The Commissioners may extend the 10-month period if it has not been possible for good reason to produce the accounts and report within that time.

The annual report will contain a report by the trustees on the activities of the charity during the year and such other information relating to the charity or to its trustees or officers as may be prescribed by regulations. The regulations will enable the Commissioners to waive the need to prepare an annual report in the case of a particular charity, class of charities or a particular financial year.

The White Paper indicated that the trustees' report will be based on SORP 2 and will:

'– set out the means employed to promote the charity's objects, noting any significant changes since the last report;
– review the charity's activities and achievements during the reporting period;
– review the transactions and financial position of the charity; and
– explain salient features of the financial report.'

4.8.2 Two categories of charity are excluded from the provisions of s 23 of the 1992 Act by s 24(2). These are exempt charities and charities with an annual income not exceeding £1,000 and which are not registered on a voluntary basis (see **4.6.1**).

Charitable companies are required to prepare an annual report to send to the Commissioners with accounts prepared under Part VII of the Companies Act 1985 and auditor's report attached.

Charities which are both excepted from the need to register by an order of the Commissioners made under s 4(4)(b) of the 1960 Act and are not registered on a voluntary basis, are partially exempt from the requirements of s 23 of the 1992 Act. Under s 24, these charities need only prepare and send an annual report when they are required to do so by the Commissioners. In such cases, the annual report should have attached to it the accounts and report of the auditor or independent examiner.

4.8.3 Section 25 of the 1992 Act provides for the annual report of a charity, including the accounts and report prepared by the auditor or independent examiner kept by the Commissioners, to be open to public inspection and for the Commissioners to supply copies of such documents on request. It is expected that regulations made under s 51 of the 1992 Act will prescribe fees for public inspection and the supply of copy documents.

4.9 Annual Returns

Section 26 of the 1992 Act requires every registered charity to prepare an annual return in such a form and containing such information as will be prescribed by regulations and to send the return to the Commissioners within 10 months of the end of the financial year to which the return relates. The White Paper indicated that the annual return would contain legal and administrative details of the charity, such as the names of the trustees and principal officers, the principal address of the charity and any changes in the charity's trusts or in the details of the individual named as the official correspondent for the charity. It will be a means of ensuring that information about every registered charity is kept up to date.

Under s 26(3), the Commissioners may waive the need to prepare an annual return in the case of a particular charity or particular class of charities or in the case of a particular financial year of a charity or class of charities.

4.10 Public Access to Accounts

Section 25(3) and (4) of the 1992 Act effects a radical change in the public accountability of charities. Sections 19 to 24 are concerned with the obligations of charity trustees to maintain accounts and, broadly speaking, in the case of registered charities, to prepare annual accounts, reports and returns to be sent to the Commissioners. The right of members of the public to inspect documents sent to the Charity Commission (see **4.8.3**) ensures that the public have access to information about registered charities.

Section 25(3) and (4) goes further. Section 25(3) confers the right on any member of the public to submit a written request to charity trustees, whether the charity is registered or not, to supply a copy of the charity's recent accounts. Provided he or she pays whatever reasonable fee the trustees require to cover the cost of supplying the accounts, the trustees must comply with the request within two months of the receipt of the request. (Section 25(4) identifies which accounts are 'the most recent accounts' of a charity.)

Therefore, any member of the public may obtain the accounts of any charity, even exempt charities which would, in the past, have been difficult to obtain.

4.11 Penalties for Non-compliance

A controversial aspect of the new accounting and reporting requirements has been the introduction of criminal sanctions for failure to fulfil the statutory obligations. This is contrary to the recommendations of the White Paper.

Section 27 of the 1992 Act provides that a person is guilty of an offence if, without reasonable excuse, he is persistently in default:

(a) in submitting the annual report with accounts attached or the annual return; or
(b) in supplying copies of the most recent accounts of the charity to a member of the public under s 25(3).

Such a person will be liable on summary conviction to a fine.

Since s 27 is subject to s 55, proceedings may not be instituted without the consent of the Director of Public Prosecutions.

The individuals likely to be prosecuted under s 27 are the charity trustees, because the statutory obligations are placed on the trustees rather than on the officers of the charity. It is the trustees' responsibility to ensure that the statutory obligations have been complied with. Where a prosecution is authorised by the Director of Public Prosecutions, it is possible that all the trustees would be prosecuted unless they could establish that they acted reasonably in delegating the obligation to send the accounts, report and return to one of their number or to an officer of the charity. This is because the charity trustees are jointly responsible for the proper conduct of the affairs of the charity. It would be less easy to establish a reasonable excuse if no steps had been taken to prepare the documents in the first place.

4.12 Summary of Requirements

The tables shown in *Fig 2* and *Fig 3* summarise the accounting and reporting requirements for registered charities and non-registered charities, respectively. Registered charities include charities registered on a voluntary basis. A charity may also be subject to another accounting and reporting regime not shown in the table, for example a registered housing association will need to comply with the requirements of the Housing Corporation.

This table shows the accounting and reporting requirements of registered charities according to the charity type. A charity may also be subject to other accounting and reporting regimes not shown in the table.

KEY TO REGISTERED CHARITIES

1 With gross income or total expenditure exceeding £100,000.
2 With gross income between £25,000 and £100,000.
3 With gross income between £1,000 and £25,000.
4 With annual income below £1,000 (voluntary registration).
5 Charitable company, regardless of income.
6 Excepted charity, registered on voluntary basis.

Fig 2 Registered Charities

Charity type	Accounting records (s 19)	Annual accounts (s 20)	Audit/independent examination (s 21)	Annual report (s 23)	Annual return (s 26)	Accounts to public (s 25)
1	Yes	Full accounts	Full audit	Yes	Yes	Yes
2	Yes	Full accounts	Independent examination	Yes	Yes	Yes
3	Yes	Simplified accounts	Independent examination	Yes	Yes	Yes
4	Yes	Simplified accounts	Independent examination	Yes	Yes	Yes
5	No, but must comply with Companies Act 1985	No, but must comply with Companies Act 1985	No, but must comply with Companies Act 1989 and subject to Charities Act 1960, s 8	Yes, in addition to Companies Act 1985	Yes, in addition to Companies Act 1985	
6	Yes	Yes. Full accounts if income in excess of £25,000	Yes. Full audit if gross income exceeds £100,000, otherwise independent examination	Yes	Yes	Yes

Fig 3 Unregistered Charities

This table shows the accounting and reporting requirements of unregistered charities according to charity type. A charity may also be subject to other statutory regimes not shown in the table.

KEY TO UNREGISTERED CHARITY TYPES
1 Exempt charity.
2 Unregistered charitable company, regardless of income.
3 Charity (other than company) with annual income below £1,000.
4 Excepted charity with annual income exceeding £1,000, but not registered on voluntary basis.

Charity type	Accounting records (s 19)	Annual accounts (s 20)	Audit/independent examination (s 21)	Annual report (s 23)	Annual return (s 26)	Accounts to public (s 25)
1	No, but must comply with Charities Act 1960, s 2	No, but must comply with Charities Act 1960, s 32	None	None	None	Yes
2	No, but must comply with Companies Act 1985	No, but must comply with Companies Act 1985	No, but must comply with Companies Act 1989 and subject to Charities Act 1960, s 8	No, but must comply with Companies Act 1985	No, but must comply with Companies Act 1985	Yes
3	Yes	None	None	None	None	Yes
4	Yes	Yes. Full accounts if gross income in excess of £25,000	Yes. Full audit if gross income exceeds £100,000	On request	None	Yes

CHAPTER 5

POWERS TO DEAL WITH ABUSE: PREVENTION, INVESTIGATION AND PROTECTION

Introduction: Disqualification: Obtaining Information: Intervention: Appointment of Receiver and Manager: Supervision of Scottish Charities: Court Proceedings

5.1 Introduction

The 1992 Act implements the recommendations of the *Efficiency Scrutiny of the Supervision of Charities* 1987 ('the Woodfield Report') and the White Paper, to give greater force to the role of the Commissioners to prevent, investigate and initiate action against abuse. Preventive powers include:

(a) the requirement in s 3 of the 1992 Act for all registered charities to declare their status on certain documents (see **2.7**);
(b) the power conferred on the Commissioners by s 4 of the 1992 Act to require a charity to change its name if it is too similar to that of another charity or otherwise misleading in some way (see **Chapter 3**); and
(c) the disqualification of individuals with convictions for fraud or dishonesty from acting as a trustee of a charity.

The status of the Commission as an investigating body is increased and they now have greater powers to obtain information and to bring civil proceedings against defaulters.

The third element of the reform is a significant change to the power of the Commissioners to initiate action for the protection of the charity. They may now take certain protective action without notice and without the need to conclude an inquiry.

5.2 Disqualification

5.2.1 The Woodfield Report recommended that any person convicted of an offence involving fraud or other dishonesty or who had previously been removed from trusteeship by the Commissioners should be disqualified from acting as a trustee of a charity without the Commissioners' permission in writing. This recommendation is implemented by ss 45 and 46 of the 1992 Act, but the grounds for disqualification have been extended.

A person is disqualified from acting as a trustee of a charity under s 45(1) of the 1992 Act, if:

(a) he has been convicted of an offence involving dishonesty or deception (including theft, fraud or forgery) provided that the conviction is not a spent conviction under the Rehabilitation of Offenders Act 1974;

(b) he has been adjudged bankrupt or sequestration of his estate has been awarded and he has not been discharged in either case;

(c) he has made a composition or arrangement with, or granted a trust deed for, his creditors and has not been discharged in respect of it;

(d) he has been removed as trustee of a charity by order of the Commissioners or the High Court on the grounds of misconduct or mismanagement in the administration of a charity for which he was responsible or to which he was privy, or which, by his conduct, he contributed to or facilitated;

(e) he has been removed under s 7 of the Law Reform (Miscellaneous Provisions) (Scotland) Act 1990 (powers of Court of Session to deal with management of charities) from being concerned in the management or control of any charity; or

(f) he is subject to a disqualification order by the Company Directors Disqualification Act 1986 or to an order made under s 429(2)(b) of the Insolvency Act 1986 (failure to pay under county court administration order) and has not obtained leave under the provisions of the appropriate Act to act as director (trustee) of the charity.

The disqualification from acting as a trustee applies to all charities, including exempt charities and other unregistered charities. It applies both to the office of managing trustee and to the office of holding trustee and is effective even if the grounds for disqualification have arisen before s 45 of the 1992 Act is implemented.

5.2.2 Disqualification is automatic unless the Commissioners exercise their power, under s 45(4) of the 1992 Act, to waive the disqualification of the individual. The waiver may authorise the individual to act as trustee of a particular charity or of a particular class of charities. For example, it may be appropriate for a convicted individual to be appointed as trustee of a charity for ex-offenders. The Commissioners may not waive the disqualification of an individual who is disqualified under the Company Directors Disqualification Act 1986 and who has not obtained leave under that Act to act as director of a company.

Since disqualification is automatic in the absence of an express waiver by the Commissioners, individuals who have been lawfully appointed as trustees, but who satisfy one of the grounds for disqualification, will automatically be disqualified on the date the section comes into force and, thereafter, their continuing trusteeship would be unlawful under ss 45 and 46. Section 45(5) provides a period of grace during which applications for waiver may be made to the Commissioners before s 45 comes into effect.

5.2.3 Section 46 imposes penalties for acting as a trustee while disqualified.

(a) Under s 46(1) it is an offence, punishable by a term of imprisonment or a fine or both, to act as a trustee while disqualified. This does not apply to a trustee who is disqualified under grounds (b) or (f) above (see **5.2.1**), in which case the offence is dealt with under company law. The proceedings may only be instituted with the consent of the Director of Public Prosecutions.

(b) Under s 46(4), the Commissioners may order an individual, who has acted as a trustee while disqualified, to repay to the charity the whole or part of any such sums received by way of remuneration or expenses or the value of any benefit received in kind. In normal circumstances, a trustee would not receive any remuneration or benefit in kind from the charity. However, out-of-pocket expenses may have been paid to the trustee.

5.2.4 Section 45(7) of the 1992 Act requires the Commissioners to keep a register, open to the public, of all individuals who have been removed from office by the Commissioners, whether before or after s 45(1) comes into force, or by the High Court after s 45(1) comes into force.

5.3 Obtaining Information

5.3.1 Sections 6 and 7 of the 1960 Act empowered the Commissioners to institute inquiries into charities (other than exempt charities), to call for documents and to search records. Sections 6 and 7 of the 1992 Act modify the procedures associated with inquiries and increase the powers of the Commissioners to obtain information.

(a) The procedure for obtaining information under s 6(3) of the 1992 Act or requiring an individual to attend to give evidence or produce documents under s 6(5) of the 1960 Act, has been simplified. Now the Commissioners (or a person appointed by them to conduct the inquiry) may direct an individual to attend to give evidence or to produce documents. Section 57 of the 1992 Act deals with the giving and enforcement of directions (see **3.5**).

(b) Section 7 of the 1992 Act extends the power of the Commissioners to acquire information so that they are entitled not only to obtain documentary evidence but also to seek an explanation of the documentary evidence before them.

(c) The offence under s 6(9) of the 1960 Act of wilfully altering, suppressing, concealing or destroying any document which might be required as part of a s 6 inquiry, is superseded by s 54(2), which removes the condition that the document may be required for a s 6 inquiry.

(d) Section 54(1) of the 1992 Act creates an offence of knowingly or recklessly providing the Commissioners (including an individual appointed to conduct a s 6 inquiry) with information which is false or misleading in a material particular. The offence exists if the information is provided supposedly in compliance with a statutory requirement (for example the requirement to provide information under s 7) or the individual providing the information intends or could reasonably be expected to know that the information would be used by the Commissioners for the purpose of discharging their statutory functions.

No proceedings may be brought under s 54 of the 1992 Act without the consent of the Director of Public Prosecutions (s 55).

The existence of a real or supposed dispute with a charity over a claim to property no longer entitles an individual to disregard a direction from the Commissioners under ss 6 or 7 of the 1992 Act (ss 6(4) and 7(3) of the 1992 Act amending ss 6(6) and 7(4) of the 1960 Act).

5.3.2 The powers of the Commissioners to obtain information from other Government departments and statutory bodies is enhanced by s 52 of the 1992 Act, which provides for an exchange of information between the Commissioners and other bodies. Section 9(3) of the 1960 Act allowed the Inland Revenue to pass information to the Commissioners where a charity appeared to the Inland Revenue to be carrying on non-charitable activities or using its funds for non-charitable purposes. This is extended by s 52 of the 1992 Act, which enables the Commissioners to exchange information with the following organisations listed in s 52(6):

(a) any government department (including a Northern Ireland department);
(b) any local authority;
(c) any constable;
(d) any other body or person discharging functions of a public nature (including a body or person discharging regulatory functions in relation to any description of activities).

Section 52(2) excludes from this list the Commissioners of Customs and Excise (who deal with VAT) and the Commissioners of Inland Revenue. However, those bodies are expressly authorised to disclose to the Commissioners information relating to:

(a) the name and address of any institution which has been treated as established for charitable purposes (so helping the Commissioners to track down unregistered charities);
(b) information about the purposes of the institution and its trusts in order to provide assistance in determining whether the institution ought to be treated as a charity (so helping the Commissioners to reach a decision on the charitable status of an organisation);

(c) information about an organisation which has been treated as a charity but which appears to be carrying on activities which are not charitable or to have applied its funds for purposes which are not charitable (so helping the Commissioners to monitor charities and check abuse).

5.4 Intervention

5.4.1 Section 20 of the 1960 Act conferred on the Commissioners a number of powers to act for the protection of charities, for example to remove trustees or charity employees and to freeze bank accounts. However, the powers were exercisable only if, as a result of a s 6 inquiry, the Commissioners were satisfied that:

(a) there had been mismanagement and misconduct in the administration of the charity; and
(b) the proposed course of action was necessary or desirable to protect the property of the charity.

There was some doubt as to whether the s 6 inquiry had to be completed before the Commissioners could exercise their powers under s 20. Certainly, it hampered the ability of the Commissioners to act swiftly to protect charity assets at risk, particularly since s 20(9) required the Commissioners to serve notice on each charity trustee in the UK before exercising their s 20 powers.

5.4.2 Section 8 of the 1992 Act amends s 20 of the 1960 Act by introducing new powers and new procedures. A distinction is drawn between temporary powers designed to enable the Commissioners to intervene swiftly to protect assets which they believe to be at risk, and remedial powers which are designed to provide a permanent solution for a charity where the Commissioners have discovered misconduct or mismanagement.

The temporary protective powers are set out in the amended s 20(1). These are:

(a) to suspend a trustee (whether a holding trustee or a managing trustee), or an officer, agent or employee of the charity, for a period of up to 12 months (previously three months under the 1960 Act) pending consideration being given to the removal of that individual;
(b) to appoint additional charity trustees if the Commissioners consider this to be necessary for the proper administration of the charity;
(c) to invest property of the charity in the official custodian of charities (whether the property consists of land or investments);
(d) to prevent a person holding property on behalf of the charity or on behalf of any trustee of the charity from parting with the property without the approval of the Commissioners;
(e) to prevent a debtor of the charity making any payment to the charity without the approval of the Commissioners;
(f) to restrict transactions which the charity may enter into without the

approval of the Commissioners (for example, transactions which exceed a specified value); and

(g) to appoint a receiver or manager in respect of the property and affairs of the charity.

The power of the Commissioners to appoint a receiver or manager is a new power, which is dealt with in greater detail in s 20A, introduced into the 1960 Act by s 9 of the 1992 Act (see **5.5**).

5.4.3 The temporary protective powers under s 20(1) may be exercised by the Commissioners if they are satisfied that either:

(a) there is or has been any misconduct or mismanagement in the administration of the charity; or

(b) it is necessary or desirable to act to protect the property of the charity.

Unlike the original s 20, only one of the conditions needs to be satisfied.

It is not necessary to have instituted an inquiry under s 6 of the 1960 Act before exercising these powers, nor is it necessary to serve charity trustees with notice of the intention to exercise the powers.

5.4.4 The permanent remedial powers of the Commissioners under the amended s 20 are:

(a) to remove a trustee (whether a charity trustee or holding trustee), officer, agent or employee of the charity who is in the view of the Commissioners responsible for or privy to misconduct or mismanagement or has by his conduct contributed to or facilitated the misconduct or mismanagement; and

(b) to make a scheme for the administration of the charity without the need for an application from the trustees or, indeed, any other person empowered to apply for a scheme under s 18 of the 1960 Act (see **10.2**).

These permanent remedial powers are exercisable only if:

(a) a s 6 inquiry has been instituted, although the inquiry need not have been concluded; and

(b) the Commissioners are satisfied both that there is or has been misconduct or mismanagement in the administration of the charity and that the course proposed is necessary to protect the property of the charity; and

(c) before exercising these powers, the Commissioners have served notice on each charity trustee in the UK.

5.4.5 The powers of the Commissioners under s 20, as amended, are exercised by order of the Commissioners. There is a right of appeal to the High Court against such orders under s 18 of the 1960 Act, although under s 18(11) it is a preliminary requirement for instituting an appeal that the Commissioners have issued a certificate stating that it is a proper case for an appeal, or leave of a judge attached to the Chancery Division has been obtained. However, this preliminary requirement does not apply to Commissioners' orders appointing a receiver or manager or to Commissioners' orders suspending or removing an officer or employee of a charity.

5.4.6 Section 20(10) imposes penalties for contravening an order of the Commissioners. Any person who contravenes an order restricting the application of charity funds will be guilty of an offence and liable on conviction to a maximum fine of £2,000. Conviction under s 20(10) does not preclude the institution of proceedings for breach of trust (s 20(10)A).

5.5 Appointment of Receiver and Manager

Section 9 of the 1992 Act introduces a new s 20(A) into the 1960 Act (to supplement the new provision in s 20) which enables the Commissioners to appoint a receiver and manager for a charity.

The order appointing the receiver and manager should specify the functions to be discharged by him. These may include all or any of the powers of the charity trustees. Furthermore, the order may provide that the receiver and manager will act in conjunction with the charity trustees or, alternatively, to the exclusion of the charity trustees.

The receiver and manager is subject to the supervision of the Commissioners to whom he may turn for advice and the Commissioners may, in turn, seek directions from the court. The costs of any such proceedings must be met by the charity.

Section 9(6) and (7) allows for regulations to be made which will deal with the appointment and removal of receivers and managers, their remuneration and reporting requirements. Remuneration will be paid out of the income of the charity and the amount may be determined by the Commissioners. In addition, the regulations may authorise the Commissioners to require security from a receiver and manager for the proper discharge of his functions, which indicates that the appointment of a receiver and manager will be a professional appointment.

5.6 Supervision of Scottish Charities

In order to prevent abuse of the system, s 12 of the 1992 Act gives the Commissioners certain powers over charities which are either established in Scotland but managed and controlled wholly or mainly in England or Wales or which are established and managed in Scotland but which have property in England.

The Commissioners may exercise their powers of inquiry under ss 6 and 7 of the 1960 Act. They may also exercise their powers to act for the protection of charity property under ss 20 and 20A of the 1960 Act in respect of a charity established in Scotland but managed or controlled wholly or mainly in

England or Wales. The Commissioners may not, however, use their power to appoint additional trustees.

The Commissioners may order an individual who holds property of a Scottish charity not to part with that property without their approval if:

(a) the charity is established in Scotland and managed or controlled wholly or mainly in Scotland; and
(b) the property is held on behalf of the charity in England or Wales; and
(c) the Commissioners are satisfied that there has been misconduct or mismanagement in the administration of the charity and that it is necessary or desirable to act to protect the property of the charity.

Finally, the 1992 Act gives the Commissioners powers in respect of persons in England or Wales who hold property for a Scottish charity, regardless of whether the charity is managed and controlled mainly in Scotland or mainly in England and Wales. In such circumstances, if the Commissioners are satisfied that there has been misconduct or mismanagement in the administration of the charity and that it is necessary or desirable to protect the property, they may order that the property held in England or Wales be transferred to another charity with purposes as similar in character as possible to those of the original Scottish charity. The transferee charity may be a Scottish charity or an English charity.

5.7 Court Proceedings

5.7.1 Under the 1960 Act the Commissioners had no power to institute proceedings against trustees. If the Commissioners were of the view that legal proceedings were desirable, they were required to refer the matter to the Attorney General under s 28(7) of the 1960 Act. The decision whether or not to institute proceedings on the basis of the information provided by the Commissioners, and the conduct of those proceedings, was entirely a matter for the Attorney General.

The White Paper recommended that in order to give new emphasis to the role of the Commissioners in dealing directly with abuse, the Commissioners should be given powers, corresponding to and concurrent with those of the Attorney General, to go direct to court for the enforcement of obligations against defaulting trustees and others. However, it was also recommended that the Commissioners should secure the Attorney General's consent before initiating litigation.

These recommendations are implemented by s 28 of the 1992 Act, which introduces a new s 26(A) into the 1960 Act. The Commissioners are given concurrent jurisdiction with the Attorney General to initiate legal proceedings relating to charities or the property or affairs of charities or, alternatively, to compromise claims with a view to avoiding such proceedings. For example, if the Commissioners are of the view that a charity has suffered loss as a result of the negligence of charity trustees, they can reach agreement with the trustees concerning what recompense the trustees, should make to the charity, without instituting proceedings.

However, the Commissioners still need the Attorney General's consent to institute proceedings and to compromise claims.

5.7.2 Section 11 of the 1992 Act, which introduces s 28A into the 1960 Act, is also relevant to the powers of the Commissioners to institute legal proceedings. Section 28A provides that a copy of the report of an inquiry under s 6 of the 1960 Act, if certified by the Commissioners to be a true copy, will be admissible in proceedings instituted by the Commissioners under s 26A of the 1960 Act or by the Attorney General. The report is evidence of any fact stated in the report and evidence of the opinion of the person appointed by the Commissioners to conduct the inquiry.

A s 6 inquiry may, therefore, be the first step towards legal proceedings instituted by the Commissioners against any one or more of the charity trustees or others involved in the administration of the charity, who are criticised in the report.

Hence, it will be important for individuals who are the subject matter of a report to challenge anything with which they disagree as soon as practicable after publication of the report.

CHAPTER 6

LAND TRANSACTIONS

Introduction: Summary of Rules on Disposals of Freehold Land and Leases
(Other than Mortgages): Disposals of Freehold Land and Leases by Charities
(Other than Mortgages): The Usual Procedure for Disposing of Land under
s 32(3) of the 1992 Act: Exemptions from the General Rule in s 32(3): Section
33 Statements: Control on Mortgages by Charities

6.1 Introduction

6.1.1 Under s 29 of the 1960 Act the trustees of registered charities require
the Commissioners' consent:

(a) to mortgage or otherwise charge any part of the charity's permanent
    endowment; or
(b) to grant leases of more than 22 years or otherwise dispose of land which
    forms part of the permanent endowment or which has, at any time, been
    occupied for the charity's purposes.

This does not apply to exempt charities and certain excepted charities.

The wide drafting of the section and, in particular, the phrase 'or otherwise
dispose of land which has at any time been occupied for the charity's
purposes', has meant that a large number of land transactions have been
subject to the Commissioners' scrutiny. For example, a simple grant of a
right of way or easement has required consent, as has the assignment of a lease
of property which has been occupied for charitable purposes.

6.1.2 The Woodfield Report recommended that trustees should be given a
general power to sell land without the Commissioners' consent, provided
that they complied with certain statutory requirements. The White Paper
accepted this recommendation. It stated, at p 39:

> 'In considering what might take the place of section 29 (the Government) have been
> concerned to provide continuing protection for charity property against mis-
> management and abuse, and to focus the Commissioners' efforts on the sorts of
> financial transaction for which closer supervision and control remain necessary.
> They have also been concerned to do as much as possible to assist purchasers in
> obtaining good title to charity land.'

6.2 Summary of Rules on Disposals of Freehold Land and Leases (Other than Mortgages)

1 Disposal to connected person – Commissioners' consent required.
2 Disposal of freehold, grant of lease of more than seven years, or other disposal – qualified surveyor's report required; advertise (if necessary).
3 Grant of lease of less than seven years – report by person with requisite ability required; no advertisement required.
4 Disposal of functional land (in cases under 1, 2 and 3 (above)) – give public notice and take into account representations, unless:

(a) a Charity Commission exemption order has been acquired; or
(b) the lease is for less than two years.

5 Leases to beneficiaries – no need for Commissioners' consent or to comply with 2, 3 or 4 (above).

6.3 Disposals of Freehold Land and Leases by Charities (Other than Mortgages)

6.3.1 Section 32(1) of the 1992 Act provides that land held by or in trust for a charity may be sold, leased or otherwise disposed of only with an order of the court or the Commissioners. Again, this applies to registered charities and charities excepted from registration only and not to exempt charities. Under the old s 29(4) of the 1960 Act, charities could be excepted from the provisions of s 29 by an order of the court or the Commissioners. A number of categories of charities were excepted, eg certain non-conformist religious charities.

Section 29 is expressly repealed by the 1992 Act. Henceforth, charities will no longer be excepted by order but will have to comply with the 1992 Act.

Section 32 of the 1992 Act does not apply to mortgages of charity land. They are dealt with in ss 34 and 35.

6.3.2 The general rule in s 32(1) (ie no disposal of land without an order of the court or the Commissioners) is subject to various exemptions set out in the rest of s 32. The exemptions do not apply if land is disposed by a charity to a connected person or a trustee of a connected person. In that case, the consent of the Commissioners must be obtained.

6.3.3 Schedule 2 to the 1992 Act defines a connected person as:

(a) a trustee of the charity;
(b) a person who is the donor of any land to the charity;
(c) a child, parent, grandchild, grandparent, brother or sister of any trustee or donor;
(d) an officer, agent or employee of the charity;
(e) the spouse of any person falling within any of the above;

(f) an institution which is controlled by any of the above defined persons or any two or more such persons together; or

(g) a body corporate in which any connected person has a substantial interest or two or more such persons have a substantial interest.

6.4 The Usual Procedure for Disposing of Land under s 32(3) of the 1992 Act

Once the 1992 Act comes into force, under s 32(3) the usual procedure which charity trustees must follow before entering into an agreement for the sale or lease or other disposition of land (other than a mortgage) will be as follows.

(a) They must obtain and consider a written report on the proposed disposition from a qualified surveyor instructed by the trustees and acting exclusively for the charity.

For these purposes, qualified surveyor means a Fellow or Professional Associate of the Royal Institution of Chartered Surveyors or the Incorporated Society of Valuers and Auctioneers, who is reasonably believed by the charity trustees to have ability in and experience of the valuation of land of the particular kind and in the particular area in question.

The report issued by the qualified surveyor will have to contain such information and deal with such matters as may be prescribed by regulations made by the Secretary of State.

It is clear that the qualified surveyor can act only for the charity and not, for example, for any other party to the transaction.

(b) The trustees must advertise the proposed disposal for such period and in such manner as the qualified surveyor advises. However, this requirement will not apply if the surveyor has advised that it would not be in the best interests of the charity to advertise the proposed disposal.

(c) The trustees must consider the surveyor's report and satisfy themselves that the proposed terms of disposal are the best that can be reasonably obtained.

As originally drafted, the Bill provided that the trustees had to meet in person to consider the disposal. That is no longer necessary. It will, therefore, be possible for the trustees to delegate the decision whether or not to dispose of land to a sub-committee of the trustees. Moreover, that sub-committee does not need to meet; it will be sufficient if its members duly consider the surveyor's report and decide in the light of the report that they are satisfied that the terms offered are the best that can be reasonably obtained.

Earl Ferrers commented for the Government:

'I have no doubt that it is right that trustees must have the final responsibility for approving the terms of any sale and in seeing that the new statutory requirements have been complied with. But this need not be at a meeting of the trustees. The governing instrument of the charity may contain powers to delegate certain

functions of the trustees to a committee of their number. We see no reason why the trustees should not set the policy for disposals and then delegate decisions in this area to a committee of their numbers who would report back to the trustee body at regular intervals.'
(HL Deb, Vol 535, col 416 (6 February 1992).)

6.5 Exemptions from the General Rule in s 32(3)

Leases under seven years

6.5.1 Charities were concerned that the requirements of s 32(3) of the 1992 Act, as originally drafted, were excessively onerous in the case of granting short-term leases. The Government agreed. Section 32(5) now provides that where a charity proposes to grant a lease of not more than seven years, the charity trustees must:

(a) obtain and consider the advice on the proposed disposition of a person (not necessarily a qualified surveyor) who is reasonably believed by the trustees to have the requisite ability and practical experience to provide them with competent advice on the proposed lease; and
(b) decide that they are satisfied, having considered that person's advice, that the proposed terms are the best that can be reasonably obtained.

Earl Ferrers commented, when introducing the amendment that led to this subsection:

'In Committee there was some anxiety that the regime that was imposed by Clause 32 [now s 32] on trustees for disposals of charity land should be more flexible in the case of short leases. I accepted then that the arguments in favour of relaxing the regime to short leases were strong. I have no wish either to be inflexible or to saddle trustees with undue and burdensome requirements which are simply not justified by transactions at hand. These amendments therefore introduce a less strict regime for those kinds of leases.

On the other hand, we need to ensure that trustees act responsibly in the administration of their trust. Therefore, their duty to get the best rent available on the grant of a lease is properly reflected in these new provisions which will replace Section 29 of the Charities Act 1960. For leases of 7 years or less these amendments will allow trustees to take advice more appropriate to the transaction concerned from someone who need not be a qualified surveyor but who they reasonably consider has the appropriate expertise to give them advice before deciding whether the terms are the best available. Such advice need not be in the form of a written report.' (HL Deb, Vol 535, cols 415–416 (6 February 1992).)

Disposals of functional land

6.5.2 Additional requirements apply by virtue of s 32(6) to land which is held by a charity to be used for the purposes or any particular purposes of the charity. This is called functional land. Section 32(5) applies to disposals of functional land held for a term of lease under seven years. In the case of other disposals s 32(3) applies.

Functional land cannot be sold, leased or otherwise disposed of unless the charity trustees have previously:

(a) given *public notice* of the proposed disposal, inviting representations to be made to them within a time specified in the public notice, being not less than one month from the date of the notice; and

(b) taken into consideration any representations made to them within that time about the proposed disposition.

There is no need for a public notice if the charity intends either to replace the land disposed of with other property which is to be held on the same trusts or if the disposal is the granting of a lease of under two years.

Questions may arise about the distinction between an advertisement of the proposed disposal under s 32(3) and the public notice of the proposed disposition of functional land under s 32(6). Clearly, a public notice is a form of advertisement, although it goes further in inviting representations to be made (s 32(6)(i)).   The form of the public notice is not prescribed by the 1992 Act nor will it be in any future regulations. Therefore, the trustees must decide on an appropriate form of public notice. No doubt the notice could incorporate the advertisement (if necessary).

Functional land – leases of less than two years

6.5.3 No public notice has to be given in the case of functional land of less than two years (s 32(7) of the 1992 Act). This was introduced by the Government after much pressure, particularly from the churches.

Functional land – Exemption orders

6.5.4 Under s 32(8), the Commissioners may direct that the charities may be exempted from the obligation to advertise disposals of functional land. The Commissioners will make the order if they are satisfied that this would be in the interests of the charity. The charity must apply in writing to the Commissioners for such a direction.

This was a late amendment to the Act and followed representations by Lord Chorley as Chairman of the National Trust, who commented, at the report stage of the Bill:

'The problems so far as concerns the National Trust can be put quite simply. The statutory objects of the Trust are to own and manage property for conservation. The great bulk of that property is held inalienably; that is to say, it may never be sold. In this respect the National Trust and the National Trust for Scotland are unique in this Bill. The Trust is now a very large landowner and I feel that I should give some figures to demonstrate the problem. We own, for example, more than 6,000 inalienable cottages; we have more than 12,000 farm tenancies and there are wayleaves, easements and so forth. Altogether we estimate that we have about 10,000 separate let properties that will be affected by sub-section (6). Properties are let for relatively short terms – the cottages, typically for eight years. What all this means is that we are dealing with up to 1,000 dispositions, to use the phrase, a year. In other words we will be required to issue about 1,000 public notices every year. That would involve heavy expenditure in advertising, in staff time, which is expensive and in management delay. And one is bound to ask; to what end? These are matters – I emphasise this – of routine property management in almost all cases of modest size; for example, cottage lease renewals. I find it hard to believe that advertising would serve in this respect any useful purpose.' (HL Deb, Vol 535, cols 418–419 (6 February 1992).)

It must be emphasised that s 32(8) only exempts charities from the requirements of s 32(6) (ie disposals of functional land). It does not exempt them from the requirements to comply with s 32(3) or 32(5).

Exemption in respect of disposals to charities

6.5.5 A charity does not need to comply with s 32 in the case of the disposal of land to another charity at a price which is not the best price that can be reasonably obtained. This exemption only applies if the disposal is in fulfilment of the trusts of the charity making the disposal.

Exemption in respect of the grant of leases to beneficiaries of a charity

6.5.6 Section 32(9)(c) makes it clear that s 32 does not apply in the case of the grant by a charity of a lease to a beneficiary of that charity where the lease:

(a) is granted otherwise than for the best rent that can be reasonably obtained; and
(b) is intended to enable the premises to be occupied for the purposes of the charity.

This subsection was introduced at the report stage of the Bill after concern had been expressed at the committee stage, particularly in relation to the grant of leases by alms houses charities to beneficiaries. Earl Ferrers commented:

'A number of charities have trusts which provide for leases to be granted to beneficiaries who occupy charity property in furtherance of its objects. Such charities may provide charitable relief for housing for the poor or other disadvantaged in society. Very often such leases are for less than a market rent.
It would be entirely inappropriate for the provisions of Section 32 to apply to those cases. The Section is designed to ensure that the trustees obtain the best price when disposing of charity property. Where the lease is to a beneficiary of the charity, that criteria clearly should not apply.' (HL Deb, Vol 535, cols 420–421 (6 February 1992).)

6.6 Section 33 Statements

6.6.1 Under s 33 of the 1992 Act, any contract for the sale or lease or other disposition of land which is held by a charity and any conveyance, transfer, lease or other instrument, eg a deed, effecting a disposal of such land must state:

(a) that the land is held by or in trust for a charity;
(b) whether the charity is an exempt charity and whether the disposition is one falling within s 32(9); and

(c) if it is not an exempt charity and the disposition does not fall within s 32(9), that the land to be disposed of is land to which the restrictions on disposition contained in s 32 apply.

Hence, to comply with s 33(1), the information contained in the following example must be given.

'BACKGROUND

(a) the vendor, which is a charity, is the beneficial owner of the land; (*or in the case where land is held by custodian trustees*) the vendor is trustee of the land for XYZ which is a charity;

(b) the vendor is/is not an exempt charity as defined in s 45(1) of the Charities Act 1960;

(c) the land does/does not fall within any of the provisions of s 32(9) of the Charities Act 1992;

(d) (*in the case of any charity which is not an exempt charity*) the land is land to which s 32 of the Charities Act 1992 applies.'

This wording is only a suggestion. The Land Registry will stipulate the form of the statement for registered land.

6.6.2 By s 33(2), the charity trustees have to certify, in the instrument by which the disposition is effected, either:

(a) that the disposition has been sanctioned by an order of the court or of the Commissioners (as the case may be); or

(b) in the case of a transaction under s 32(2), that the charity trustees have power under the trusts of the charity to effect the disposition and that they have complied with the provisions of that section so far as applicable to it.

Does the certificate in the conveyance, transfer, lease or deed disposing of the land have to be signed by all the trustees? Section 33(2) requires that the 'charity trustees shall certify in the instrument etc'. This is different from the requirement under the stamp duty legislation, where the instrument must contain a statement concerning the value of the transaction.

Do the charity trustees have to sign the certificate themselves or is it sufficient for the instrument to contain a certificate which could read as follows?

'It is certified that the charity trustees of the vendor have power under the trusts of the vendor to effect the provisions of this deed and that they have complied with the provisions of s 32 of the Charities Act 1992 so far as applicable to this deed.'

Under s 34 of the Charities Act 1960, trustees of an unincorporated trust may sanction two or more trustees to execute documents in the names and on behalf of the trustees. Hence, trustees so empowered should be able to sign the s 33(2) certificate. In the case of an incorporated charity, two trustees can usually witness the execution of documents. The implication of this must be that the certificate can be in the deed and requires no additional signatures from the trustees.

6.6.3 If s 33(2) has been satisfied, any person who later acquires an interest in the land for money or money's worth may presume that the facts were as stated in the certificate.

6.6.4 If land is disposed of which is subject to s 32(1) or s 32(2), but s 33(2) has not been complied with, ie the charity trustees have not given a certificate, the disposal of the land is still valid in favour of a person who, in good faith, acquires an interest in the land for money or money's worth. This is so notwithstanding that the requisite court order or Commissioners' order has not been obtained or that the charity trustees have failed to comply with s 33(2).

6.6.5 If, on a disposal of land by a charity, the land will be *acquired* by a charity or held in trust for a charity, both the contract for the sale or lease or other disposition and any conveyance, transfer, lease or other instrument has to state:

(a) that the land will, as a result of the disposition, be held by or in trust for a charity;
(b) whether the charity is an exempt charity; and
(c) if it is not an exempt charity, that the restrictions on disposition imposed by s 32 will apply to the land.

Hence, if charity A is disposing of land to charity B, the conveyance or other documents of transfer, as well as the contract, will, in addition to the other requirements (see **6.6.1**), have to contain words such as:

'BACKGROUND

(a) the purchaser is/is not an exempt charity;

(b) (*if it is not an exempt charity*) the restrictions on disposition of land imposed by s 32 of the Charities Act 1992 will apply to the land hereby conveyed.'

This wording is only a suggestion. The Land Registry will stipulate the form of the statement for registered land.

6.7 Controls on Mortgages by Charities

6.7.1 The Woodfield Report made no recommendation for mortgages and charges by trustees. Section 29 of the 1960 Act applied equally to mortgages as to other disposals of land.

In the White Paper, the Government proposed to give trustees a general power to borrow money on the security of a mortgage without the Commissioners' consent. Before creating any mortgage or charge, however, the

Government wished trustees to be obliged to obtain and consider 'proper advice' on:

(a) whether the terms of the proposed borrowing are reasonable having regard to the charity's circumstances;
(b) the charity's ability to repay the sum borrowed on the terms proposed; and
(c) whether the borrowing is properly needed for the purposes of the charity.

6.7.2 As in s 32, with disposals of land under s 34(1) the general rule is that there can be no mortgage of land held by a charity without an order of the court or of the Commissioners. This rule does not apply to exempt charities.

6.7.3 Equally, the rule in s 34(1) does not apply if s 34(3) (see below) has been complied with. This derogation applies only to a mortgage of land by way of security for the repayment of a loan. It would not apply to the grant of a mortgage to secure any other obligation, eg a guarantee. If s 34(3) has been complied with, the charity trustees do not need the Commissioners' consent. However, before executing the mortgage they must obtain and consider proper written advice.

Under s 34(3) that advice must cover:

(a) whether the proposed loan is necessary;
(b) whether the terms are reasonable; and
(c) the ability of the charity to repay, on those terms, the sum proposed to be borrowed.

6.7.4 Who can give the proper advice? It need not be a qualified surveyor (as defined in s 32(4)). Instead, the advisor must:

(a) be reasonably believed by the charity trustees to be qualified by his ability in and practical experience of financial matters; and
(b) have no financial interest in the making of the loan in question. The person who gives the advice can be an employee, a trustee or an officer of the charity.

6.7.5 Surprisingly, the restrictions on disposals of land to connected persons do not apply in the case of mortgages to secure moneys borrowed from a connected person. Accordingly, such a transaction does not require the consent of the Commissioners if s 34(3) is complied with.

6.7.6 Under s 34(5), s 34 does not apply to any mortgage which has been authorised under s 32(9)(a). That refers to matters authorised by any statutory provision contained in or having effect under an Act of Parliament or by any scheme. Hence, if a category of mortgages for charities is exempted either by an Act of Parliament or by statutory instrument in the future or by a scheme, the requirements of s 34 will not apply to those types of mortgages.

Section 35 statements

6.7.7 Under s 35, any mortgage of land held by or in trust for a charity must state:

(a) that the land is held by or in trust for a charity;
(b) whether the charity is an exempt charity and whether the mortgage falls within s 34(5) (see **6.7.6**); and
(c) if it is not an exempt charity and the mortgage is not within s 34(5) that the mortgage is one to which the restrictions imposed by s 34 apply.

6.7.8 The Land Registry will stipulate the form of statement in the case of registered land. In the case of unregistered land the statement might read as follows:

'(a) the land hereby mortgaged is held by a charity;
(b) the charity is/is not an exempt charity as defined in s 45(1) of the Charities Act 1960;
(c) the mortgage does/does not fall within s 34(5) of the Charities Act 1992; and
(d) the mortgage falls within s 34 of the Charities Act 1992' (*this only applies if the charity is not an exempt charity or the mortgage does not fall within s 34(5)*).

6.7.9 By s 35(2), if the provisions in either s 34(1) or (2) apply, then the charity trustees have to certify in the mortgage either:

(a) that the mortgage has been sanctioned by an order of the court or the Commissioners; or
(b) that the charity trustees have power under the trusts of the charity to grant the mortgage and that they have obtained and considered such advice as is mentioned in s 34(2).

The certificate could read as follows:

'It is hereby certified that the charity trustees of the vendor have power under the trusts of the vendor to grant this mortgage and that they have complied with the provisions of s 34(2) of the Charities Act 1992.'

Section 35(3) and (4) provides for good title to be given to anyone who acquires an interest in charity land where s 34(2) has been complied with. If it has not been complied with, but a person acquires the charity land in good faith and for money's worth, the mortgage shall be deemed valid notwithstanding a breach of s 34.

CHAPTER 7

CHARITY INVESTMENTS AND THE OFFICIAL CUSTODIAN FOR CHARITIES

Introduction: Common Deposit Funds: Trustee Investments Act 1961: Apportionment of Funds: Permitted Investments: Application to Scotland: The Official Custodian for Charities: Divestment from the Official Custodian

7.1 Introduction

The 1992 Act makes important changes to the investment powers of charities and to the legal and administrative arrangements for holding charity investments. An attempt was also made to secure an amendment to the Charities Bill to give charity trustees power to delegate the exercise of their investment powers, subject to conditions to be specified in regulations made by the Secretary of State. However, the amendment was lost. Trustees still lack a power of delegation unless it is provided for in the governing instrument of their charity.

7.2 Common Deposit Funds

7.2.1 The Commissioners have made a number of schemes, under s 22(1) of the 1960 Act, to set up common investment funds. These are essentially pooling arrangements, enabling charities to transfer property into a common investment fund which is invested under the control of the trustees of the fund. A common investment fund operates in much the same way as a unit trust fund. Surprisingly, s 22 did not permit the Commissioners to set up free-standing, common deposit funds, by which charities could pool money to be placed on deposit at a more advantageous rate of interest.

7.2.2 This omission is rectified by s 16 of the 1992 Act, which introduces a new s 22A into the 1960 Act, permitting the court or the Commissioners, on the application of two or more charities, to make schemes to establish common deposit funds. The provisions of s 22 of the 1960 Act, relating to common investment funds, are extended to the new common deposit funds. As a result, every charity is empowered to invest in common deposit funds, unless their trusts specifically exclude such investment.

7.3 Trustee Investments Act 1961

7.3.1 The Trustee Investments Act 1961 ('the 1961 Act') extended the scope of authorised investments for trusts, with statutory powers of investment, whether private trusts or charitable trusts. Under that Act, it was possible for trustees to invest in equities, provided that they first divided the trust fund into two equal parts, the 'narrower range' part and the 'wider range' part. The trustees could invest the wider range part in equities, but such investments were restricted to securities issued in the UK, in a company incorporated in the UK with a total issued and paid-up share capital of at least one million pounds. The company must also have paid a dividend on all shares issued by it, in each of the five years immediately preceding the calendar year in which the investment was made.

7.3.2 The operation of the 1961 Act has been the subject of increasing criticism over the years. Comparative studies of the performance of equities and gilts indicated that the value of fixed interest assets had been undermined by high levels of inflation, whereas equities had, by and large, kept pace with inflation. A charity required by the statutory powers of investment to divide capital into two equal parts before investing in equities was bound to see its capital devalued. The provisions of the 1961 Act had also failed to take account of the developments in investment practice which had taken place since 1961. This was recognised by Sir Robert Megarry in *Trustees of the British Museum v Att-Gen* [1984] 1 All ER 337. There was mounting pressure to amend the provisions of the Act, particularly in their application to charities which were more likely than private trusts to be restricted to the statutory powers of investment. The Government conceded to pressure during the passage of the Charities Bill through the House of Lords, to include provisions which would enable the 1961 Act to be modified by subordinate legislation in so far as they applied to charities.

7.4 Apportionment of Funds

Section 38 of the 1992 Act empowers the Secretary of State (in this case the Secretary of State for the Home Department – the Home Secretary) by order to vary the apportionment required by s 1(2) of the Trustee Investments Act in so far as it applies to charities. The order might, for example, permit charity trustees to apportion their fund on a 25:75 basis between respectively narrower range and wider range investments. (Any such order will not alter the investment powers of any private trust caught by the restrictive investment powers of the 1961 Act.)

Section 38(2) provides that the revised apportionment will apply to future and existing charitable funds restricted to the statutory power of investment. Newly acquired capital, for example a legacy, may be divided according to the new ratio. Equally, funds which have already been divided 50:50 between narrower and wider range may be re-divided according to the new ratio.

Example

> Trustees may have divided the property of the charity into two equal parts, in accordance with the 1961 Act, in order to invest one half in wider-range investments. As a result of the better performance of equities, the wider-range part may have grown to represent 60 per cent of the trust fund, so that the actual apportionment between narrower- and wider-range is 40:60. (There is no obligation under the 1961 Act to maintain equality between the two halves.) If an order is made by the Home Secretary under s 38(1) to permit an apportionment of 25:75 between narrow- and wider-range, the trustees may re-divide their fund according to the new ratio, so freeing a further 15 per cent of the fund for investment in equities.

7.5 Permitted Investments

7.5.1 As mentioned in **7.3.2**, the range of investment permitted by the 1961 Act failed to take account of developments in investment practice since 1961 or the new range of investment opportunities open to charity trustees with wider powers of investment, for example direct investment in land, investment in shares of newly privatised state undertakings and investment overseas, particularly in the other states of the European Community.

Section 39 of the 1992 Act empowers the Secretary of State, by regulations (with the consent of the Treasury), to extend the range of investments authorised for charity investment beyond the range permitted for trustee investment in the 1961 Act. The regulations may specify what proportion of a charity's property may be invested in the new range or in any particular investment within the new range and may impose requirements for obtaining and considering advice before investment. For example, regulations might permit investment in the European Community on the same basis as investment in UK Equities but:

(a) restrict the proportion of a charity's funds which may be invested in this way;

(b) restrict the percentage of funds which may be invested in any one state; and

(c) require the trustees to obtain specialist advice on investing overseas.

The underlying purpose would be to ensure that the funds were diversified and that the trustees received proper advice when making and reviewing their investments.

7.5.2 Under s 39(4), the new forms of investment envisaged by the regulations will be open to any charity unless its trusts specifically exclude such investment or unless it is prohibited from making such investment by a contrary intention in an Act of Parliament or in a statutory instrument under an Act. For example, the trusts of a charity may specifically exclude any form of investment other than investment in ethical unit trusts. This charity could not take advantage of any new forms of investment permitted by the regulations. The regulations themselves, introducing the new forms of investment, may also exclude certain categories of charity from exercising the new powers. For example, if regulations permitted investment overseas, charities below a certain size might be excluded.

7.5.3 The power to make regulations under s 39 of the 1992 Act relates to the powers of investment of charities generally, rather than to any particular charity. If the charity trustees of a charity wish to extend the range of investment open to them and have no power to amend the administrative provisions of their trust, they should seek a scheme from the Commissioners under s 18 of the 1960 Act.

7.6 Application to Scotland

The Trustee Investments Act 1961 applies to trusts throughout the UK, whereas the Charities Act 1992 is, for the most part, concerned with charities in England and Wales. Sections 38 and 39 are two of the few exceptions. Any order or regulations made under those sections will apply to charities in Scotland (a charity being defined as a recognised body within the meaning of s 1(7) of the Law Reform (Miscellaneous Provisions) (Scotland) Act 1990).

7.7 The Official Custodian for Charities

7.7.1 The official custodian for charities was established by s 3 of the 1960 Act as a corporation sole, with the functions of holding land and investments for charities. As the holder of investments, the official custodian provided useful services to charity trustees. These included avoiding the need to transfer title to newly appointed trustees, receiving and paying to trustees dividends and interest without deduction of tax (so that there was then no need for the trustees to reclaim tax), informing trustees when investments were due for redemption and being a source of general advice on investment matters. The official custodian was not, however, permitted to advise on any particular investment decision.

The services of the official custodian were provided free of charge.

7.7.2 At the time of the White Paper, it was estimated that the official custodian's holdings amounted to approximately 1.25 billion pounds, involving almost 40,000 charities. The White Paper recommended that the official custodian should cease to hold investments on behalf of charities except in special circumstances but that the land-holding function should continue, as should the function of holding investments in order to protect a charity.

7.8 Divestment from the Official Custodian

7.8.1 Despite opposition to these proposals, ss 29 and 30 of the 1992 Act provide statutory authority to divest the official custodian of investments held on behalf of charities.

(a) Section 29(1) authorises the official custodian to divest himself of all property except land or property vested in him by an order made under s 20 of the 1960 Act for the protection of a charity.

(b) The investments may be returned to the charity trustees or to a person nominated by the charity trustees to receive and hold the property.

 A nominee must be either an individual resident in England and Wales or a body corporate which has a place of business in England and Wales.

 It is inadvisable to transfer investments to one single individual. The trustees should request that investments be transferred instead to two or more of their number, to a holding company or to a body corporate entitled to act as a custodian trustee under the Public Trustee Act 1906. A body corporate entitled to act as custodian trustee will be entitled, by s 4(3) of the 1906 Act, to charge fees not exceeding those chargeable by the Public Trustee. In all other cases, unless the trusts of the charity authorise the remuneration of a trustee, no payment may be made. This follows the rule established since *Robinson v Peet* (1734) 3 P Wms 249, that a trustee should act gratuitously.

(c) Section 29(4) empowers the Commissioners to make directions for the process of divestment to be effected in stages and to make directions for dealing with different types of holding in different ways. Some types of holding can be transferred in kind to the charity trustees or their nominees and others can be realised and the proceeds of the sale returned to the charity trustees or their nominees.

7.8.2 The Charity Commission will publish guidance for trustees, advising on how the programme of divestment is to be achieved. It is expected to start on 1 January 1993 and to last for three years. The White Paper proposed the following.

(a) The programme of divestment would proceed stock by stock, rather than dealing with each charity in turn.

(b) Equities and holdings in common investment funds would be returned in kind.

(c) Undated fixed interest securities (for example 3.5 per cent War Loan) would be realised and the proceeds remitted to each charity's bank account for re-investment. The justification for this apparent interference in the management role of charity trustees was that substantial amounts were held in undated fixed interest securities offering no prospect of capital growth and a reducing income in real terms. This indicated that the charity trustees had not regularly reviewed the investments of their charity. To realise the holdings would speed up and minimise the cost of divestment and encourage trustees of small charities to reconsider their investment policy.

(d) A middle course should be adopted for dated-fixed-interest securities, with the trustees of each charity being asked to state whether they wished the holding to be returned in kind or to be realised and the proceeds remitted for re-investment.

7.8.3 The White Paper recognised that one of the problems of divestment would be the discovery of a number of dormant charities where it would not be possible to trace the charity trustees in order to seek instructions or transfer holdings. Section 29(7) to (11) makes provision for dealing with the assets of dormant charities (see **9.5**).

7.8.4 When the Commissioners are satisfied that the official custodian has completed the programme of divestment, any remaining funds (excluding, of course, land and any property transferred for protection to the official custodian under s 20 of the 1960 Act) are to be paid by the official custodian into the consolidated fund.

7.8.5 The trusts of many charities provide for the property of the charity to be vested in the official custodian. Similarly, the Commissioners may have made schemes or orders requiring trustees to recoup permanent endowment, which has been expended for the purposes of the charity, by making payments into an accumulation account maintained by the official custodian. Section 30 of the 1992 Act overrides those provisions so that nothing in the trusts of a charity or in an order or scheme of the Commissioners will prevent the process of divestment in s 29. Furthermore, as soon as ss 29 and 30 come into force, a requirement in the trusts of a charity that the investments be held in the name of the official custodian will cease to have effect. The trustees will be able to transfer the investments of the charity (but not the interests in land) to a nominee or into the names of the trustees, without waiting for the official custodian's programme of divestment to run its course. The right of the Commissioners to require property to be transferred to the official custodian by order under s 20 of the 1960 Act, for the protection of the charity, is preserved.

CHAPTER 8

INCORPORATION: TRUSTEES AND CHARITABLE COMPANIES

Introduction: Incorporation and Trustee Liability: The Charitable Trustees Incorporation Act 1872: The 1872 Act Updated: Trust Companies: Status of Charitable Companies

8.1 Introduction

Incorporation may be relevant to a charity in one of two different ways. The trustee body may be incorporated, either under the Charitable Trustees Incorporation Act 1872 ('the 1872 Act') or as a company under the Companies Act 1985. Alternatively, the charity itself may be incorporated, either by royal charter or under statute, as a company or industrial and provident society. Incorporation of the charity, rather than the trustee body, is the more usual arrangement.

The 1992 Act amends the 1872 Act to facilitate the incorporation of the trustee body, but without limiting the liability of the individual trustees. It also develops the special body of law relating to charitable companies, setting them apart from commercial companies which operate for the benefit of shareholders.

8.2 Incorporation and Trustee Liability

8.2.1 An incorporated body has a legal identity of its own. It may acquire property, enter into contracts and incur liabilities in its own name, even though its affairs are managed by individuals. However, the issue of legal identity is distinct from the question of legal liability. Limited liability is not an automatic consequence of incorporation.

For charities, the issue of trustee liability is of increasing concern. This is partly because of a greater awareness among charity trustees of their responsibilities, but also because of the increased responsibilities being placed on trustees, as charities extend their activities to fulfil functions formerly undertaken by local authorities and other statutory bodies.

Where a body of charity trustees – as distinct from the charity – is incorporated as a company, the individuals will have the same protection from personal liability as they would if the charity itself were incorporated. If, however, the trustee body is incorporated under the Charitable Trustees Incorporation Act 1872, s 5 of that Act makes it clear that the trustees continue to be liable as if there were no incorporation (see **8.3.1**).

8.2.2 The White Paper addressed the issue of incorporation. However, its primary purpose was not to minimise the risk of personal liability for trustees but to ensure that charitable companies would be subject to regulation and supervision by the Attorney General and Charity Commission. It considered two possibilities.

(a) The creation of a new charity structure, fully under the Commissioners' jurisdiction but involving some form of incorporation coupled with limited liability.
(b) Provisions for the trustee body to be incorporated, with limited liability, but with the charity itself remaining as a charitable trust.

In fact, the 1992 Act adopts neither course. The Act amends the Charitable Trustees Incorporation Act 1872, to facilitate the incorporation of charity trustees, but without the benefits of limited liability. This meets a need created by the withdrawal of the investment-holding function of the official custodian for charities but does not answer questions about the potential liability of trustees.

However, during the passage of the Bill through the House of Lords, Earl Ferrers indicated that the Government was committed to exploring the problem of liability and possible solutions to it.

8.3 The Charitable Trustees Incorporation Act 1872

8.3.1 The 1872 Act provided a mechanism for trustees of an unincorporated charity, whether a trust or an association, to apply to the Commissioners for a certificate of incorporation, registering the trustee body as a corporate body. The power of the Commissioners to issue the certificate was discretionary and they could include, in the certificate, conditions and directions relating to the trustee body, eg the number of trustees, the method of appointment and term of office.

Section 5 of the 1872 Act made it clear that incorporation did not diminish the liability of trustees, stating:

> 'After a certificate of incorporation has been granted under the provisions of this Act all trustees of the charity, notwithstanding their incorporation, shall be chargeable for such property as shall come into their hands, and shall be answerable and accountable for their own acts, receipts, neglects, and defaults, and for the due administration of the charity and its property, in the same manner and to the same extent as if no such incorporation had been effected.'

8.3.2 The Act was little used. It was largely superfluous in view of the possibilities of:

(a) vesting property, whether land or investments, in the official custodian;
(b) incorporating the charity as a company limited by guarantee; or
(c) relying on the procedure in s 34 of the 1960 Act by which only two trustees need execute documents on behalf of all the trustees.

There was no advantage to be gained from incorporation under the 1872 Act.

8.4 The 1872 Act Updated

8.4.1 Section 48 and Sch 4 to the 1992 Act amend the 1872 Act, correcting the technical flaws and updating the provisions in the following ways.

(a) The Commissioners may issue a certificate of incorporation to charity trustees on the written application of the trustees, if they are satisfied that incorporation is in the best interests of the charity. The certificate may set out the conditions and directions relating to the constitution of the incorporated trustees and the method of appointing new trustees.

The Commissioners' powers under the 1872 Act apply to all charities, including exempt charities. However, the amended s 1(2) of the Act prevents a certificate being granted to the trustees of a charity which is required to be a registered charity under the 1992 Act, but which is not registered. No certificate is available for charity trustees who have failed in their statutory duty to register their charity.

(b) There is now power for the Commissioners to amend the certificate of incorporation. Under the new s 6 of the 1872 Act, they have power to initiate an amendment, provided that they inform the trustees of the proposed change and allow one month for the trustees to make representations. A new certificate of incorporation will be issued following the amendment. Although s 6 gives the Commissioners power to initiate an amendment, in the normal course of events change would be initiated at the request of the trustees, eg seeking some change in the constitution of the incorporated trustees, such as the number of trustees or length of term of office.

(c) Schedule 4, para 9, inserts a new s 12A into the 1872 Act. This gives the Commissioners power to dissolve an incorporated trustee body on the application of the trustees, if they are satisfied that this course is in the interests of the charity. Alternatively, the Commissioners may dissolve a trustee body on their own initiative if the incorporated trustee body has no assets or has ceased to operate or to exist. Section 12A provides that any assets held by the trustee body immediately before dissolution will be transferred either to the individuals who constituted the incorporated trustee body as trustees for the charity or to a person nominated by the trustees to receive the property.

8.4.2 Arrangements for the execution of documents on behalf of incorporated trustees are set out in the new s 12. There are three possible methods.

(a) If there is a seal, by affixing the seal.
(b) Whether or not there is a seal, a deed may be expressed to be executed by the incorporated trustees and signed by at least a majority of the trustees.
(c) Whether or not there is a seal, s 12(4) of the 1872 Act introduces a procedure similar to the procedure in s 34 of the 1960 Act, enabling the trustees to confer on any two or more of their number, power to execute a document on behalf of the incorporated trustees. This authority may be general, relating to any transaction approved by the incorporated trustees or it may be restricted to a particular transaction. The authority may be restricted to named trustees or it may require the signature of any two of the trustees.

A document which is executed by individual trustees under s 12 should make clear the basis on which they act, since a document which purports to be signed by a majority of the trustees or by two of the trustees acting under the authority of a resolution of the incorporated trustees is deemed to be properly executed in favour of any purchaser in good faith for valuable consideration. Appropriate clauses would be:

> 'This deed has been approved and ordered to be executed by resolution passed at a duly constituted meeting of the Incorporated Trustees of . . . and is intended to be executed by a majority of them.'

or

> 'This deed has been approved and ordered to be executed by resolution passed at a duly constituted meeting of the Incorporated Trustees of . . . and is intended to be executed by two of the trustees on whom acting under s 12 of the Charitable Trustees Incorporation Act 1872 the Incorporated Trustees of . . . have duly conferred a general authority to execute in the name of that body and on its behalf documents for giving effect to transactions to which it is a party.'

8.5 Trust Companies

8.5.1 Although it is rare for charity trustees to be incorporated, it is more common for a charity to have a company to act as nominee, to hold land and investments.

The trust company holds the assets of the charity to deal with in accordance with the instructions of the charity trustees. However, an ordinary trust company incorporated with power to act as trustee and to hold land, does not come within the statutory definition of a trust corporation. If charity land held by a trust company is sold, the payment of the proceeds of sale to the trust company does not, in itself, satisfy the rule of trust law that either two trustees or a trust corporation are required to give a good receipt for capital monies.

This problem does not arise when property is held by the official custodian (which is still a possibility where land is involved), nor to a corporate body authorised to act as custodian trustee under the Public Trustee Rules 1912, SR&O 1912/348. Paragraph 30 of those Rules includes any corporation incorporated under the Charitable Trustees Incorporation Act 1872 and any corporation authorised by the Lord Chancellor to act in relation to any charitable trusts as a trust corporation. However, few trust companies set up by individual charities to act as nominees, will satisfy these conditions.

8.5.2 Section 14 of the 1992 Act provides a solution to these difficulties. It introduces a new s 21A into the 1960 Act whereby a corporation appointed to act as trustee by an order of the Commissioners under s 18 or s 20 of the 1960 Act, will be included in the definition of trust corporations.

If charity trustees have appointed a trust company to act as nominee to hold property on behalf of the charity, it is advisable for the trustees to seek an order from the Commissioners under s 18 of the 1960 Act, to ensure that the nominee company is a trust corporation able to give a valid receipt for capital money arising on the sale of land.

An order would also be necessary in those cases where a corporate body, which is not a trust corporation, is to act as charity trustee, but an order is not required if the charity itself is a company. In those circumstances, the company is not acting as trustee but as the owner of the property.

8.6 Status of Charitable Companies

8.6.1 The White Paper expressed concern at the ability of the Attorney General and the Charity Commission to exercise their full supervisory role over charitable companies.

The 1960 Act had acknowledged the special status of charitable companies to some extent. Section 30(1) of that Act conferred on the Attorney General power to apply to the court to wind up a charitable company. Section 30(2) ensured that a company could not exercise its statutory power to amend its memorandum and articles of association, in order to divert property dedicated for the charitable purposes of the company to some other purpose.

Section 111 of the Companies Act 1989 went further by introducing three new sections into the 1960 Act: ss 30A, 30B and 30C.

Section 30A restricts the power of a charitable company to amend its objects without the prior approval of the Charity Commission.

Section 30B effectively excludes charities from the relaxation of the ultra vires rule, which enabled other companies in certain circumstances to undertake activities otherwise unauthorised by their memorandum and articles of association.

Section 30C requires a charitable company to declare its status on business letters and other documents.

8.6.2 The 1992 Act continues the special treatment of charitable companies in the following ways.

(a) Section 40 of the 1992 Act amends s 30A of the 1960 Act. It is now necessary to obtain prior written approval to amend the objects of a charitable company or any provision in the memorandum or articles of association which directs or restricts the manner in which the property of the charitable company may be used or applied (eg an amendment of the memorandum of association to permit the remuneration of a charity trustee). It is necessary to obtain the written consent of the Commissioners before the special resolution effecting the amendment is put to the general meeting and to send a copy of the Commissioners' written approval to the Registrar of Companies when filing a copy of the special resolution.

(b) Section 41 of the 1992 Act introduces a new s 30BA into the 1960 Act. A charitable company now requires the prior written approval of the Commissioners before approving certain arrangements for the benefit of directors or persons connected with a director, which are authorised by the Companies Act 1985 but which would be inconsistent with the normal rules of charity law. Normally, such arrangements will be contrary to the rule of charity law that trustees should not benefit from their charity (*Re French Protestant Hospital* [1951] Ch 567).

(c) Section 42 of the 1992 Act rectifies an anomaly by amending the Companies Act 1985 so that charitable companies are required to comply with s 349(1) of that Act to publish the company's name on business letters and other documents.

CHAPTER 9

SMALL CHARITIES AND DORMANT CHARITIES

Introduction: Amalgamation, Division and Amendment: Power to Spend Permanent Endowment: Dormant Bank Accounts: Dormant Investment Accounts

9.1 Introduction

9.1.1 There has been concern for many years about the effectiveness of small charities which have a small endowment fund, producing what is, in real terms, an ever-decreasing income. The Charities Act 1985 was intended to facilitate the modernising and amalgamation of small charities and in some cases the winding up of charities. However, the Act has been of limited use. Sections 43 and 44 of the 1992 Act now replace the 1985 Act.

9.1.2 There has also been concern about the existence of dormant charities which have ceased to function. The updating of the register, the increased reporting requirements and the process of divesting the official custodian are all likely to reveal numbers of dormant charities. Arrangements for disposing of the assets of dormant charities are set out in ss 18 and 29 of the 1992 Act.

9.2 Amalgamation, Division and Amendment

9.2.1 Section 43 of the 1992 Act confers on charity trustees the power to transfer property of a charity to one or more other charities, to amend the objects and administrative powers of a charity. Section 43 does not enable the trustees to spend the permanent endowment of their charity. This is dealt with in s 44 (see **9.3**).

9.2.2 Section 43 applies to a charity if the following three conditions are all satisfied.

(a) The gross income of the charity in its last financial year does not exceed £5,000. Gross income, as defined by s 1 of the Act, includes gross income from all sources, including special trusts (see **4.5.2**). (Section 43(11) confers on the Secretary of State power by order to amend the £5,000 threshold.)

(b) The charity does not hold any land subject to trusts which stipulate that the land must be used for the purposes of the charity (eg an almshouse charity or a village hall charity would be excluded, whereas a charity which holds land as an investment, producing income for the charity, would satisfy the condition).

(c) The charity is not an exempt charity or a charitable company.

Section 43(12) defines a charitable company to include a charity incorporated by royal charter. Industrial and provident societies are exempt charities. These charities do not need to rely on s 43, since they have mechanisms for amendment and dissolution in their governing instruments.

9.2.3 Section 43(2)(a) and (b) empowers charity trustees to resolve to transfer their charity's property to another charity or to divide the property among two or more charities if they are satisfied both that:

(a) the purposes of their charity have ceased to be conducive to a suitable and effective application of the charity's resources; and
(b) the purposes of any transferee charity are as similar in character to the purposes of their charity as is reasonably practicable.

A transferee charity must be a registered charity or an unregistered charity which does not require registration. A charity which should be registered, but is in breach of that statutory requirement, cannot benefit.

Section 43(2)(c) empowers charity trustees to resolve to modify all or any of the purposes of their charity or to change the purposes to other charitable purposes if they are satisfied both that:

(a) the existing purposes of the charity have ceased to be conducive to a suitable and effective application of the charity's resources; and
(b) the purposes specified in the resolution are as similar in character to those existing purposes as is practical in the circumstances.

Section 43(2)(d) empowers charity trustees to resolve to modify their administrative powers and procedures.

A resolution passed by charity trustees under s 43(2) must be approved by a majority of not less than two-thirds of those trustees voting on the resolution.

9.2.4 When a resolution has been passed in accordance with s 43, the charity trustees are required by s 43(7):

(a) to give public notice of the resolution in such manner as they think reasonable in the circumstances; and
(b) to send a copy of their resolution to the Commissioners, together with a statement of their reasons for passing it.

There is no prescribed form of notice, although guidance on an appropriate form may be given by the Commissioners and they are likely to do so in a booklet describing the s 43 procedures.

The Commissioners must indicate, within three months of receiving the resolution, that either they concur with the resolution or they do not. If they concur with the resolution to modify or replace the purposes of the charity or to amend the administrative powers or procedures of the trustees, the Commissioners should also specify the date when the resolution is to take effect. In reaching their conclusion, the Commissioners are entitled to call for further information or explanation from the trustees. They must also take into consideration any representations made to them by any person who appears to them to be interested in the charity (for example a trustee or potential beneficiary) and which are made within six weeks of the Commissioners receiving the resolution.

9.2.5 Where a resolution to transfer the property of the charity to one or more other charities has been passed, the trustees must make arrangements to effect the transfer. The Commissioners may assist in this process, at the request of the transferor charity, by making orders under s 43(10) to vest the property in the new trustees or in their nominees. The new trustees will hold the property on the trusts of their charity, but subject to any restrictions on expenditure which applied when the property was held by the transferor charity. So, if the property was permanent endowment of the transferor charity, it will remain permanent endowment in the hands of the transferee charity, even though the transferee charity has no other permanent endowment.

9.3 Power to Spend Permanent Endowment

9.3.1 Section 44 of the 1992 Act empowers trustees of certain small charities with a permanent endowment to spend the permanent endowment and so bring the charity to an end. To come within the scope of s 44, a charity must satisfy the following three conditions.

(a) The permanent endowment of the charity must not consist of any land. It does not matter whether the land is used for the charitable purposes of the charity or is only a source of income.
(b) The gross income in the last financial year of the charity must not have exceeded £1,000. Gross income is defined in s 1 of the 1992 Act to mean gross recorded income from all sources, including special trusts. Section 44(9) confers on the Secretary of State power, by order, to amend the threshold figure of £1,000.
(c) The charity must not be an exempt charity or a charitable company. As in s 43, a charitable company is defined to include a charity which is incorporated by royal charter (see **9.2.2(c)**).

9.3.2 Section 44 empowers charity trustees to resolve that their charity shall be free from restrictions against spending permanent endowments:

(a) if they are satisfied that the property of the charity is too small, in relation

to its purposes, for any useful purpose to be achieved by the expenditure of its income alone; and
(b) they have considered whether there is any reasonable possibility of transferring the property of the charity to one or more other charities, under s 43.

For this purpose the charity trustees must disregard the issue of whether the transfer to other charities, under s 43, would impose on the charity an unacceptable burden of costs. In fact, any costs of transfer should be minimal if the transfer is made by order of the Commissioners under s 43(10) (see **9.2.5**).

A resolution passed by charity trustees must be approved by a majority of not less than two-thirds of those trustees voting on the resolution.

9.3.3 Having passed the resolution, the trustees and the Commissioners must then follow a procedure similar to that set out in s 43 for giving public notice of the resolution and for obtaining confirmation that the Commissioners concur with the resolution (see **9.2.5**). The trustees' resolution is effective on the date specified by the Commissioners in their notification to the trustees that they concur with the resolution. The trustees may then apply both capital and income for the purposes of the charity and bring the charity to an end. If the charity is a registered charity, the Commissioners would remove the charity from the register, having received from the trustees their final report and accounts confirming that all capital has been expended.

9.4 Dormant Bank Accounts

9.4.1 A number of financial institutions, including banks and building societies, hold accounts in the name of a charity, but no transactions have been initiated in the account by the charity trustees for a number of years and the financial institution is unable to trace any of the trustees. The funds lie dormant, without achieving the purpose for which they are held. Section 18 of the 1992 Act provides a mechanism for these funds to be released for use by an active charity. For s 18 to apply the following conditions must be satisfied.

(a) The charity must not be an exempt charity.
(b) The account must have been dormant for five years immediately preceding the date on which the financial institution informs the Commissioners of the existence of the account. The account will be treated as dormant if no transaction has taken place in the account other than a payment into the account or a transaction initiated by the financial institution itself. For example, an account might exist which receives income on a regular basis, which is accumulated in the account. If no transaction takes place apart from the receipt of income and possibly the deduction of charges made by the financial institution holding the account, it is a dormant account.

(c) The financial institution must be unable, after making reasonable inquiries, to locate the charity or any of its trustees.

9.4.2 If these conditions are satisfied the financial institution should inform the Commissioners of the existence of the account and of its inability to trace the trustees or the charity. (Section 18(7) of the 1992 Act removes the normal obligation of confidentiality which would bind the financial institution and which might otherwise be an impediment to the operation of s 18.)

The Commissioners may direct the financial institution to transfer the funds to one or more charities specified by the Commissioners. In identifying transferee charities, the Commissioners are required to have regard to the purposes of the original charity if those purposes are known to them and to obtain written confirmation from the trustees of a transferee charity that they are willing to accept the property.

A transferee charity will hold the funds received from a dormant account for its purposes, but subject to any restrictions on expenditure (for example, as permanent endowment) which applied to the original charity. This assumes that the Commissioners will have sufficient knowledge about the transferor charity to know whether the funds were permanent endowment or not. Section 18 does not indicate whether there should be a presumption for or against permanent endowment when the status of the funds is unknown.

The receipt of the funds by the trustees of the transferee charity is a complete discharge to the financial institution.

9.4.3 There may be occasions when the procedure under s 18 is implemented, but the circumstances change subsequently, so that a transaction takes place in the dormant account, or the financial institution now has the means to trace the transferor charity or its trustees. Section 18(5) provides that if the Commissioners have made a direction under s 18, but it has not been implemented, the financial institution has a duty to inform the Commissioners, in writing, of the changed circumstances.

If it appears to the Commissioners that the account is no longer dormant, they are required to revoke the direction, so that no funds are transferred to the intended transferee charity. However, s 18 does not make any provision for the recovery of funds by the transferor charity if the financial institution has already implemented the Commissioners' direction. In those circumstances, the funds have become the property of the transferee charity and cannot be recovered.

9.5 Dormant Investment Accounts

The White Paper recognised that in the process of transferring investments from the official custodian to trustees, the official custodian would be unable to contact trustees of a number of charities. In order to complete the process of divesting investments, arrangement for dealing with the investments of dormant charities would be needed. The White Paper concluded that the most appropriate solution would be for the Commissioners to transfer the assets to some other charity with similar purposes, in accordance with the cy-près doctrine. The Commissioners' powers are contained in s 29(7) to (10) and are similar in many respects to the arrangements dealing with dormant bank accounts set out in s 18 (see **9.4**). Section 29(7) to (10) provides as follows.

(a) If the official custodian holds property in trust for a charity, but after making reasonable inquiries is unable to locate the charity or any of its trustees, he is required to sell the property, unless it is already money, and to hold the proceeds of sale or money pending instructions from the Commissioners.

(b) The Commissioners may direct the official custodian to transfer the money or proceeds of sale to one or more charities whose purposes are as similar in character to those of the dormant charity as is reasonably practicable. Before making their direction, the Commissioners must obtain written confirmation from the trustees of the transferee charity that they are willing to receive the amount proposed.

(c) The trustees of the transferee charity hold the funds for the purposes of the recipient charity, but subject to any restrictions on expenditure (for example, a permanent endowment), which applied to the funds in the hands of the transferor charity.

Section 29 does not make provision for the dormant charity, should it come to life, to recover property which has been transferred to another charity under the provisions of s 29(7) to (10).

CHAPTER 10

SCHEME-MAKING AND OTHER REFORMS

Introduction: Scheme Applications: Failed Charity Appeals: Ex Gratia Payments: Almshouse Contributions: Reverter of Sites Act 1987: Redundant Churches

10.1 Introduction

The impetus for the 1992 Act came from an acknowlegement that the role of charities had changed substantially since 1960. To minimise the possibility of abuse, the accounting and reporting procedures needed urgent improvement and a modern central data base was required to facilitate the monitoring of charities. At the same time, the opportunity was taken to modernise a number of procedures and statutory provisions affecting charities.

10.2 Scheme Applications

10.2.1 Section 18 of the 1960 Act confers on the Commissioners concurrent jurisdiction with the High Court for the following purposes:

(a) for establishing a scheme for the administration of a charity;
(b) for appointing, discharging or removing a charity trustee or trustee of the charity, or removing an officer or servant; and
(c) for vesting or transferring property, or requiring or entitling any person to call for or make any transfer of property or any payment.

The Commissioners cannot act on their own initiative, but only on an order of the court or on an application to apply under s 18 of the 1960 Act. Most applications are made by the trustees under s 18(4). This may not be possible if, for example, the trustees disagree among themselves or with the Commissioners over the need for a scheme, or if there are insufficient trustees to make a valid decision. Section 18(5) and (6) permitted applications from other sources, in certain circumstances, to overcome these difficulties, but its provisions had become outdated.

10.2.2 Section 13 of the 1992 Act amends the provisions of s 18 to facilitate the scheme-making process.

A scheme or order under s 18 of the 1960 Act may now be made by the Commissioners in the following circumstances.

(a) On the application of the charity trustees.

(b) In pursuance of an order of the court.

(c) On the application of the Attorney General, provided that the charity is not an exempt charity.

(d) If the total income of the charity from all sources does not exceed £500 a year, on the application of:

   (i) any one or more of the charity trustees;
   (ii) any person interested in the charity, for example a potential beneficiary;
   (iii) any two or more of the inhabitants of the area of benefit of the charity if the charity is a local charity.

   The sum of £500 may be varied by order of the Secretary of State either to take account of inflation or to bring more charities within the scope of this provision. As to the meaning of 'income from all sources', see **2.5**.

(e) A scheme for the administration of the charity (as distinct from an order appointing or removing trustees or removing an officer of the charity or an order dealing with property) may be made under s 18, as amended, in the following circumstances:

   (i) if charity trustees are willing to apply for a scheme, but are prevented from doing so because of a vacancy in their number, or the absence or incapacity of any of them, the Commissioners may make a scheme on an application of such number of the charity trustees as the Commissioners think appropriate. This avoids the need for the Commissioners to make a preliminary order to appoint trustees to comply with the requirements of the trusts of the charity, and then to invite those trustees to apply for a scheme to alter the trusts of the charity. The appointment of trustees and the alteration of the trusts can be dealt with in one document;

   (ii) if the Commissioners are satisfied that the charity trustees ought, in the interests of the charity, to apply for a scheme, but have unreasonably refused or neglected to do so and if the Commissioners have given the trustees an opportunity to make representations to them, the Commissioners may proceed to make a scheme on their own initiative without an application being made to them (s 18(6) of the 1960 Act as amended).

Section 18(6) does not apply to exempt charities.

If the charity trustees dispute the need for a scheme, they may either:

(a) institute proceedings in the High Court to seek directions as to whether they should apply for a scheme or not. (These proceedings would be charity proceedings under s 28 of the 1960 Act and would need to be authorised by an order of the Commissioners, although the trustees could appeal to the High Court against a refusal of the Commissioners to make an order.); or

(b) the trustees may wait until the Commissioners have made a scheme under s 18(6) and then exercise the statutory right to appeal to the High Court within three months of the making of the scheme under s 18(2). (Such an appeal requires a certificate from the Commissioners that the case is a proper one for an appeal (unlikely to be forthcoming in the circumstances) or the leave of one of the judges of the High Court attached to the Chancery Division.)

10.3 Failed Charity Appeals

10.3.1 From time to time a public charitable appeal fails to raise sufficient funds to carry out the intended purpose. Often, the trustees omit to include a provision to enable the funds which have been raised to be used for another charitable purpose.

Section 14 of the 1960 Act enables the Commissioners to make a scheme to apply the proceeds of a failed appeal for charitable purposes similar to those of the appeal. Section 15 of the 1992 Act supplements that procedure. A scheme may be made if:

(a) the funds fall within s 14(2) or (3) of the 1960 Act, so that the donor is presumed to be unidentifiable (for example, funds raised by street collections or through lotteries or competitions); or

(b) the donor cannot be traced after the trustees have published advertisements and inquiries. The Commissioners will, in subsequent regulations, prescribe the form of advertisement and inquiry; or

(c) the donor has executed a written disclaimer. That, too, will be in a form prescribed by regulations to be made by the Commissioners.

If a scheme is made, the charity trustees will not be liable to any donor who makes a claim outside any time limit prescribed by the regulations.

10.3.2 Unidentified donors have a right to reclaim property falling into category (b) above within six months of the date of a scheme (s 14(4) as amended by s 15(4) of the 1992 Act). Section 14(4) also enables the Commissioners to direct charity trustees to set aside a specific amount to meet such claims. If the amount set aside is insufficient to meet the claims, the Commissioners may authorise the trustees to reduce proportionately the amount paid to each claimant and to deduct expenses properly incurred by the trustees in dealing with claims. New s 14(4A) ensures that neither the expenses nor any shortfall become the personal liability of the trustees, but are deducted from the donors' funds.

10.4 Ex Gratia Payments

10.4.1 There are occasions when charity trustees believe they are under a moral obligation to make a payment to an individual, although the payment is not consistent with the purposes of the charity. These are known as ex gratia payments. In *Re Snowden and Re Henderson* [1969] 3 WLR 273, Cross J established that such payments could be authorised by the Attorney General or the court, and laid down an appropriate procedure to be followed to obtain authority.

10.4.2 Section 17 of the 1992 Act inserts a new s 23A into the 1960 Act, conferring on the Commissioners the power to authorise ex gratia payments. Their power is, however, subordinate to that of the Attorney General in three ways.

(a) The exercise of the power is subject to the supervision of the Attorney General, and must be exercised in accordance with any directions he may give. For example, he may direct the Commissioners not to exercise the power in particular cases (perhaps according to the value of the payment) or require them to consult him before they exercise their power.
(b) The Commissioners may, of their own accord, decide that a case should be referred to the Attorney General for decision.
(c) There is a right of appeal to the Attorney General against a decision by the Commissioners to refuse authorisation.

Any charity trustees wishing to make an ex-gratia payment should, in the first place, seek the consent of the Commissioners.

10.5 Almshouse Contributions

10.5.1 Almshouse charities are occupied by their residents under licence. The residents do not pay a rent, but make a weekly payment to the charity as a contribution to the cost of maintaining the almshouses and meeting the cost of essential services. In many cases, the authority for the trustees to charge weekly maintenance contributions has been conferred by a scheme made by the Commissioners, which also requires any changes in the weekly amount to be approved by the Commissioners.

The White Paper recommended an end to this practice. It took the view that the work of the Commissioners in approving increases in weekly maintenance contributions had become a matter of routine and was inappropriate, since it involved the Commissioners in management decisions which were a matter for the trustees.

10.5.2 Section 50 of the 1992 Act implements the recommendations of the White Paper. Any condition in the trusts of an almshouse charity requiring the Commissioners to specify, approve or authorise the amount (or the maximum amount) of weekly maintenance contributions, ceases to have effect. The basic power to make such charges continues, free of the condition. However, s 50 does not confer power to make charges where no power exists at present. Any almshouse charity in that position would need a scheme from the Commissioners to give the charity trustees power to charge.

10.5.3 Section 50(2) defines an 'almshouse charity' as a charity which is authorised, under its trusts, to maintain almshouses. 'Almshouse' is defined as any premises maintained as an almshouse, whether they are called an almshouse or not. These definitions are not particularly helpful. An almshouse charity is traditionally a charity providing housing for the poor, particularly the elderly poor.

If any charity trustees are in doubt about the status of their charity and whether they may rely on s 50, they may formally seek the advice of the Commissioners under s 24 of the 1960 Act.

10.6 Reverter of Sites Act 1987

10.6.1 The School Sites Act 1841, the Literary and Scientific Institutions Act 1854 and the Places of Worship Act 1873 encouraged landowners to give land for charitable purposes by granting a statutory right of reverter.

If, at any time in the future, the land ceased to be used for the purpose for which it had been given, the land would revert to the original owner or to his successors. In practice, the right gave rise to significant difficulties. When land ceased to be used for the charitable purpose for which it was given the trustees of the charity became trustees for the successors of the original landowner, who could not usually be identified or traced. The trustees were without power to sell the property or the means to repair it. The Reverter of Sites Act 1987 ('the 1987 Act') overcame this difficulty in part, by replacing the statutory right of reverter with a statutory trust for sale for the benefit of the successors of the original landowner, including powers to manage, repair and sell the land.

10.6.2 There is, however, a problem in relation to the statutory right of reverter and the statutory trust for sale under the 1987 Act. If the legal title to the land has been transferred to the official custodian, the official custodian becomes a trustee of land held subject to private non-charitable trusts as soon as the land ceases to be used for the charitable purpose for which it was given. This is inconsistent with the function of the official custodian to act as trustee of charity property. Section 31 of the 1992 Act provides that the Commissioners may, on their own initiative, make an order under s 18 of the 1960 Act if either of two conditions are fulfilled. These are:

(a) where a trust for sale has arisen under the 1987 Act; or
(b) in the opinion of the Commissioners a trust for sale under the 1987 Act is likely to arise at a particular time or in particular circumstances (ie a trust for sale is foreseeable).

The Commissioners' order will:

(a) discharge the official custodian; and
(b) transfer the title of the property into the names of the charity trustees or, if
    the trust for sale has already arisen, into the names of the individuals who
    were the charity trustees immediately before the trust for sale arose.

The Commissioners may, at the request of the charity trustees, transfer the
title into the names of other persons.

10.6.3 If a trust for sale has arisen under the 1987 Act, but the official
custodian has not yet been discharged by an order of the Commissioners,
s 31(5) makes clear that the powers of management and the liabilities under
the trust for sale fall on the trustees of the charity rather than on the official
custodian. The trustees may exercise all powers of management in the name
of the official custodian. However, s 31(6) also makes clear that the trustees
cannot sell the land while it remains vested in the name of the official
custodian. No sale can take place until the Commissioners have made an
order under s 18 of the 1960 Act to transfer the property into the names of
individual trustees, who will then receive the proceeds of sale.

10.7 Redundant Churches

10.7.1 As a general rule, trustees of a charity have a duty to dispose of land or
buildings which have been used by the charity, but which have ceased to be
suitable for its purposes, and to obtain the best price reasonably obtainable.
At one time, this rule presented a particular difficulty for buildings which
were classified as ancient monuments or buildings of historic or architectural
interest and which were used as places of public worship by religious
charities. If the building fell into disuse or was otherwise unsuitable for the
purposes of the charity, the trustees were required to sell to the highest
bidder, even though this might not be in the best interests of the continued
preservation of the building and public access to the building.

10.7.2 Sections 4 and 5 of the Redundant Churches and Other Religious
Buildings Act 1969 (amended by the National Heritage Act 1983) overcame
this problem, empowering the court or the Commissioners to make a scheme
to permit charity trustees to give or sell at an undervalue a redundant church
or place of public worship to the Secretary of State (acting under his power to
preserve buildings of historical or architectural interest and ancient monuments) or to the Historic Buildings and Monuments Commission for
England.
    There are a number of ancillary provisions enabling:

(a) adjacent land, for example a churchyard, to be disposed of in the same way;
(b) rights of way to be granted by the trustees to give necessary access,
    including public access;

(c) the Commissioners to make schemes to permit public worship to continue in the building, even if it is not by the original charity or according to its tenets of faith; and

(d) ancillary charities, whose purposes were to maintain and repair a redundant church, to continue to be used for the repair and maintenance of the building.

10.7.3 Section 49 of, and Sch 5 to, the 1992 Act, amend ss 4 and 5 of the 1969 Act. The power to give or sell premises at an undervalue to the Secretary of State or Historic Buildings or Monuments Commission for England, is extended to such a charity as may be prescribed by the Secretary of State. It is now open to the Secretary of State to transfer to certain charities the function of preserving redundant churches which are listed buildings of historical or architectural interest or ancient monuments.

Redundant churches and chapels of the Church of England situated in England are not governed by the 1969 Act, but by the Pastoral Measure 1983.

CHAPTER 11

CONTROL OF FUND-RAISING: PROFESSIONAL FUND-RAISERS

Introduction: Proposals for Reform: Control of Professional Fund-raisers: Charitable Institutions: Summary of Exemptions from the Definition of Professional Fund-raiser: What is a Professional Fund-raiser?: Examples of Professional Fund-raisers: Section 59 Agreements: Section 60 Statements: Future Regulations

11.1 Introduction

11.1.1 Until the 1992 Act comes into force there will have been only limited controls on fund-raising by or on behalf of charities. The 1939 House to House Collections Act regulated (as one might expect) house-to-house collections. Different rules applied, however, to street collections under the Police, Factories etc (Miscellaneous Provisions) Act 1916. In the background lurked the criminal law, in particular the Theft Act 1968. Under that Act any person guilty of abusing fund-raising can be prosecuted for:

(a) theft (defined as dishonestly appropriating property belonging to another); and
(b) fraud (defined as obtaining a financial advantage by deception).

11.1.2 Parliament has not addressed itself specifically to the problems of charity fund-raising since 1939. A huge number of new charities have been established. In 1965, when the compulsory registration of charities under the 1960 Act was underway, the number of registered charities was 57,500. At the date of the Charity Commissioners' 1991 Report (May 1992) the figure was 166,503.

11.1.3 Many of these charities are unendowed and are dependent on a wide range of sources of income, fund-raising being one. Many of the great household names in the voluntary sector (not just charities) are unendowed – for example Oxfam, World Wide Fund for Nature, Greenpeace and Friends of the Earth, which have all been started since 1939.

11.1.4 Fund-raising practices have developed and become more sophisticated in response to this rising tide of demand. Examples are the telethon, TV and radio appeals, sponsored activities etc, direct mail and telephone campaigns and mass charity concerts like Band Aid.

11.2 Proposals for Reform

11.2.1 Public concern about malpractice in fund-raising by charities has prompted a number of independent reviews of fund-raising practice. A working party of the National Council for Voluntary Organisations (NCVO) in 1985 reviewed the means currently available for protecting charities from dubious fund-raising practices and made recommendations. Its report was quoted, with approval, by the Woodfield Report of 1988. The working party identified the following abuses in particular:

(a) excessive sums retained by some fund-raising practitioners;
(b) claims that part of the proceeds from the sale of goods or services will go to charity when, in fact, the share given to charity is much smaller than donors might suppose; and
(c) dubious fund-raising practices, carried on in a charity's name but without its knowledge or approval.

The Woodfield Report and the White Paper

11.2.2 These particular abuses were considered by the Woodfield Report, which made the following recommendations.

(a) That it should be a criminal offence for fund-raising practitioners to deduct their remuneration (however calculated) from donations received before paying them to the charity, unless they could prove that their intention to do so was made clear to every donor. The White Paper rejected this but recommended that 'all those who receive funds raised for or on behalf of a charity should remit the full amount to the charity without deducting fees or expenses' (at p 56).

(b) That whenever goods or services were offered for sale with the indication that some part of the proceeds was to be devoted to charity, there should be specified:

(i) the charity or charities that were to benefit (and, if more than one, in what proportion);
(ii) the *manner* in which the sums they were to receive would be calculated.

In the White Paper, the government expressed its concern about the practicability of these proposals, and commented (at p 56):

'Basic details of the agreement reached between charity and the "co-venturer", should be provided, however, with some latitude being allowed as to the form of expression chosen. Under the kind of provision envisaged charity catalogues, for example, would be required to incorporate a simple, single, statement to the effect that X per cent of net profits, gross profits or receipts would go to the named charity or charities. Some formulae may be more complex. Even so, it should be possible to give some indication of their effect, by reference, for example, to the minimum proportion going to charity.'

(c) That a charity should be able, in certain circumstances, to obtain an injunction against the use of its name by a named person or organisation.

There was concern that this recommendation did not go far enough because the onus of detecting the abuse of its name and the initial liability for legal costs would fall on the charity. The charity might be able to recover some of its legal costs but this would be by no means certain, as it would depend, in each case, on the financial strength of the defendant. An alternative might have been a blanket ban on all fund-raising in a charity's name without its written consent. This alternative was rejected. If implemented, it would doubtless have destroyed local grassroots fund-raising initiatives – many people are moved, especially in cases of emergencies, to 'do their bit', raise money and send it off to the relevant charity. If such heartfelt responses had to be first processed through a bureaucratic mill they would no doubt be frequently stifled by the time the requisite written consent came through.

11.3 Control of Professional Fund-raisers

The recommendations of the Woodfield Report are important, for they form the basis of Part II of the 1992 Act. Part II is concerned to control, to a certain extent:

(a) the activities of professional fund-raisers;
(b) certain types of fund-raising practice (TV, radio and telephone appeals);
(c) the activities of people who sell goods or services and represent that a proportion is to go to charity; and
(d) the use of a charity's name by unauthorised fund-raisers.

It must also be emphasised that the 1992 Act only applies (save in certain very limited cases) to England and Wales. It does not apply to Scotland or Northern Ireland.

11.4 Charitable Institutions

11.4.1 It is vital to understand that Part II of the 1992 Act does not apply simply to charities but to *charitable institutions* as defined by the 1992 Act.
Section 58(1) defines a 'charitable institution' as:

'a charity or an institution (other than a charity) which is established for charitable, benevolent or philanthropic purposes.'

This wording follows the House to House Collections Act 1939. The definition includes registered charities and those charities which are *exempt* from registration under the Charities Act 1960 (such as Universities) and those charities which are *excepted* by statutory instrument from registration as charities (such as the Boy Scouts). Section 46 of the 1960 Act defines 'charitable purposes' as 'purposes which are exclusively charitable according to the laws of England and Wales'. An organisation established under the laws of another country, eg France, could qualify as an institution established for charitable purposes *provided* its objects were exclusively charitable under English law.

Hence, it must be emphasised that there is a very important and clear distinction between the two phrases, 'charitable purposes' and 'charitable institution'. When coupled with 'purposes', 'charitable' means exclusively charitable according to the laws of England. But when 'charitable' is joined with 'institution' it does *not* mean that. It means something much wider. It encompasses 'benevolent and philanthropic purposes' as well.

Benevolent

11.4.2 There is a dearth of reported cases on the meaning of 'benevolent and philanthropic' under the 1939 Act. The word 'benevolent' has been held to include purposes which are not exclusively charitable. It is defined in the Shorter Oxford Dictionary as 'of a kindly disposition, charitable, generous'. In 1891, Lord Branwen distinguished 'benevolent' and 'charitable' in *Income Tax Commissioners v Pemsel* (1891) AC 531.

> 'I think there is some fund for providing oysters at one of the Inns of Court for the Benchers. This, however benevolent, would hardly be called charitable.'

In Australia, a public benevolent institution has been construed to mean institutions which promote the relief of poverty, sickness, destitution or helplessness (see *Perpetual Trustee Co Ltd v FCT* (1931) 45 CLR 224).

This case is quoted in P Luxton 'Public Charitable Collections: the New Regime' *Charity Law & Practice Review* Vol 1992/93, Issue 1.

Philanthropic

11.4.3 In *Re Macduff* [1896] 2 Ch 481, a name whose Shakespearian connections hardly evoke philanthropy, Stirling J said (at p 481):

> '"Philanthropic" is no doubt a word of narrower meaning than "benevolent". An act may be benevolent if it indicates goodwill to a particular individual only; whereas an act cannot be said to be philanthropic unless it indicates goodwill to mankind at large. Still, it seems to me that "philanthropic" is wide enough to comprise purposes not technically charitable.'

Philanthropic is defined in the Shorter Oxford Dictionary to mean 'benevolent, humane'. Would this and the judgment in *MacDuff* be wide enough to include organisations such as Greenpeace or Friends of the Earth, which are primarily dedicated to preserving the environment (rather than 'mankind') as benevolent or philanthropic organisations? The phrase should be wide enough to cover the non-charitable work of Amnesty International or charitable-type organisations established in other jurisdictions concerned with mankind, eg Médecins sans Frontières, which, if not charitable under English law (see **11.4.1**), should fall within the definition of 'philanthropic'.

If, for example, Friends of the Earth is not a philanthropic organisation, then Parts II and III of the 1992 Act will not apply to it. However, in the discussions in the House of Lords on Part III of the 1992 Act, it was clear that their Lordships thought that Greenpeace was a philanthropic institution.

11.5 Summary of Exemptions from the Definition of Professional Fund-raiser

Fund-raising by any of the following is exempt from the controls of Part II of the 1992 Act.

(a) Charitable institutions (see **11.5.1**).
(b) Companies connected with charitable institutions (see **11.5.2**).
(c) Low-paid workers (see **11.5.3**).
(d) Collectors (see **11.5.4**).
(e) Celebrities (see **11.5.5**).

Exemption for charitable institutions

11.5.1 It is important to note that the controls introduced by Part II of the 1992 Act do not apply to direct fund-raising undertaken by a charitable institution. Equally, fund-raising by one charitable institution on behalf of other charitable institutions, eg the BBC's 'Children in Need Appeal' (itself a registered charity), is outside the 1992 Act. The definition of professional fund-raiser (s 58(1)) expressly excludes 'a charitable institution'.

Exemption for connected companies

11.5.2 This exemption of charitable institutions is further extended by s 58(2)(a) of the 1992 Act to *any company connected with a charitable institution* provided that company is not carrying on a fund-raising business (see **11.6.1**). If a company is connected with a charitable institution as defined in s 58(2)(a) but carries on a fund-raising business as defined in the first part of the definition of professional fund-raiser, that company can be a professional fund-raiser and subject to the controls set out in the Act even though it is connected with a charitable institution.

A company is defined in s 46 of the 1960 Act (as amended by the Companies Act 1989), as being 'a company formed and registered under the Companies Act 1985, or to which the provisions of that Act apply as they apply to such a company'.

A company is 'connected with' a charitable institution if the institution or the institutions and one or more other charitable institutions taken together, is or are entitled (whether directly or through one or more nominees) to exercise, or control the exercise of, the whole of the voting power at any general meeting of the company (s 58(5)).

Hence, trading subsidiaries or trading companies owned by a number of charitable institutions, eg to co-ordinate the sale of Christmas cards, are outside the scope of Part II of the 1992 Act. As originally defined, the Bill would have made charities' trading subsidiaries comply with the disclosure requirements in what is now s 60. As Lord Allen of Abbeydale pointed out in the Public Committee, National Trust Enterprises Limited sold over 11 million individual items and 1,600 lines of products in 1990. If the proposals in the Bill had been enacted this would have imposed a very considerable bureaucratic burden on the National Trust in particular and the charity sector in general.

Exemption for low-paid workers

11.5.3 When the Bill was first published there was considerable concern that the definition of 'professional fund-raiser' was so wide that it would include people who collected money for charity and were paid expenses and a nominal fee. The Government addressed these concern in s 58(3), which provides that a person is not a professional fund-raiser if he does not receive more than £5 per day or £500 per year by way of remuneration in connection with soliciting money or other property. The person paid £5 a day or less for 'rattling his tin' in the street is not, therefore, a professional fund-raiser. If someone is paid less than £5 per day or £500 per year *plus* expenses, he or she will still be within the exemption.

Section 58(3)(b) excludes from the definition anyone paid a small fee (£500 or less) for organising or otherwise undertaking other kinds of fund-raising events or activities for a charitable institution. So, for example, if a person is paid £400 for organising a garden fete at which he solicits money or other property for the benefit of a charitable institution he is not a professional fund-raiser.

However, some difficult questions could arise.

Example

Mrs Jones organises a garden fete for XYZ charity. She is paid £600 for doing so. At the garden fete solicitations for money are made by the stall holders who are not themselves professional fund-raisers. The fete is run by the charity and not by Mrs Jones. Mrs Jones is not responsible for the money. She has, therefore, not solicited money herself and s 58(3) of the 1992 Act requires her to solicit money, for that section to apply and for her to be treated as a 'professional fund-raiser'. Hence, even though Mrs Jones has been paid more than £500 per year she is not a professional fund-raiser. If, on the other hand, she was responsible for receiving the money under an arrangement with XYZ charity, she would be deemed to have solicited (see s 58(7)(b)), and (by virtue of being paid more than £500), would be treated as a professional fund-raiser.

Exemption for collectors

11.5.4 If a professional fund-raiser uses paid collectors or agents to solicit funds for a charitable institution, those collectors or agents are not themselves professional fund-raisers. They are, in effect, sheltered by the professional fund-raiser who contracts their services (s 58(2)(c)).

Exemption for appeals by celebrities

11.5.5 The first draft of the Bill caused concern that celebrities employed by professional fund-raisers or charitable institutions to make appeals on radio and television would be caught in the net of the professional fund-raiser definition. The Bill was amended.

Section 58(2)(d) excludes from its definition of professional fund-raiser for the purposes of s 58(1):

'any person who in the course of a relevant programme, that is to say a radio or television programme in the course of which a fund-raising venture is undertaken by:

(i)   a charitable institution; or
(ii) a company connected with such an institution,

makes any solicitation at the instance of that institution or company.'

Hence, even if a celebrity is paid to make an appeal on behalf of a charity, he will not be a professional fund-raiser.

11.6 What is a Professional Fund-raiser?

11.6.1 A professional fund-raiser is defined in s 58(1) as:

'(a) any person (apart from a charitable institution) who carries on a fund-raising business, or
(b) any other person (apart from a person excluded by virtue of subsection (2) or (3)) who for reward solicits money or other property for the benefit of a charitable institution, if he does so otherwise than in the course of a fund-raising venture undertaken by a person falling within paragraph (a) above.'

A *fund-raising business* is defined in s 58(1) as 'any business carried on for gain and wholly or primarily engaged in soliciting or otherwise procuring money or other property for charitable, benevolent or philanthropic purposes'.

Hence, the definition of professional fund-raiser includes people who for *gain* specialise 'wholly or primarily' in soliciting money, etc, for charitable institutions or who for *reward* solicit money otherwise than in the course of a 'fund-raising venture' undertaken by someone who runs a fund-raising business.

For the purposes of determining whether a business is a fund-raising business, 'wholly or primarily' engaged in soliciting, etc, money for charitable etc, purposes, presumably one must consider the overall activities of that business in the course of its financial year.

On the other hand, the person who is paid £501 for soliciting money or other property for a charitable institution will be a professional fund-raiser even if he does not carry on a 'fund-raising business', because he will be soliciting for reward. Equally, the business which carries on fund-raising activities for charitable institutions for reward but which does not do this 'wholly or primarily', will be caught under this second test.

'Otherwise procuring'

11.6.2 The phrase 'otherwise procuring' in the definition of fund-raising business requires consideration. Concern was expressed by Lord Swinfen at the report stage of the Bill that the definition could include outside agencies in support of charitable fund-raising. For example, is a direct mail house, which specialises in carrying out work for charitable institutions, 'otherwise procuring' money for the charitable institutions and, hence, a professional fund-raiser? Alternatively, is a company which specialises in writing advertising copy for charitable institutions a professional fund-raiser because it 'otherwise procures' money for charitable institutions through the power of its design of advertisements?

Earl Ferrers had earlier stated in the committee stage of the Bill on 11 December 1991:

> 'We do not want to catch as a professional fund-raiser the marketing consultant, for example, who gives advice to a charity on how it should prepare its fund-raising pamphlet, or indeed a direct mailing firm which might simply send out appeal letters on behalf of a charity, or another firm which might put the appeal notices in the envelopes. This type of indirect involvement does not fall within Clauses 57 to 60 [now ss 58 to 61] as they are currently drafted. These people, such as the ones who print the document, put it in the envelope and mail it are acting as contractors. They are providing a service to the charity in the same way as a catering contractor might provide food for the charity. It is not intended that those people should be caught. Only when a person falling within the definition of professional fund-raiser makes the solicitation himself will he be regulated by the Bill and rightly so.' (Public Bill Committee, Fifth Sitting, col 220 (11 December 1991).)

This statement begs a number of questions. The fact that a particular supplier is acting as a contractor is irrelevant. Professional fund-raisers are contractors. The crucial issue is: where does the boundary lie between a professional fund-raiser and someone who helps raise money for a charitable institution but who does not solicit money or other property? In other words, what does 'otherwise procure' mean? Lord Swinfen sought to have the words removed. He commented:

> 'In Committee my noble friend Lord Ferrers clarified the Government's intention with respect to that aspect of the Bill. He indicated that outside agencies contracting services to charities and other voluntary organisations in the course of their fund-raising activities would not be regulated under the Bill . . . In order to ensure that that intention is properly clarified on the face of the Bill and so as to allay the considerable anxiety which still exists within the charity sector in that respect, [this] amendment seeks to remove the words "or otherwise procuring" from the definition of the type of activity undertaken by fund-raising businesses.' (HL Deb, Vol 535, col 1201 (18 February 1992).)

Viscount Astor replied:

> 'The words are intended to deal with a situation where, although an appeal or a campaign is undertaken solely by a professional fund-raiser, the appeal literature appears to come from the charity itself with the name and address of the fund-raiser appearing, sometimes inconspicuously, as the recipient of donations and so forth. The key factor is that the fund-raiser is the agent who makes the appeal and gathers

in the funds. In such a case the reference to soliciting alone would probably be inadequate because the solicitation would appear to come from the charity even if, in reality, it was from the fund-raiser. The expression 'procuring' is used in preference to 'obtaining' in order to make clear that the fund-raiser in question must actively achieve the obtaining of funds for charitable purposes and not simply be a passive recipient by accident.' (HL Deb, Vol 535, col 1202–1203 (18 February 1992).)

One can sympathise with the Government's desire to ensure that professional fund-raisers do not try to avoid the Act's requirements by following the common practice of putting out fund-raising literature in the charity's name. On the other hand, there can be no doubt that the phrase 'otherwise procuring' could sweep up into the definition of professional fund-raiser certain types of activity which were not intended to be included, eg the writing of advertising copy if it is undertaken by a business which is 'wholly or primarily' engaged with the charitable sector. We must wait and see how the courts will interpret this phrase.

11.7 Examples of Professional Fund-raisers

A covenant renewal agency

11.7.1 Some charities employ the services of outside firms to organise their covenant renewals. These firms telephone covenantors to explain that their covenants have lapsed and ask them to renew. The donors send no money to the agency. It could be argued that the agency was merely performing a service on behalf of the charity, ie like a contractor. Clearly it is. But one needs to go further and ask 'what is the nature of that agency?'. Is the agency soliciting money for charitable purposes? The answer must be 'yes'. In soliciting covenants it is soliciting money. If that is the case, the agency is a professional fund-raiser and its relationship with the charity and the donors must comply with the 1992 Act.

Telephone appeals

11.7.2 A telephone appeal for charitable donations carried out by a telemarketing organisation will amount to fund-raising. The telemarketing organisation will be caught under the definition of 'fund-raising business' if it is 'wholly or primarily' engaged in soliciting money '. . . for charitable, benevolent or philanthropic purposes' (s 58(1)). What is the position if it is not 'wholly or primarily' engaged in soliciting money for charitable, etc, purposes, eg if it mainly does telemarketing on behalf of non-charitable institutions? The telemarketing organisation will still be subject to the 1992 Act, because the second limb of the definition of professional fund-raiser includes any other person who is not running a fund-raising business (see **11.6.1**) but 'who for reward solicits money or other property for the benefit of a charitable institution' (s 58(1)).

This is the case even if (as is usual) the telemarketing organisation requests that all payments be made to the charity or, alternatively, if a donor responds positively to the telephone appeal, that the agency sends the donor appeal literature and asks the donor to send the donation direct to the charity. It could be argued that the agency is like the contractor who prints a document, addresses it and posts it, and whom Earl Ferrers did not consider to be a professional fund-raiser (see **11.6.2**). As Earl Ferrers said in the same speech:

> '. . . only when a person falling within the definition of professional fund-raiser makes the solicitation himself will he be regulated by the Bill.' (Public Bill Committee, Fifth Sitting, col 220.) (11 December 1991).

'Solicitation' is extremely widely drafted in s 58(6) (see **11.9.3**) and must cover the telemarketing agency which will, therefore, be a professional fund-raiser for the purposes of the Act.

Secondees

11.7.3 Some organisations, eg banks, second their staff to work for charities. The bank continues to employ (and pay) the secondee. If the secondee solicits funds on behalf of the charity with whom he is working, is he a professional fund-raiser? He will be soliciting money and will be being paid (by his employer). Therefore, will he be soliciting money *for reward* (see **11.6.1**)? It could be that the secondee, in these circumstances, will be classified as a professional fund-raiser.

11.8 Section 59 Agreements

11.8.1 Broadly speaking, the 1992 Act introduces controls on professional fund-raisers which follow the recommendations of the White Paper (see **11.2**).

By s 59(1), 'it shall be unlawful for a professional fund-raiser to solicit money or other property for the benefit of a charitable institution unless he does so in accordance with an agreement with the institution satisfying the prescribed requirements'.

Hence, once the 1992 Act is in force, all professional fund-raisers will need to have an agreement with a charitable institution before they can attempt to solicit money or property for the benefit of that charitable institution. That agreement will have to conform to, as yet, unpublished regulations.

Section 59(1) uses the word 'unlawful'. Something may be unlawful in two senses:

(a) unenforceable by law; and
(b) punishable by law.

It is clear from the rest of s 59 that 'unlawful' is used here to denote unenforceability.

Breach of s 59

11.8.2 By s 59(3), the court may grant an injunction on the application of a charitable institution if it is satisfied:

(a) that any person has breached s 59(1) (ie a professional fund-raiser is soliciting money for the benefit of a charitable institution without having entered into a s 59(1) agreement); and
(b) that unless restrained, such a contravention is likely to continue or be repeated.

The court in question is either the High Court or a county court. In injunction cases, either court could be used.

11.8.3 Note that an agreement is not enforceable if a charitable institution enters into a s 59(1) agreement with a professional fund-raiser and the agreement does not comply with the prescribed requirements set out in the regulations. In that case, the agreement can only be enforced by the professional fund-raiser to such an extent (if any) as may be provided by an order of the court. Hence, it is imperative for professional fund-raisers that all agreements with charitable institutions conform exactly with the requirements of the regulations.

11.8.4 This is equally vital for charity trustees. For example, if a charity was to make payments to a professional fund-raiser under an agreement which breached s 59(1), that agreement would not be enforceable against the charitable institution without the order of the court (see s 58(4)), but the charity, nonetheless, might make payments under it. Could the trustees be held personally liable to reimburse the charity for payments made in breach of s 59(1) on the basis that the charity has suffered as a result of their negligence? The argument would be that, but for their negligence (in permitting payments under a non-enforceable agreement), the charity could have resisted paying out under the agreement, unless payment had been sanctioned by the court.

Enforceability

11.8.5 Section 59(5) makes it clear that any provision under an agreement between a charitable institution and a professional fund-raiser is only enforceable by the professional fund-raiser if:

(a) the agreement satisfies the prescribed requirements (ie it conforms to the regulations required by s 59(1)); or
(b) a court orders that the provision of the agreement can be enforced.

11.9 Section 60 Statements

11.9.1 Section 60(1) of the 1992 Act requires that where a professional fund-raiser solicits money or other property for the benefit of one or more particular charitable institutions, the solicitation shall be accompanied by a statement clearly indicating:

(a) the name or names of the institutions concerned, eg 'XYZ charity';
(b) if there is more than one institution concerned, the proportions in which the institutions are respectively to benefit, eg 'XYZ charity 50 per cent, ABC charity 50 per cent'; and
(c) (in general terms) the method by which the fund-raiser's remuneration in connection with the appeal is to be determined, eg 'the organisers of this appeal will be paid X per cent of the proceeds of the appeal'.

11.9.2 Section 60(2) deals with the situation where a professional fund-raiser is soliciting money or other property for charitable, benevolent or philanthropic purposes of any description, rather than for the benefit of one or more particular charitable institutions. Thus, it covers, for example, an appeal for 'Victims of Famine' or 'The Handicapped' rather than an appeal for Oxfam or Mencap (which falls within s 60(1)).

In this case, the professional fund-raiser has to accompany his solicitation with a statement clearly indicating:

(a) the fact that he is soliciting money or other property for those purposes, eg 'Famine' and not for any particular charitable institution;
(b) the method by which it is to be determined how the proceeds of the appeal are to be distributed between different charitable institutions; and
(c) (in general terms) the method by which his remuneration in connection with the appeal is to be determined.

11.9.3 Subsections (1) and (2) of s 60 raise similar issues and can be dealt with together.

It is worth emphasising the meaning of 'solicit'. Under s 58(6), soliciting can occur:

(a) by speaking directly to the person being solicited (whether in his presence or not) [hence, a solicitation can be made face to face, or by telephone]; or
(b) by means of a statement published in any newspaper, film, radio or television programme;
(c) 'or otherwise'.

Therefore, solicitations can be made in many different ways. Whenever a solicitation is made, a s 60(1) or (2) statement has to accompany it. If, for example, a professional fund-raiser organises a street collection, the collector will have to display the statement. If a professional fund-raiser arranges a charity ball, the tickets will have to bear the statement. If a professional fund-raiser arranges a telephone appeal, the statement will have to be given on each call. It will not be enough to send the statement with the appeal documentation to the potential donor.

11.9.4 How detailed does the s 60 statement have to be?
Earl Ferrers clarified the position:

> 'As regards the statement it will have to be true and correct. That is the first point. It need not go into the detail and precision that a test of accuracy would impose.
>
> I accept that such a test would be too rigid given the variety of fund-raising methods used. That is why I introduced the element of flexibility which is contained in these amendments. I appreciate that Clause 60 places new duties on professional fund-raisers and commercial participators. They will be at the bottom of what one might call a fairly daunting learning curve. It is only right that the Government should help fund-raisers along that new curve. I am happy to undertake that we shall, in consultation with practitioners, give appropriate help and guidance to them so that they do not fall into any unfortunate traps.' (HL Deb, Vol 535, cols 1206–1207 (18 February 1992).)

It should be noted that the 1992 Act is drafted in such a way that the form of statement will not be prescribed in regulations. However, by s 64(1) the Secretary of State may make such regulations as appear to him to be necessary or desirable for any purposes connected with Part II of the 1992 Act. In years to come, the Government might issue regulations laying down guidelines on the contents of s 60 statements. At the report stage of the Bill, Lord Swinfen moved an amendment requiring the government to issue guidelines on the content of s 60 statements. Earl Ferrers rejected this. He did not consider statutory guidance would be helpful because it would have to deal with every contingency. Instead, he reiterated that the government would consult with practitioners on this issue. In the interim, it is for the professional fund-raiser to draw up the statement.

Example of s 60(1) statement

11.9.5 A possible format for a statement under s 60(1) might be as follows.

Charity Appeal

For XYZ charity, a registered charity★ and ABC Charity, a registered charity.

XYZ and ABC will each receive 50 per cent of the net proceeds of this appeal.

Scrouge and Co, the organisers of this appeal, will be paid a flat fee by XYZ and ABC.

[or]

Scrouge and Co, the organisers of this appeal, will receive 10p for every £ raised by the appeal.

If you make a donation of more than £50 by credit or debit card, you have the right to cancel your donation within seven days of this broadcast.★★

NOTES

* Under s 3 of the 1992 Act, if a registered charity had an income of more than £5,000 in its last financial year, it must state the fact that it is a registered charity in legible characters on all notices, advertisements, etc, issued by or on behalf of the charity and soliciting money or other property. As already explained (see **2.8**) breach of s 3 can give rise to criminal liabilities – and this could include liability on a professional fund-raiser.

** If the appeal is made in the course of a radio or television programme and in association with an announcement that payment may be made by credit or debit card, the statement must include details of the donor's right to cancel his donation and demand a refund so long as the demand for a refund, is made within seven days of the broadcast.

Is it necessary to state that XYZ and ABC will each receive 50 per cent 'of the net proceeds of this appeal'? The 1992 Act merely requires a statement 'of the proportions in which the institutions are respectively to benefit'. That begs the question: from what shall the institutions benefit? The total proceeds of the appeal? If that is the case, how does the fund-raiser get his reward? But if one uses the phrase 'net proceeds', that raises the question, 'net of what'? Should the fund-raiser, in the example above, in order to make the statement a clear indication, state '50 per cent of the net proceeds after deduction of Scrouge and Co's remuneration'?

If the public becomes aware that professional fund-raisers are receiving large proportions of moneys ostensibly raised for charitable institutions, the effect on public generosity could be dramatic. The degree of disclosure needed about the fund-raiser's remuneration could be crucial. The 1992 Act only calls for a statement in general terms about the *method* by which the fund-raiser's remuneration is to be determined. Is it sufficient to state that Scrouge and Co is being paid a flat fee (of an unspecified amount)? It seems that that would comply with the Act. It shows the *method* by which the fund-raiser is to be paid. Equally, in the case of a telephone appeal, a fund-raiser might be paid £1 per call. Does the fund-raiser have to state that he is being paid £1 per call (which might be a considerable turn-off for potential donors) or is it sufficient to state that he is being paid a flat rate per call? It would appear that the latter would suffice. But what happens if the potential donor then asks 'how much per call?'? Does the fund-raiser have to reply? It seems not. His obligation under the 1992 Act is to give a statement clearly indicating the method by which his remuneration is to be determined and it would seem that the statement 'We are being paid a flat rate per call' would comply with that requirement.

It must be emphasised that these conclusions are tentative. As Earl Ferrers recognised, there is much learning to be done. The precise meaning and requirements of the statement will have to await judicial scrutiny or possible regulations.

Example of s 60(2) statement

11.9.6 A possible format for a statement under s 60(2) might be as follows.

Save the Whale Appeal

This is an appeal on behalf of whales and not for the benefit of any particular charitable institution.

Ninety per cent of the proceeds of this appeal shall go to such charitable institutions as are chosen by the management committee of this appeal.

Scrouge and Co, as organisers of this appeal, will receive 10p for every £1 raised by the appeal.

If you make a donation of more than £50 by credit or debit card you have the right to cancel your donation within seven days of this broadcast.

The same notes concerning the statement under s 60(1) which are mentioned above apply to this statement.

The right to cancel – ss 60 and 61

11.9.7 Reference has already been made (see **11.9.5**) to the obligation of a professional fund-raiser, under s 60(4), to notify potential donors who may give more than £50 in response to a radio or TV appeal, of their right to demand a refund if the donation is made by credit or debit card. By s 60(5), if a solicitation is made by a professional fund-raiser *by telephone*, the fund-raiser must notify, within seven days, the donor of:

(a) the full details of the s 60 statement (see **11.9.1**); and
(b) his right to cancel the donation within seven days and demand a refund if he pays more than £50 to the professional fund-raiser.

This does not apply if the payment is made to a charitable institution (s 60(5)) even if the solicitation has been made by a professional fund-raiser. It must be noted that in the case of a telephone appeal, the donor has the right to cancel irrespective of how he has paid the £50 or more. In the case of a TV or radio appeal, the right to cancel only applies if payment is made by a debit or credit card.

11.9.8 The professional fund-raiser must give the donor who has paid more than £50 in response to a telephone appeal details of the donor's right to cancel within seven days. This seven-day period is determined as follows (s 60(6)):

(a) if the donor pays in person – the seven days run from the time of payment;
(b) if the donor pays by post – the seven days run from the time of posting the donation;
(c) if the donor pays via telephone or fax or other telecommunication apparatus and orders an account to be debited – the seven days run from the time when such authority is given.

The donor then has seven days from the date he is *given* the written statement (s 61(2)(b)) to exercise, if he so wishes, his right to cancel the donation.

Does that mean that the donor has literally to be given the notice, ie, must it be physically *handed* to him, or is the statement given when it is posted through his letter box or when it is put into the post (if posted)?

11.9.9 Section 7 of the Interpretation Act 1978 provides that where an Act authorises or requires any document to be served by post (whether the expression 'serve' or the expression 'give' is used) then, unless the contrary intention appears, the service is deemed to be effected by properly addressing, prepaying and posting a letter containing the document and, unless the contrary is proved, to have been effected at the time when the letter would be delivered in the ordinary course of post. The implication is that 'to give' is synonymous with 'to serve'. This is confirmed by a case under the Law of Property Act 1925, s 36(2), which uses the phrase 'give . . . notice in writing' in which it was held that 'give' meant the same as 'serve' (*Re 88 Berkeley Road, Rickwood v Turnesk* [1971] Ch 648).

Section 76 of the 1992 Act states that any notice or other document to be given or served under Part II may be served on or given to a person by:

(a) delivering it to that person;
(b) leaving it at his last known address in the UK; or
(c) sending it by post to him at that address.

In the case of a body corporate (eg a limited company, or a body incorporated by Royal Charter) notice is effected by delivering it or sending it by post:

(a) to the registered or principal office of the body in the UK; or
(b) if it has no such office in the UK, to any place in the UK where it carries on business or conducts its affairs.

The right to cancel notice is deemed to be effected under the Interpretation Act 1978 'at the time at which the letter would be delivered in the ordinary course of post' (s 7). This means that delivery will be presumed to have taken place on the next working day or the next but one, depending on whether first or second class post is used. The court will normally assume that second class mail is used.

Example

Gullible responds to a telephone appeal run by Scrouge and Co on behalf of the XYZ charity and sends £100 by post on 1 May to Scrouge. Scrouge receives the donation on 3 May. Scrouge has to give to Gullible the right to cancel notice within seven days (s 60(5)) of the postmark on Gullible's letter – (s 60(6) states that payment shall be regarded as made at the time when it is posted) ie by 7 May.

Scrouge posts the right to cancel notice on 7 May. Gullible will be deemed to have received the notice two working days after the 7 May unless the 'contrary is proved' (Interpretation Act 1978, s 7). If he receives the notice, Gullible must exercise his right to cancel within seven days of being given the right to cancel notice. If he receives the notice on 9 May, he will have to post his notice exercising his right to cancel by 16 May (letter posted on 7 May and served on 9 May).

There is no approved format for the notice exercising the right to cancel. It merely has to indicate the donor's intention to cancel.

How much refund?

11.9.10 The Bill allowed no right for the professional fund-raiser to deduct any administrative costs before refunding any donation over £50 where the donor had exercised the right to cancel. This was criticised. As a result, s 61(4) allows the fund-raiser to deduct 'administrative expenses reasonably incurred' in connection with making the refund. Viscount Astor explained:

> 'administrative expenses' is intended to cover the direct costs of refunding the payment, for costs such as staff time, postage, bank charges and so forth. It will also cover the costs of dealing with any notice of cancellation of an agreement to make payment.' (HL Deb, Vol 535, col 1215 (18 February 1992).)

Breach of s 60

11.9.11 Section 60(7) imposes a strict criminal liability on a professional fund-raiser who is in breach of s 60, ie a professional fund-raiser who fails to give the statements required under s 60(1), (2), (4) or (5). The maximum fine is currently £2,000.

It will be a defence for a person charged with any offence under s 60 'to prove that he took all reasonable precautions and exercised all due diligence to avoid the commission of the offence' (s 60(8)). This is similar to a phrase used in the Trade Descriptions Act 1968, s 24. It shifts the burden of proof from the prosecution, who would, under normal rules of criminal law, have to prove that the defendant had mens rea and committed the offence, onto the defendant, who has to show that he took all reasonable precautions, etc. That is a heavy burden. In one case under the Trade Descriptions Act 1968, *Tesco Supermarkets v Nattrass* [1972] AC 153, the House of Lords ruled that the defendants had exercised all due diligence by devising a proper system for the operation of their supermarket and by securing its implementation as far as was reasonably practicable.

Thus, professional fund-raisers will need to ensure that they have proper procedures, adequately monitored, to ensure that their staff comply with the requirements of s 60. If they do not, they will be unable to establish that they have taken all reasonable precautions and exercised all due diligence. Viscount Astor commented on behalf of the Government:

> 'In order to avail himself of this defence the person charged must establish, on the balance of probabilities, that he was not negligent in failing to avoid the commission of the offence.' (HL Deb, Vol 535, col 1210 (18 February 1992).)

11.9.12 Section 60(9) contains a sting. It provides that where there is a breach of s 60 which is due to the act or default of some other person, that other person shall be guilty of the offence. The same defence of having taken all reasonable precautions, etc, can be pleaded. The subsection is principally designed to allow charges to be brought against employees who break the requirements of the Act, in breach, for example, of their employer's rule book. But the subsection could have wider implications. The original clause 4 of the Bill (now s 3) contained a similar subclause (4(5)). The Law Society was most concerned about its effect because it feared that solicitors who failed to advise their clients of the requirements of what is now s 3, could have been guilty of a criminal offence. The solicitor who failed to advise might have been guilty of a 'default' under the section. The Government was persuaded to drop clause 4(5) but s 60(9) remained.

Viscount Astor commented:

> 'The provision [s 60(9)] is designed to ensure that, where a professional fund-raiser's employees or agents go off on a frolic of their own and neglect to make the necessary disclosures, they are guilty of an offence whether or not the fund-raiser is prosecuted. Of course if the employer has taken steps to institute a proper system to ensure the making of the statement he will be able to rely on sub-section (8).
>
> It has been suggested that the wording of subsection (9) could catch solicitors or accountants who advise professional fund-raisers or commercial participators. We have looked at this matter again and I have to say we do not see how that could be so. The duty placed on the professional fund-raiser is to disclose certain information when soliciting funds. The act or default relates to the failure to disclose that information when soliciting funds.
>
> Sub-section (9) of Clause 60 cannot render solicitors liable to prosecution under this clause if they advise their client incorrectly about when the provisions of Clause 60 apply. They are under no duty to make any disclosure. The offence relates to the failure to make the required statements of disclosure.' (HL Deb, Vol 535, col 1210 (18 February 1992).)

11.10 Future Regulations

11.10.1 Section 64 gives the Secretary of State authority to introduce regulations to cover a number of matters under Part II of the 1992 Act.

These may cover:

(a) the contents of s 59 agreements;

(b) requirements on professional fund-raisers who have entered into a s 59 agreement with a charitable institution to make available to the institution books, documents or other records (however kept) which relate to the institution;

(c) regulations on professional fund-raisers to transmit moneys or property acquired for a charitable institution to that institution. Under the Act, there is no obligation that a professional fund-raiser must pay the total proceeds of an appeal over to the charitable institution(s) concerned. This is somewhat surprising given that the Woodfield Report identified this as a major area of abuse. We must await the regulations to see how the Government intends to handle this; and

(d) criminal sanctions for breach of any regulations – the maximum fine will be £100.

Charities

11.10.2 It is worth reiterating that Part II of the 1992 Act does not apply to charitable institutions or companies controlled by them. However, the Government did consider applying the right to cancel in the case of donations over £50 to appeals made directly by charitable institutions. In the end the Government decided not to. In part, this was because the Home Office has given financial support towards the development of a voluntary code of practice for broadcast appeals. The charities involved in broadcast appeals had indicated their willingness to include in that voluntary code a requirement that donors of money over a certain sum should be informed in writing or by telephone of the right to cancel the donation.

However, the Government has reserved the right to introduce regulations to extend the statutory right to cancel to radio or television appeals made by charitable institutions or their connected companies (as defined in s 58). Indeed, s 64(2)(e) is much wider. It states:

> 'Any such regulations may . . . make other provision regulating the raising of funds for charitable, benevolent or philanthropic purposes (whether by professional fund-raisers or commercial participators or otherwise).'

These are wide powers and could cover far more than the imposition of the right to cancel upon appeals made by charitable institutions or their connected companies.

CHAPTER 12

CONTROL OF FUND-RAISING: COMMERCIAL PARTICIPATORS AND OTHER MATTERS

Introduction: What is a Commercial Participator?: Application of the Definition: Section 59 Agreements: Section 60 Statements: Criminal Sanctions: Commercial Participators – Conclusion: Right of Charitable Institutions to Prevent Unauthorised Fund-raising: Section 63

12.1 Introduction

12.1.1 As noted (see **11.2.2**) one of the recommendations of the Woodfield Report was that whenever goods or services were advertised or offered for sale, with an indication that some part of the proceeds was to be devoted to charity, there should be specified:

(a) the charity or charities that were to benefit; and
(b) the manner in which the sums they were to receive would be calculated.

12.1.2 The White Paper endorsed this. There had been some doubts about the practicability of the Woodfield proposal but the authors of the White Paper were sure that 'the public, when being encouraged to make a purchase on the grounds that it will benefit charity, have a right to certain basic information, which should not be difficult to provide' (at para 10.20).

The Government followed that when drafting the Act.

12.2 What is a Commercial Participator?

12.2.1 The 1992 Act introduces a new phrase to the dictionary of the voluntary sector: 'the commercial participator'. In essence, a commercial participator is someone who encourages purchases of goods or services on the grounds that some of the proceeds will go to charity.

12.2.2 Section 58(1) defines a commercial participator as:

'in relation to any charitable institution . . . any person who:

(a) carries on for gain a business other than a fund-raising business, but

(b) in the course of that business, engages in any promotional venture in the course of which it is represented that charitable contributions are to be given to or applied for the benefit of the institution.'

A number of the expressions used in this definition are also defined in the Act. The definition of 'a charitable institution' and the definition of 'a fund-raising business' have been considered (see **11.4** and **11.6**, respectively). 'Promotional venture' is defined by s 58(1) of the Act as 'any advertising or sales campaign or any other venture undertaken for promotional purposes'. 'Venture' has not, apparently, been defined in any statute or, remarkably, considered in any judgment. The Oxford English Dictionary defines a venture as: 'that which is ventured or risked in a commercial enterprise or speculation'.

'Represent' is defined by s 58(6) as meaning to represent 'in any manner whatever, whether done by speaking directly . . . or by means of a statement published in any newspaper, film or radio or television programme or otherwise . . .'; 'charitable contributions' is defined by s 58(1) as meaning 'in relation to any representation made by any commercial participator or other person . . .

(a) the whole or part of –

    (i) the consideration given for goods or services sold or supplied by him, or
    (ii) any proceeds (other than such consideration) of a promotional venture undertaken by him, or

(b) sums given by him by way of donation in connection with the sale or supply of any such goods or services (whether the amount of such sums is determined by reference to the value of any such goods or services or otherwise)'.

'Services' is defined by s 58(9) as including facilities and in particular:

(a) access to any premises or event;
(b) membership of any organisation;
(c) the provision of advertising space; and
(d) the provision of any financial facilities;

and references to the supply of services shall be construed accordingly.'

12.2.3 In debate at the committee stage of the Bill, Viscount Astor, referring to the definition of commercial participator, stated:

'It is a wide definition drafted to ensure that a broad range of types of facility or service that may be offered by a person acting as a commercial participator are encompassed within the Bill.' (Public Bill Committee, Fifth Sitting, col 221 (11 December 1992).)

12.3 Application of the Definition

The following questions arise on the definition of commercial participator.

Companies controlled by charitable institutions

12.3.1 The exclusion of companies connected with a charitable institution (see **11.5.2**) from, in part, the definition of a professional fund-raiser, does not extend to commercial participators. Therefore, a trading company owned by a charitable institution will fall within the definition of commercial participator.

This is very much at odds with the discussion on the Bill that took place at the committee stage. At that point, it was generally believed that trading subsidiaries of charitable institutions would not be treated as commercial participators and would be outside the scope of Part 2.

However, as drafted, the Act applies the rules relating to commercial participators to a trading company owned by a chariable institution. This means that the obligations under ss 59(2) and s 60(3) (see **12.4** and **12.5**) will apply to such companies.

12.3.2 Section 58(1) defines a commercial participator as '. . . any person who carries on for gain a business *other than a fund-raising business*'. A fund-raising business is defined (see **11.6.1**) as any business carried on for gain and wholly or primarily engaged in soliciting, etc, money for charitable, etc, purposes. Any person who carries on a fund-raising business is a professional fund-raiser – see the definition in s 58(1) (**11.6.1**). Charitable institutions are excluded from the definition of professional fund-raiser – see **11.6.1**. But a company controlled by a charitable institution is only excluded from the second part of the definition of professional fund-raiser which reads:

'any other person . . . who for reward solicits money or other property for the benefit of a charitable institution, if he does so otherwise than in the course of a fund-raising venture undertaken by a person falling within paragraph (a) above.'

A person falling within paragraph (a) is a person who carries on a fund-raising business.

Hence, if a trading subsidiary carries on a fund-raising business it cannot enjoy the exemptions from being a professional fund-raiser. But if it is a professional fund-raiser then it is carrying on a fund-raising business. If so, it cannot be a commercial participator.

There is an advantage for a charity to establish its trading subsidiary as a professional fund-raiser, rather than as a commercical participator. The reason lies in the comparison of s 60(1) and 60(3) of the Act.

Under 60(1) the statement has to show (in general terms) 'the method by which the fund-raiser's remuneration in connection with the appeal is to be determined'.

In the case of a trading subsidiary selling Christmas cards, it gets no remuneration from the charity on whose behalf it sells cards. The trading company's remuneration is derived solely from its own efforts. Hence, would it be sufficient to state:

'No remuneration is paid by XYZ charity to its trading subsidiary XYZ Trading Limited'

in order to comply with s 60(1)?

Such a general statement is much simpler to make and organise than the statement under s 60(3), which has to be tied to the proportion of the consideration paid for goods sold which is given to the charitable institution. The s 60(1) statement can be made on a poster in each shop run by a charity's trading subsidiary. The s 60(3) statement has to be tailor-made to each different item sold or service supplied – a much more demanding proposal.

It is suggested that trading subsidiaries should adopt an objects clause in their memorandum of association which is drafted to conform to the definition of fund-raising business in s 58(1).

Broadcast appeals

12.3.3 Much concern was expressed in the House of Lords about broadcast appeals, where all the contributions go to the charitable institution on whose behalf the broadcast appeal is made. The appeals use building societies and credit card companies which provide facilities for the receipt of donations and charge for their services. Are they commercial participators? Viscount Astor confirmed:

> 'the definition [   ] of commercial participator [is] not intended to include commercial organisations providing services for broadcast appeals as part of their normal business.' (Public Bill Committee, Fifth Sitting, col 222 (11 December 1992.)

This clearly accords with the definition of commercial participator which requires the participator to be engaged in a 'promotional venture' in the course of which it is represented that charitable contributions will be given. If a bank charges a charity for running pledge lines during a broadcast appeal, it is not engaging in a 'promotional venture' (as defined in s 58(1)).

What if a bank gave its facilities free of charge and this was mentioned in the appeal? This would not alter the position. The bank would not be a commercial participator – it would not be representing that 'charitable contributions' (as defined) would be made. In advertising that it was donating free services to the charity, it could be argued that the use of the charity's name was consideration given for the free service. But s 58(1) requires that the representation must be in relation to 'the whole or part of the consideration given . . . for services sold'. In this case, although the charity is giving consideration for the free service (ie use of its name) no part of *that* consideration is being given to the charity.

Affinity cards

12.3.4 Under this system, banks issue credit cards dedicated to a particular charity and donate a percentage of the customer's monthly payments to a charity. Clearly, in this situation, the bank is:

(a) engaging in a business (banking) which is not a fund-raising business; but
(b) in the course of that, is engaging in a promotional venture in which it is representing that a percentage of the consideration paid for the services provided by the bank will go to a charitable institution.

Hence, the bank is a commercial participator.

This is made clear by s 58(9)(d) of the 1992 Act where the definition of 'services' includes 'the provision of any financial facilities'.

Christmas cards

12.3.5 Many commercial organisations sell charity Christmas cards, ie cards which state 'sold in aid of XYZ charity'. Is a high street retailer who sells such cards a commercial participator? The retailer carries on, for gain, a business other than fund-raising. In the course of his business, is he engaging in a promotional venture of any sort? Since a promotional venture includes a sales campaign (s 58(1)) displaying the cards for sale constitutes a promotional venture. But it is also necessary to establish that in the course of that promotional venture it is represented that charitable contributions (as defined) will be made. Like a solicitation (see **11.9.3**), a representation can be made in any manner whatever, expressly or impliedly. Hence, the sale of a Christmas card stating 'sold in aid of XYZ charity' is an implied representation that part of the price paid for the card will go to XYZ charity. Therefore, on this analysis, the retailer is a commercial participator with the consequences analysed below (see **12.4** and **12.5**).

Is the position different if the Christmas card merely states 'XYZ charity'? This is more difficult, but it may be an implied representation that part of the price paid will go to the charity.

Other examples of commercial participators

12.3.6 Other examples of commercial participators include the following.

(a) The maker of a product who prints a charity's logo on the product and states:

'1p will go to XYZ charity for each packet sold'.

(b) The events organiser (eg the Glastonbury Festival) who states that the net proceeds of the event will go to a charitable institution.

Glastonbury raises an interesting issue. The proceeds used to go to the Campaign for Nuclear Disarmament. Is that a benevolent or philanthropic institution? Probably not, as it is established for political purposes. The proceeds now go to Greenpeace. Is that a benevolent or philanthropic institution? (For a discussion, see **11.4**.)

(c) The travel company which offers to pay one per cent of the price of a holiday to a named charitable institution.

12.4 Section 59 Agreements

12.4.1 Just as the professional fund-raiser has to have an agreement with a charitable institution before it can solicit money for its benefit, so too must the commercial participator. Section 59(2) states that it is unlawful for a commercial participator to represent that charitable contributions are to be given to a charitable institution 'unless he does so in accordance with an agreement with the institution satisfying the prescribed requirements'.

The consequences of a breach of s 59(1) (see **11.8.2–11.8.5**), apply equally to a breach of s 59(2), ie in summary, any agreement which does not comply is unenforceable without the sanction of the High Court or county court.

Possible problems with s 59 agreements

12.4.2 Under s 59(2), the commercial participator has to have the charitable institution's consent before he can engage in a promotional venture in the course of which it is represented that charitable contributions will be given. An interesting question arises in terms of the tax treatment of any payment made by the commercial participator to a charity. This point does not apply to any payments made by a commercial participator to a benevolent or philanthropic institution because such organisations are not charities and do not enjoy the tax benefits available to charities. Will the payment received by the charity from a commercial participator be treated as an implied licence fee paid by the commercial participator to the charity for the use and exploitation of the charity's name?

One could take the example of a pen manufacturer, which encourages the public to buy its pens by saying that five per cent of the purchase price will be donated to a named charity. The charity's name and logo is used in connection with the marketing of the pen. Is the charity, therefore, engaged in a business of exploiting its name and logo commercially? If it is, then the receipts from that exploitation could be treated by the Inland Revenue as profits of a business which has not been carried on in fulfilment of the charity's main objects. If that is the case, the Inland Revenue will be entitled to levy corporation or income tax (depending on how the charity is constituted) upon those profits, under s 505 of the Income and Corporation Taxes Act 1988.

Similar problems have already arisen in connection with affinity cards. In these cases, the Inland Revenue has approved treating such income as Schedule D, Case III royalty income in the hands of charities. This is on the basis that the royalties will be paid under a legal obligation, will be annually recurring and will be pure income profit (as opposed to a licence fee). Hence, the agreement with the commercial participator will need to be structured to ensure that all payments are treated as pure income profit.

However, if the agreement with the commercial participator covers more than use of the charity's name and logo, eg use of a mailing list, any payments will not be susceptible to being treated as pure income profit.

One method which has been adopted by charities to get round this problem is to appoint its trading subsidiary as its licensee to exploit the other commercial activities, eg mailing lists. The trading subsidiary negotiates with commercial partners for use of the mailing list, and payments are then made to the trading subsidiary in respect of those activities.

12.4.3 The rest of s 59 (which is discussed at **11.8**) applies to commercial participators just as it does to professional fund-raisers. Therefore, in summary, the position is as follows.

(a) A commercial participator who represents that charitable contributions will be made, without having entered into a s 59(2) agreement, can be restrained by injunction.
(b) If a charitable institution makes an agreement with a commercial partici-pator but the agreement does not satisfy the prescribed requirements, the agreement is unenforceable unless a court orders that it is enforceable.

12.5 Section 60 Statements

12.5.1 Section 60(3) makes similar provisions, in terms of statements to be made by commercial participators, as s 60(1) and (2) makes for professional fund-raisers.

12.5.2 Section 60(3) provides that where any representation is made by a commercial participator to the effect that charitable contributions are to be given to or applied for the benefit of one or more particular charitable institutions the representation shall be accompanied by a statement clearly indicating:

(a) the name or names of the institution or institutions concerned;
(b) if there is more than one institution, the proportions in which the institutions are respectively to benefit; and
(c) in general terms, the method by which it is to be determined:

   (i) in what proportion the consideration given for goods or services sold or supplied by him, or of any other proceeds of a promotional venture undertaken by him, is to be applied for the benefit of the institution or institutions concerned; or
   (ii) what sums, by way of donations by him in connection with the sale or supply of any such goods or services, are to be so given or applied,

   as the case may require.

12.5.3 This closely parallels s 60(1). Surprisingly, there is nothing to parallel s 60(2) which deals with fund-raising for a general cause, rather than a specific charitable institution (see **11.9.2**). This seems to imply that it will be legitimate for a commercial participator to seek to sell goods accompanied by a statement to the effect that part of the proceeds of sale will be spent on general charitable, benevolent or philanthropic purposes, without having to comply with something similar to s 60(2). Therefore, the seller of a pen could state that five per cent of the proceeds of sale would go to relieve poverty in the Third World and the controls in s 60 would not apply!

12.5.4 Section 60(3) requires that any representation made by a commercial participator has to be accompanied by a statement. A representation, as we have already seen, can be made expressly or impliedly and can be made by speaking directly or by means of a statement published in a newspaper, film, radio or television programme or otherwise. Whenever the representation is made, the statement has to accompany it. In the case of an oral representation, the statement has to be made at the same time or be visible; in the case of a newspaper advertisement, the advertisement must contain the statement. In shops, it will be sufficient that the statement is made by a clear and legible sign, provided it is readily visible when the representation is made.

12.5.5 The statement has to include details 'in general terms' of the method by which it is to determine what proportion of the consideration, etc, is to be given to the institution(s) concerned or what donation will be given. This seems contradictory. How can one have a general statement of a method to determine a proportion? It is not sufficient to say that 'five per cent of the net profits of the organisation will be given to XYZ charity'. The statement has to state in general terms the method of calculating the proportion of the consideration (ie the price for the individual items sold or services rendered), which is to go to the charitable institution(s) concerned. Alternatively, the statement has to say what donation will be paid to the charitable institution(s).

Examples of a s 60(3) statement

(a) *In a shop*

'These cards are sold on behalf of XYZ charity. Five per cent of the retail price will be given to XYZ charity'

[or]

'In respect of each card sold, five pence will be given to XYZ charity'

(b) *A statement made on radio or TV – sale of goods, eg a lawnmower*

'Five per cent of the price you pay for your lawnmower will be given to XYZ charity. If you pay for goods which cost more than £50 by credit or debit card you have the right to cancel your purchase within seven days of this broadcast.'*

NOTE

* By s 60(4), if a representation under s 60(3) is made in the course of a radio or television programme and payment can be made by credit or debit card, the broadcast has to include details of the right to cancel under s 61(1). In the case of goods purchased by virtue of s 61(4)(b), any right to cancel and have a refund paid is conditional upon restitution being made by the purchaser of the goods in question.

Telephone sales

If a representation under s 60(3) is made by telephone, the commercial participator is obliged, within seven days of any payment of £50 or more to the commercial participator, to give any person making a payment in response to the telephone appeal the s 60(3) statement and details of the right to cancel under s 61(2) (see **11.9.7**).

12.6 Criminal Sanctions

Just as the professional fund-raiser who breaches s 60(1) to (5) is guilty of a criminal offence, so also is the commercial participator. The same points concerning the criminal sanctions for breaching s 60 which applied to professional fund-raisers, also apply to commercial participators (see **11.9.11**).

12.7 Commercial Participators – Conclusion

The new law relating to commercial participators could cause a number of problems. Charitable organisations have a myriad of different types of relationships with various commercial organisations, some of which may fall within the definition of commercial participator. Each of these will need to be analysed to see whether or not the 1992 Act applies to them.

Particular problems could arise with the sale of charity Christmas cards. Some retailers will stock a large number of different charity Christmas cards. The retailer will need to comply with the 1992 Act in relation to each charity whose Christmas cards it sells. The retailer will need a s 59 agreement and make the necessary s 60(3) statement in relation to each charity. This will undoubtedly cause a large amount of paperwork. It may, therefore, be sensible for charities to co-ordinate the sale of Christmas cards through one company, which could act as a clearing house for all charities and deal with the high-street retailers on their behalf. The clearing house would be appointed the charities' agent for the purposes of negotiating s 59 agreements with the retailers. This would mean that the retailer would only need to deal with the clearing house to get one s 59 agreement for all the charities whose cards the retailer sells (provided that all those charities are members of the clearing house).

The s 60(3) statement will also present problems. Will the same price per card be paid to each charity? Presumably not. It will probably depend upon the price and size of each card. Hence, a retailer selling three types of card, all priced differently, produced by 20 different charities, would have to make the s 60(3) statement in respect of each type of card sold for each charity. It may be sensible, therefore, for charities to set up a clearing house charity so that the s 60(3) statement could refer to all charitable donations or proportions of the consideration being given to the clearing house charity. This could, in turn, refer to those charities which were constituent members of the clearing house charity, to encourage the public to purchase those cards.

12.8 Right of Charitable Institutions to Prevent Unauthorised Fund-raising

As mentioned at **11.2.2**, the Woodfield Report and the White Paper both considered that there should be some mechanism for charities to prevent unauthorised fund-raising being carried on in their name. This is reflected in s 62 of the 1992 Act, which applies not only to charities but to charitable institutions.

By s 62(1), where the court (ie the High Court or county court) is satisfied that any person has, or is, either soliciting money or other property for the benefit of a charitable institution or representing that charitable contributions are to be given, and that unless restrained he is likely to do further acts of that nature, if the court is satisfied as to one or more of the matters set out in s 62(2) it may grant an injunction restraining the unauthorised fund-raising.

The charitable institution has to establish, to the court's satisfaction, one or more of the following under s 62(2):

(a) that the person in question is using methods of fund-raising to which the institution objects;
(b) that that person is not a fit and proper person to raise funds for the institution; and
(c) in the case where it is represented that charitable contributions (as defined in s 58(1)) are to be given, that the institution does not wish to be associated with the particular promotional or other fund-raising venture in which that person is engaged.

Before the charitable institution can obtain an injunction it must have given not less than 28 days' notice in writing to the person in question. The notice must request him to cease forthwith and state that if he does not comply with the notice the institution will make an application for an injunction. The form of the notice may be prescribed by regulations to be issued under s 64(2).

To help charitable institutions which may be plagued by unauthorised fund-raisers, where a charitable institution has given the 28-day notice under s 62(3), but the person, having initially complied with the notice, subsequently begins to carry on the same activities, the charitable institution can immediately apply for an injunction without having to serve a further notice. This only applies if the application for the injunction is made not more than 12 months after the date of service of the relevant notice upon the fund-raiser. Service can be effected by complying with s 76 of the 1992 Act. (For further details, see **11.9.9**.)

12.9 Section 63

Criminal offences

Section 63 makes it a criminal offence for a person who is representing that an institution is a registered charity to solicit money or other property for the benefit of that institution when it is not a registered charity.

Therefore, for example, it would be a criminal offence under s 63 for a person to solicit money on behalf of Eton coupled with the representation that Eton is a registered charity. Eton is not a registered charity, although it is a charity which is exempt from registration. Equally, it would be a criminal offence for a person to solicit money on behalf of the Girl Guides together with a representation that the Girl Guides are a registered charity. The Girl Guides are an excepted charity, ie excepted from registration and are, therefore, not registered. These fine distinctions may be lost on fund-raisers, particularly in the case of such charities as the Girl Guides, Boy Scouts and other excepted charities.

The maximum fine that can be imposed under this section is currently £2,000.

CHAPTER 13

PUBLIC CHARITABLE COLLECTIONS: PART III OF THE 1992 ACT

Background: Static Collecting Boxes: What is a Public Charitable Collection?: Definition of Public Place: Exceptions to the Public Place Definition: Charitable Appeals: Controls on Public Charitable Collections: Obtaining a Local Authority Permit: Section 68 Permits – Conditions: Appeal Against Conditions Contained in a Permit: Refusal of a Local Authority Permit: Appeal Against Refusal to Grant a Permit: Withdrawal of a Local Authority Permit: Criminal Offences: Section 72 Orders: Conclusion

13.1 Background

Street and house to house collections prior to the implementation of the 1992 Act are controlled by s 5 of the Police, Factories etc (Miscellaneous Provisions) Act 1916 and the House to House Collections Act 1939 (both as amended by the Local Government Act 1972). Both Acts involve the issue of licences or permits by District Councils, Metropolitan Police or the Common Council of the City of London. Both contain detailed regulations covering the conduct of collections with submission of accounts and so forth. Oddly, there are significant differences between the two pieces of legislation and the associated regulations. The Woodfield Report saw no reason why the two sorts of collection should be regulated differently. The White Paper endorsed this and proposed combining the provisions in a single piece of legislation accompanied by standard regulations to apply throughout England and Wales. Part III of the 1992 Act does this.

Schedule 7 of the Act repeals most of the old legislation. Section 5 of the 1916 Act and all of the 1939 Act are repealed, although the 1916 Act will still apply in Northern Ireland.

13.2 Static Collecting Boxes

The 1992 Act does not extend the controls on public charitable collections to static collecting boxes found in shops, public houses or elsewhere – which is made clear by s 65(2)(c). This caused some concern in the debate at the committee stage. The Government responded that the amount of money collected by static collection boxes was usually relatively small and such collections did not have the potential to cause inconvenience to the public. The Government clearly hopes that a code of practice on static collecting boxes covering the kinds of container to be used, the appointment of an individual as responsible for each container and the identification to be carried by a static box, will be sufficient to deal with such problems as they arise. The Institute of Charity Fundraising Managers has produced a guidance note on the management of static collecting boxes.

In addition, the Charity Commissioners do have the power to transfer abandoned funds to the official custodian for safekeeping while an inquiry is underway. This function of the official custodian will continue (see s 29(2)(b)).

13.3 What is a Public Charitable Collection?

13.3.1 When the Bill was first published there was an outcry from the voluntary sector because the definition of a public charitable collection was so wide that it would have encompassed coffee mornings and jumble sales.

13.3.2 As Earl Ferrers said at the committee stage of the Bill:

> 'During the debate on Second Reading a number of members of the Committee expressed anxiety that the scope of the definition of public place cast the net of regulation too wide. It was argued that the Bill would require charity shops to have a permit in order to be able to trade and that permits might also be necessary for coffee mornings in private houses. I undertook to consider the drafting of the Bill in order to ensure that inappropriate regulations such as this were not imposed by the Bill . . . The amendments will ensure that the Bill will regulate collections that are taken in places which, although technically private, are for many purposes, including access by members of the public, no different to purely public places. I have in mind the forecourts of railway stations and privately owned shopping centres. Such places can be lucrative sites for public collections.' (Public Bill Committee, Sixth Sitting, col 243 (11 December 1992).)

13.3.3 A public charitable collection means a charitable appeal which is made (s 65(1)(a)):

(a) in any public place; or
(b) by means of visits from house to house.

13.4 Definition of Public Place

A public place is defined (s 65(8)) as:

(a) any highway; and
(b) any other place to which at any time when the appeal is made members of the public have or are permitted to have access and which is either:

    (i) not within a building; or

(ii) if within a building, is a public area within any station, airport or shopping precinct or any other similar public area.

As Earl Ferrers stated (see **13.3.2**), s 65(8)(b) is designed to cover railway stations and shopping precincts, etc. Lord Swinfen was most concerned about the phrase 'or any other similar public area' and introduced a probing amendment on the report stage of the Bill to ascertain what the phrase meant. Viscount Astor responded:

> 'In general terms the answer to my noble friend's first question is that the words in sub-section (7) of Section 65 [now s 65(8)] are designed to ensure that collections in places which are buildings but to which the public has already access are regulated by Part III of the Bill. These places include railway stations, airports or ports for ferries to which the public has access without the need for a ticket, covered and uncovered shopping precincts and so on. Places such as the interiors of shops or theatres would certainly be excluded.
>
> As to the question of who will know whether an area is similar or not I think that the specific examples in sub-section (7) [now (8)] of the public areas within a station, airport or shopping precinct sufficiently indicate the types of areas which fall within sub-section (7)(b)(ii) [now subsection (8)(b)(ii)]. The characteristics of these areas are that, even though they are within buildings and not privately owned, the public has unrestricted access for much of the day.
>
> It will of course be for the local authority to judge in the first instance whether the proposed site for a public collection falls within the scope of the sub-section.' (HL Deb, Vol 535, col 1231 (18 February 1992).)

13.5 Exceptions to the Public Place Definition

13.5.1 The definition of public place excludes, by implication, any building, except for public areas such as stations, etc. Hence, collections in hospitals, schools or offices are not public charitable collections. An interesting question arises with public houses. Presumably a collection within one public house is not a public charitable collection but moving from one pub to another would be, if the public house was a 'dwelling' or contained a 'dwelling', ie if people lived in the building. If no one did, the public house would not be a dwelling and, therefore, the controls on 'house-to-house' collections would not apply.

13.5.2 By s 65(9), the definition of public place does not apply:

(a) to any place to which members of the public are permitted to have access only if any payment or ticket required as a condition of access has been made or purchased [eg a jumble sale]; or
(b) to any place to which members of the public are permitted to have access only by virtue of permission given for the purposes of the appeal in question [eg a coffee morning].

13.5.3 Collections in a churchyard or in the course of a public meeting are excluded (s 65(2)).

13.6 Charitable Appeals

13.6.1 A charitable appeal is defined (s 65(1)(b)) as an appeal to members of the public to give money or other property (whether for consideration or otherwise) which is made in association with a representation that the whole or any part of its proceeds is to be applied for charitable, benevolent or philanthropic purposes (see **11.4**). If, for example, Greenpeace is not established for 'benevolent or philanthropic' purposes, it will be outside the scope of the 1992 Act and will be able to conduct public appeals without local authority control.

13.6.2 The definition covers not only the donation of money but also property. This means that collections of jumble, books, newspapers, stamps, old clothes or milk bottle tops will be charitable appeals if it is stated that the whole or any part of the proceeds is to be applied for charitable, etc, purposes.

13.6.3 A charitable appeal can also take place if goods or services are offered for sale or to be supplied in any public place or by means of visits from house to house and is coupled with a representation that the whole or any part of the proceeds of sale is to be applied for charitable, benevolent or philanthropic purposes (s 65(7)). Hence, the itinerant salesperson going from door to door, selling goods made by handicapped people for the purposes of selling those goods to benefit a charity for the handicapped, will be conducting a public charitable collection. So, too, will the jumble sale, unless it does not take place in a public place by virtue of s 65(9) (see **13.5.2**).

13.7 Controls on Public Charitable Collections

13.7.1 Under s 66(1) no public charitable collection shall be conducted in the area of any local authority except in accordance with:

(a) a permit issued by the authority under s 68; or
(b) an order made by the Charity Commissioners under s 72.

For these purposes, a local authority means a District Council or a London borough, the Common Council of the City of London or the Council of the Isles of Scilly. The promoter of any public charitable collection which is conducted in breach of s 66(1) shall be guilty of a criminal offence and liable on conviction to a fine not exceeding £1,000.

This is a major change so far as London is concerned. Hitherto, the Metropolitan Police have been the licensing authority, which role will be taken over by the London Boroughs, once Part III of the 1992 Act is in force. Therefore, planning public charitable collections in London will be difficult in the interim period, until the take-over occurs.

13.7.2 Section 66(1) states that no public charitable collection can take place without either a local authority permit or a Charity Commissioner's order. In view of the wide definition of public charitable appeal, Lord Allen of Abbeydale made strenuous attempts for local authorities to be given the power to waive these requirements in certain cases. As he commented at the report stage of the Bill:

'People undertaking all kinds of collections, whether for funds or goods, are required under the Bill to obtain licences. It seems that that could include people who call around to collect for a jumble sale for charity, groups singing carols for children's charities or scouts for washing parked cars to raise funds. They could face the threat of criminal sanctions if no licence is obtained. It may be worth nothing that the DPP's consent would not be required . . . The wording of the amendment may be susceptible to improvement but there is a case for giving some discretion over the need for permits for fund-raising activities. The Secretary of State should have the ability, perhaps after a more detailed consultation than has so far been possible with local authorities and voluntary organisations to prescribe circumstances under which some of the requirements for permits might be waived.' (HL Deb, Vol 535, col 1232 (18 February 1992).)

For the Government, Earl Ferrers commented:

'. . . there is a balance to be struck here between public accountability and private inconvenience. I do not think that the need to obtain a permit is an onerous one for small local groups. They are collecting from local people, and I see no reason why they should not be accountable locally for the moneys which they raise.
    The noble Lord, Lord Allen of Abbeydale, referred to jumble sales. He said people are always conducting house to house jumble collections. That is perfectly true and bags are left outside people's houses and people are invited to put all kinds of things in the bags which have to be sold for the benefit of the charity involved. A rag-and-bone merchant may then sell the items collected on behalf of a charity. However, a rag-and-bone merchant or whoever it may be may retain 95% of the proceeds and send the charity concerned only a small percentage of the proceeds. That is precisely the kind of thing that we wish to stop. The noble Lord . . . referred to carol singers. If I wished to collect for a charity in the street, I would need a permit. I would feel fairly miffed if all someone else did was to go down the street and sing a carol outside someone's door and that obviated the need for a permit. It is important that the same regulations apply in every case. The responsibility we are discussing is not an onerous one.' (HL Deb, Vol 535, col 1234 (18 February 1992).)

On the Third Reading the question came up again. Lord Allen returned to the attack. But Earl Ferrers resisted any amendment, principally because he considered that drafting the kind of regulations would be very difficult to accomplish, without either creating absurdities or loopholes for the less scrupulous.

'It would be easy enough to specify carol singing as an exempt activity. But if one did so the group which sings "The Holly and the Ivy" would be able to take advantage of the concession but the group which sang "White Christmas" would not because that is not a carol. It will be difficult to think of a more absurd situation than one in which the application of the criminal law depends on the classification of the item sung.
    Likewise it ought to be possible to cover what is known as Bob-a-Job Week. But

a detailed provision of this kind would create its own anomalies since similar activities by groups other than scouts would not be covered . . . Exception seems at odds with what Part III is trying to do. It serves two purposes. First it ensures that those who raise money or collect property locally are also accountable locally for what they collect. That is why it requires local authorities to give permission for public charitable collections and why the regulations to be made under the Bill will require promoters to keep proper accounts.

Secondly, Part III serves to ensure that public charitable collections do not cause a nuisance to the public as a result of their sheer number or the places in which they are conducted. Both of those purposes might be undermined by the system of waivers which are suggested by the amendment.' (HL Deb, Vol 535, col 217 (25 February 1992).)

A system of supervision along the lines set out in the 1992 Act has been operating in Scotland by virtue of the Civic Government (Scotland) Act 1982. There is no exemption or waiver system in the Scottish legislation.

13.8 Obtaining a Local Authority Permit

13.8.1 The promoter of a collection has to apply for a permit to the relevant local authority (see **13.7.1**). Hence, a different permit has to be obtained from each separate local authority area in which a public charitable collection is to be conducted, unless a Charity Commission order is obtained under s 72 (see **13.15**).

13.8.2 The promoter is defined, in s 65(3), as the person who organises or controls the conduct of the charitable appeal in question. Hence, this could be (but is probably not) a charity trustee.

13.8.3 The application for the permit will have to comply with regulations to be issued under s 73 of the 1992 Act. The application has to specify the period for which it is desired that the permit will last, up to a maximum of 12 months.

13.8.4 The application normally has to be made at least one month before the day on which the collection is to be conducted or, if it is to be collected on more than one day, on the first of those days. However, in cases of emergency, the local authority can allow an application to be made less than a month before the day of the collection. No application can be made more than six months before the first day of the collection. It will be a criminal offence knowingly or recklessly to furnish false information in an application (s 74(3)).

13.8.5 The local authority is obliged to consult the chief officer of police for the police area which comprises or includes the local authority area.

Having enquired of the chief officer of police, the local authority then, by s 68, has either to:

(a) issue a permit; or
(b) refuse the application in accordance with s 69.

If a local authority fails to determine an application for the issue of a permit then the applicant would have the right to seek an order of judicial review from the High Court in respect of the local authority's failure to determine the application.

13.9 Section 68 Permits – Conditions

13.9.1 A local authority may attach such conditions as it thinks fit to any permit (s 68(2)). However, all such conditions have to be consistent with the requirements of any regulations issued by the Secretary of State under s 73(2). Those regulations may make provision:

(a) about the keeping and publication of accounts;
(b) for the prevention of any annoyance to members of the public;
(c) to provide for the use by collectors of badges and certificates of authority including in particular a provision:

  (i) prescribing the form of badges and certificates; and
  (ii) requiring a collector, on request, to permit his badge or certificate to be inspected by a constable or a duly authorised officer of a local authority or by an occupier of any premises visited by him in the course of the collection;

(d) prohibiting persons under a prescribed age from acting as collectors.

13.9.2 By s 68(3), a local authority may, in particular, attach conditions on a permit:

(a) specifying the day of the week, date, time or frequency of the collection;
(b) specifying the locality or localities within their area in which the collection may be conducted; and
(c) regulating the manner in which the collection is to be conducted.

Where a local authority attaches any condition to a permit it must serve notice in writing on the applicant of their decision and of the reasons for their decision. The notice also has to state the right of appeal, set out in s 71(2).

13.10 Appeal Against Conditions Contained in a Permit

A person to whom a permit has been issued under s 68 may appeal to a magistrates' court against the decision of the local authority to attach a condition to the permit (s 71(2)). The appeal has to be lodged within 14 days of the date of service on the person of a notice under s 68. An appeal can be made from the decision of the magistrates' court to the Crown Court.

13.11 Refusal of a Local Authority Permit

Under s 68(1)(b), the local authority can refuse to issue a permit provided it is on the basis of one or more of the grounds specified in s 69. Written notice of the refusal has to be given to the applicant, together with the reasons for the decision. The notice also has to state the right of appeal conferred by s 71(2). The grounds for refusal by a local authority to grant a permit are set out in s 69 of the 1992 Act.

They are as follows:

(a) If it appears to the local authority that the collection would cause undue inconvenience to members of the public by reason of:

    (i)   the day of the week or date on which;
    (ii) the time at which;
    (iii) the frequency with which; or
    (iv) the locality or localities in which;
    it is proposed to be conducted.

(b) If the collection falls on the same day or within one day of another public charitable collection already authorised. This is qualified by s 69(2) whereby the local authority cannot refuse to issue a permit if it appears to them that the collection will only be conducted in one location, which is on land to which members of the public will have access only by virtue of the permission of the occupier of the land.

(c) If the amount likely to be applied for charitable, benevolent or philanthropic purposes would be inadequate, having regard to the likely amount of the collection proceeds. This is similar to s 2(3)(a) of the House to House Collections Act 1931. The local authority's judgment on this was questioned in the committee stage of the Bill, but Viscount Astor pointed out that a similar test had been applied for 50 years under the 1939 Act and it had not given rise to any problems.

(d) If the applicant or any other person is likely to receive an excessive amount by way of remuneration in connection with the collection. This ground also appeared in the 1939 Act.

(e) If the applicant has been convicted:

    (i) of an offence under s 5 of the Police, Factories, etc, (Miscellaneous Provisions) Act 1916, under the House to House Collections Act 1939, under s 119 of the Civic Government (Scotland) Act 1982 or regulations made under it, or under Part III of the 1992 Act or regulations made under s 73 of the 1992 Act; or
    (ii) of any offence which involves dishonesty or an offence which would, in the opinion of the local authority, be likely to be facilitated by the issuing to him of a permit.

(f) If the applicant is a person other than a charitable, benevolent or philanthropic institution for whose benefit the collection is proposed to be conducted, but the local authority are not satisfied that the applicant is authorised by the relevant institution,

(g) If the local authority consider that the applicant, when promoting any collection authorised under Part III of the 1992 Act or under s 119 of the Civic Government (Scotland) Act 1982, did not exercise due diligence:

   (i)   to ensure that persons authorised by him to act as collectors were fit; and

   (ii) to ensure that those persons complied with the provisions of regulations under s 73 of the 1992 Act or s 119 of the Civic Government (Scotland) Act; or

   (iii) to prevent badges or certificates of authority being obtained by persons other than those he had so authorised.

13.12 Appeal Against Refusal to Grant a Permit

If the local authority refuses to issue a permit, the applicant may appeal to the magistrates' court against the decision of the authority within 14 days of the date of the service of the notice under s 68(4). An appeal against the decision of the magistrates' court can be brought to the Crown Court.

13.13 Withdrawal of a Local Authority Permit

13.13.1 Under s 70 of the 1992 Act, a local authority has power to withdraw the permit, to attach any condition to the permit or to vary any existing condition of the permit.

The local authority can do this only if it satisfies s 70(1), ie that it has reason to believe:

(a) that there has been a change in the circumstances which prevailed at the time when it issued the permit and is of the opinion that if the application for the permit had been made in the new circumstances of the case the permit would not have been issued by them; or

(b) that any information furnished to it by the promoter for the purposes of the application for the permit was false in a material particular.

13.13.2 If the local authority decides to impose conditions on an existing permit, they must comply with s 68(2) – ie be in accordance with regulations to be issued under s 73. It does not appear that the local authority can, at this stage, impose any of the conditions set out in s 68(3) and in particular s 68(3)(c), regulating the manner in which the collection is to be conducted. Any notice imposing new conditions has to be advised to the promoter in writing. The notice has to state the right of appeal conferred by s 71(2) and the 14-day period within which such appeal must be brought.

13.13.3 The local authority can also, by s 70(3), withdraw a permit if it has reason to believe that there has been or is likely to be a breach of any condition of the permit. The permit holder has the right to appeal to the magistrates' court within 14 days of the date of service of written notice withdrawing the permit (s 71(2)(b)).

The permit continues to have effect as if it had not been withdrawn or, in the case of an additional condition, if the condition had not been attached until either:

(a) the time for bringing an appeal under s 71(2) has expired; or
(b) until the determination or abandonment of the appeal, if such an appeal is brought.

13.14 Criminal Offences

13.14.1 Under s 73(3), the regulations that will be issued under s 73 may provide that any failure to comply with any part of the regulations will be an offence punishable by a fine on summary conviction, not exceeding £100. This will cover, inter alia, the keeping and publication of accounts, the use of badges and certificates and the banning of persons under a prescribed age from acting as collectors.

13.14.2 It will be an offence, under s 74, to use any badge or certificate or authority which is not being used in accordance with an appeal or to use any false badge or certificate or article to deceive a member of the public. Breach of this section can give rise to a fine not exceeding £1,000 on conviction.

13.14.3 Any person who makes an application under s 67 for a local authority licence and knowingly or recklessly furnishes any information which is false in a material particular, shall be guilty of a criminal offence and on conviction will be liable to a fine not exceeding £1,000.

13.15 Section 72 Orders

Introduction

13.15.1 The obligation to obtain a local authority permit to conduct a public charitable collection is reduced to an extent by s 72 which states:

'(1) Where the Charity Commissioners are satisfied, on the application of any charity, that that charity proposes –
   (a) to promote public charitable collections –
        (i)   throughout England and Wales, or
        (ii) throughout a substantial part of England or Wales,
   in connection with any charitable purposes pursued by the charity, or
   (b) to authorise other persons to promote public charitable collections as mentioned in paragraph (a),
the Commissioners may make an order under this subsection in respect of the charity.'

13.15.2 It must be noted that the capacity to give a national order only applies to charities, ie registered, exempt or excepted charities. It does *not* apply to institutions established for benevolent or philanthropic purposes. This gave rise to great debate in the House of Lords where certain of their Lordships pressed the Government to allow such national organisations as Amnesty International or Greenpeace to be able to benefit from some similar national exemption. The Government refused on the grounds that such benevolent or philanthropic organisations were not susceptible to supervision by the Charity Commissioners and the Government was not prepared to set up a special regime for those organisations.

13.15.3 What is meant by 'throughout England and Wales or throughout a substantial part of England and Wales'? Unless the public charitable collections are to be conducted throughout England and Wales or throughout a substantial part of England and Wales, no exemption order will be issued.

In the House of Lords debate on the report stage of the Bill, Earl Ferrers commented:

> 'My Lords, there is an inherent flexibility in the phrase: "a substantial part of England and Wales".
>
> In the first instance it will be for the Charity Commissioners and ultimately for the courts to decide whether a proposed public charitable collection covers a substantial part of England and Wales. That is an alternative to a collection throughout England and Wales. I suggest that the collection will need to take place in a majority of the districts in England and Wales. For example, collections in association with a long distance sponsored walk will be unlikely to cover a substantial part of England and Wales. To do so the walk would have to pass through at least the majority of districts of England and Wales. A walk around the coastline of England and Wales will probably just about satisfy the requirements; a walk across the Pennines would not.
>
> My noble friend Lord Swinfen was worried about Exemption Orders for disaster appeals. The amendment will allow disaster appeals which are established for charitable purposes to apply for an exemption order under this Clause. They will be eligible for such an Order whether they were concerned with the disaster in this country or abroad. The amendment would not allow disaster appeals established for benevolent or philanthropic purposes to obtain an Exemption Order.' (HL Deb, Vol 535, cols 1241–1242 (19 February 1992).)

Hence, it appears that it will be extremely difficult to obtain an exemption order if the applicant charity has to show that collections will take place in a majority of the districts in England and Wales.

13.15.4 What will be the position with a charity with a number of branches? The position will vary according to how the charity is established. If the branches are part of one national charity so that the branches and the national organisation comprise one legal entity, it could be that the charity will be able to seek an exemption order if it can comply with the terms of s 72(1). On the other hand, a charity whose branches are each independent, separate, legal entities will almost certainly not be able to comply with the Act because it will rely upon the local branches to carry out collections in their localities and, therefore, each local branch will have to obtain the necessary permit from the relevant local authority.

It may be possible, in this case, for the national charity to authorise the independent local branches to collect on the national charity's behalf. In this case, the collection would be carried out by persons authorised by the national charity and might then fall within s 72. The moneys would all have to be paid to the national charity, but it could then (depending on the terms of the appeal) make grants to the local branches.

13.15.5 The exemption order can apply to a collection not only made directly by the charity but by other persons authorised by the charity to promote a public charitable collection. This will cover a collection organised by a professional fund-raiser.

13.15.6 The area covered by the exemption order will be decided by the Charity Commissioners. Section 72(2) gives the Commissioners the power to order that the collections be conducted 'in such an area or areas as may be specified in the order'.

In addition, by s 72(3) an order under s 72(1) may:

(a) include such conditions as the Commissioners think fit, eg to notify the relevant local authorities;
(b) be expressed to have effect without limit of time or for a specified period only; or
(c) be revoked or varied by a further order of the Commissioners.

13.15.7 If the Commissioners decide to revoke or vary an order they have to serve written notice of their reasons for making a further order on the charity. However, this is qualified by the words 'unless it appears to them (ie the Commissioners) that the interests of the charity would not be prejudiced by the further order'. Whether or not the Commissioners' judgment on any such question is fair or not will be an interesting question. What will be the position if the Commissioners revoke an order but decide that the interests of the charity would not be prejudiced by the revocation of the order and, therefore, do not give reasons? There is no right of appeal against a decision of the Commissioners in this regard. An aggrieved charity could apply to the High Court for an order of judicial review against the Commissioners in these circumstances.

13.15.8 Any collections conducted in accordance with an order from the Charity Commissioners under s 72 will have to comply with regulations to be issued by the Secretary of State under s 72(1). An obligation to inform and consult local authorities may be included.

13.16 Conclusion

The provisions of Part III of the 1992 Act cover a very large range of fund-raising activities, undertaken directly by or on behalf of charitable, benevolent or philanthropic institutions. It must be emphasised that, unlike Part II, Part III not only applies to professional fund-raisers and commercial participators. It regulates fund-raising directly, by charitable institutions (as defined). Although the definition of public place was considerably narrowed after debate in the House of Lords, many fund-raising activities by or on behalf of charitable institutions are covered by the Act. Accordingly, the following activities all require either a local authority permit or, in the case of charities, a Charity Commission exemption order under s 72.

(a) All forms of collection on highways and in public places, including railway forecourts, shopping precincts, airport lounges, etc.
(b) House to house collections.
(c) Jumble collections.
(d) All sales of goods on behalf of charities in a public place.

This list is illustrative only.

APPENDIX 1

CHARITIES ACT 1992

(1992 c 41)

ARRANGEMENT OF SECTIONS

PART I
CHARITIES
Preliminary

PART I

CHARITIES

Preliminary

1. Interpretation of Part I etc

(1) In this Part –
'the 1960 Act' means the Charities Act 1960;
'financial year' –

    (a) in relation to a charity which is a company, shall be construed in accordance with section 223 of the Companies Act 1985; and

    (b) in relation to any other charity, shall be construed in accordance with regulations made by virtue of section 20(2);

'gross income', in relation to a charity, means its gross recorded income from all sources, including special trusts;

'independent examiner', in relation to a charity, means such a person as is mentioned in section 21(3)(a);

'the official custodian' means the official custodian for charities;

'the register' (unless the context otherwise requires) means the register of charities kept under section 4 of the 1960 Act, and 'registered' shall be construed accordingly;

'special trust' means property which is held and administered by or on behalf of a charity for any special purposes of the charity, and is so held and administered on separate trusts relating only to that property.

(2) Subject to subsection (3) below, sections 45 and 46 of the 1960 Act (interpretation) shall have effect for the purposes of this Part as they have effect for the purposes of that Act.

(3) A special trust shall not, by itself, constitute a charity for the purposes of sections 19 to 26.

(4) No vesting or transfer of any property in pursuance of any provision of this Part, or of any provision of the 1960 Act as amended by this Part, shall operate as a breach of a covenant or condition against alienation or give rise to a forfeiture.

Registration of charities

2. The register of charities

(1) Section 4 of the 1960 Act (the register of charities) shall be amended as follows.

(2) For subsection (1) there shall be substituted –

    '(1) The Commissioners shall continue to keep a register of charities, which shall be kept by them in such manner as they think fit.'

(3) In subsection (2), after 'so excepted' there shall be inserted '(other than one excepted by paragraph (a) of that subsection)'.

(4) After subsection (2) there shall be inserted –

    '(2A) The register shall contain –
        (a) the name of every registered charity; and

(b) such other particulars of, and such other information relating to, every such charity as the Commissioners think fit.'

(5) In subsection (4), for paragraph (c) there shall be substituted –
  '(c) any charity which has neither –
    (i) any permanent endowment, nor
    (ii) the use or occupation of any land,
    and whose income from all sources does not in aggregate amount to more than £1,000 a year;'.

(6) After subsection (7) there shall be inserted –

'(7A) Where any information contained in the register is not in documentary form, subsection (7) above shall be construed as requiring the information to be available for public inspection in legible form at all reasonable times.
(7B) If the Commissioners so determine, that subsection shall not apply to any particular information contained in the register and specified in their determination.'

(7) After subsection (8) there shall be inserted –

'(8A) If he thinks it expedient to do so –
    (a) in consequence of changes in the value of money, or
    (b) with a view to extending the scope of the exception provided for by subsection (4)(c) above,
the Secretary of State may by order amend subsection (4)(c) by substituting a different sum for the sum for the time being specified there.

(8B) Any such order shall be made by statutory instrument subject to annulment in pursuance of a resolution of either House of Parliament.'

(8) Where an exempt charity is on the register immediately before the time when subsection (3) above comes into force, its registration shall cease to have effect at that time.

(9) Section 4 of the 1960 Act, as amended by this section, and with the omission of repealed provisions, is set out in Schedule 1 to this Act.

3. Status of registered charity (other than small charity) to appear on official publications etc

(1) This section applies to a registered charity if its gross income in its last financial year exceeded £5,000.

(2) Where this section applies to a registered charity, the fact that it is a registered charity shall be stated in English in legible characters –
    (a) in all notices, advertisements and other documents issued by or on behalf of the charity and soliciting money or other property for the benefit of the charity;
    (b) in all bills of exchange, promissory notes, endorsements, cheques and orders for money or goods purporting to be signed on behalf of the charity; and
    (c) in all bills rendered by it and in all its invoices, receipts and letters of credit.

(3) Subsection (2)(a) has effect whether the solicitation is express or implied, and whether the money or other property is to be given for any consideration or not.

(4) If, in the case of a registered charity to which this section applies, any person issues or authorises the issue of any document falling within paragraph (a) or (c) of subsection (2) in which the fact that the charity is a registered charity is not stated as required by that subsection, he shall be guilty of an offence and liable on summary conviction to a fine not exceeding the third level on the standard scale.

(5) If, in the case of any such registered charity, any person signs any document falling within paragraph (b) of subsection (2) in which the fact that the charity is a registered charity is not stated as required by that subsection, he shall be guilty of an offence and liable on summary conviction to a fine not exceeding the third level on the standard scale.

(6) The Secretary of State may by order amend subsection (1) by substituting a different sum for the sum for the time being specified there.

Charity names

4. Power of Commissioners to require charity's name to be changed

(1) Where this subsection applies to a charity, the Commissioners may give a direction requiring the name of the charity to be changed, within such period as is specified in the direction, to such other name as the charity trustees may determine with the approval of the Commissioners.

(2) Subsection (1) applies to a charity if –
  (a) it is a registered charity and its name ('the registered name') –
    (i) is the same as, or
    (ii) is in the opinion of the Commissioners too like,
    the name, at the time when the registered name was entered in the register in respect of the charity, of any other charity (whether registered or not);
  (b) the name of the charity is in the opinion of the Commissioners likely to mislead the public as to the true nature –
    (i) of the purposes of the charity as set out in its trusts, or
    (ii) of the activities which the charity carries on under its trusts in pursuit of those purposes;
  (c) the name of the charity includes any word or expression for the time being specified in regulations made by the Secretary of State and the inclusion in its name of that word or expression is in the opinion of the Commissioners likely to mislead the public in any respect as to the status of the charity;
  (d) the name of the charity is in the opinion of the Commissioners likely to give the impression that the charity is connected in some way with Her Majesty's Government or any local authority, or with any other body of persons or any individual, when it is not so connected; or
  (e) the name of the charity is in the opinion of the Commissioners offensive;
and in this subsection any reference to the name of a charity is, in relation to a registered charity, a reference to the name by which it is registered.

(3) Any direction given by virtue of subsection (2)(a) above must be given within 12 months of the time when the registered name was entered in the register in respect of the charity.

(4) Any direction given under this section with respect to a charity shall be given to the charity trustees; and on receiving any such direction the charity trustees shall give effect to it notwithstanding anything in the trusts of the charity.

(5) Where the name of any charity is changed under this section, then (without prejudice to section 4(6)(b) of the 1960 Act (notification of changes in particulars of registered charity)) it shall be the duty of the charity trustees forthwith to notify the Commissioners of the charity's new name and of the date on which the change occurred.

(6) A change of name by a charity under this section does not affect any rights or obligations of the charity; and any legal proceedings that might have been continued or commenced by or against it in its former name may be continued or commenced by or against it in its new name.

(7) Section 26(3) of the Companies Act 1985 (minor variations in names to be disregarded) shall apply for the purposes of this section as if the reference to section 26(1)(c) of that Act were a reference to subsection (2)(a) above.

(8) Any reference in this section to the charity trustees of a charity shall, in relation to a charity which is a company, be read as a reference to the directors of the company.

(9) Nothing in this section applies to an exempt charity.

5. Effect of direction under s 4 where charity is a company

(1) Where any direction is given under section 4 of this Act with respect to a charity which is a company, the direction shall be taken to require the name of the charity to be changed by resolution of the directors of the company.

(2) Section 380 of the Companies Act 1985 (registration etc. of resolutions and agreements) shall apply to any resolution passed by the directors in compliance with any such direction.

(3) Where the name of such a charity is changed in compliance with any such direction, the registrar of companies –
    (a) shall (subject to section 26 of the Companies Act 1985 (prohibition on registration of certain names)) enter the new name on the register of companies in place of the former name, and
    (b) shall issue a certificate of incorporation altered to meet the circumstances of the case;
and the change of name has effect from the date on which the altered certificate is issued.

Supervision and control by Commissioners

6. General power to institute inquiries

(1) Section 6 of the 1960 Act (general power to institute inquiries) shall be amended as follows.

(2) In subsection (3) –
    (a) for the words from 'may by order' to 'require' there shall be substituted ', or a person appointed by them to conduct it, may direct'; and

(b) for paragraph (b) there shall be substituted –

'(b) to furnish copies of documents in his custody or under his control which relate to any matter in question at the inquiry, and to verify any such copies by statutory declaration;

(c) to attend at a specified time and place and give evidence or produce any such documents.'

(3) In subsection (5), for 'an order or precept under paragraph (b)' there shall be substituted 'a direction under paragraph (c)'.

(4) Subsection (6) (exemption for person claiming to hold property adversely to a charity) shall be omitted.

(5) For subsection (7) there shall be substituted –

'(7) Where an inquiry has been held under this section, the Commissioners may either –

(a) cause the report of the person conducting the inquiry, or such other statement of the results of the inquiry as they think fit, to be printed and published, or

(b) publish any such report or statement in some other way which is calculated in their opinion to bring it to the attention of persons who may wish to make representations to them about the action to be taken.'

(6) Subsection (9) (which is superseded by section 54(2) below) shall be omitted.

7. Power of Commissioners to obtain information and documents

(1) Section 7 of the 1960 Act (power to call for documents and search records) shall be amended as follows.

(2) For subsection (1) there shall be substituted –

'(1) The Commissioners may by order –

(a) require any person to furnish them with any information in his possession which relates to any charity and is relevant to the discharge of their functions or of the functions of the official custodian for charities;

(b) require any person who has in his custody or under his control any document which relates to any charity and is relevant to the discharge of their functions or of the functions of the official custodian for charities –

(i) to furnish them with a copy of or extract from the document, or

(ii) (unless the document forms part of the records or other documents of a court or of a public or local authority) to transmit the document itself to them for their inspection.'

(3) Subsection (4) (exemption for person claiming to hold property adversely to a charity) shall be omitted.

(4) At the end of the section there shall be added –

'(6) The rights conferred by subsection (2) above shall, in relation to information recorded otherwise than in legible form, include the right to require the information to be made available in legible form for inspection or for a copy or extract to be made of or from it.'

8. Power to act for protection of charities

(1) Section 20 of the 1960 Act (power to act for protection of charities) shall be amended as follows.

(2) For subsection (1) there shall be substituted –

'(1) Where, at any time after they have instituted an inquiry under section 6 of this Act with respect to any charity, the Commissioners are satisfied –

(a) that there is or has been any misconduct or mismanagement in the administration of the charity; or

(b) that it is necessary or desirable to act for the purpose of protecting the property of the charity or securing a proper application for the purposes of the charity of that property or of property coming to the charity;

the Commissioners may of their own motion do one or more of the following things, namely –

(i) by order suspend any trustee, charity trustee, officer, agent or employee of the charity from the exercise of his office or employment pending consideration being given to his removal (whether under this section or otherwise);

(ii) by order appoint such number of additional charity trustees as they consider necessary for the proper administration of the charity;

(iii) by order vest any property held by or in trust for the charity in the official custodian for charities, or require the persons in whom any such property is vested to transfer it to him, or appoint any person to transfer any such property to him;

(iv) order any person who holds any property on behalf of the charity, or of any trustee for it, not to part with the property without the approval of the Commissioners;

(v) order any debtor of the charity not to make any payment in or towards the discharge of his liability to the charity without the approval of the Commissioners;

(vi) by order restrict (notwithstanding anything in the trusts of the charity) the transactions which may be entered into, or the nature or amount of the payments which may be made, in the administration of the charity without the approval of the Commissioners;

(vii) by order appoint (in accordance with section 20A of this Act) a receiver and manager in respect of the property and affairs of the charity.

(1A) Where, at any time after they have instituted an inquiry under section 6 of this Act with respect to any charity, the Commissioners are satisfied –

(a) that there is or has been any misconduct or mismanagement in the administration of the charity; and

(b) that it is necessary or desirable to act for the purpose of protecting the property of the charity or securing a proper application for the purposes of the charity of that property or of property coming to the charity;

the Commissioners may of their own motion do either or both of the following things, namely –

(i) by order remove any trustee, charity trustee, officer, agent or employee of the charity who has been responsible for or privy to the misconduct or mismanagement or has by his conduct contributed to it or facilitated it;

(ii)   by order establish a scheme for the administration of the charity.'

(3) In subsection (2), after 'subsection (1)' there shall be inserted 'or (1A)'.

(4) In subsection (3), for paragraph (a) there shall be substituted –

'(a) where, within the last five years, the trustee –
  (i)   having previously been adjudged bankrupt or had his estate seques-
        trated, has been discharged, or
  (ii) having previously made a composition or arrangement with, or
        granted a trust deed for, his creditors, has been discharged in respect
        of it;
(aa) where the trustee is a corporation in liquidation;
(ab) where the trustee is incapable of acting by reason of mental disorder within
     the meaning of the Mental Health Act 1983;'.

(5) For subsection (7) there shall be substituted –

'(7) Subject to subsection (7A) below, subsections (10) and (11) of section 18 of
this Act shall apply to orders under this section as they apply to orders under that
section.
(7A) The requirement to obtain any such certificate or leave as is mentioned in the
    proviso to section 18(11) shall not apply to –
  (a) an appeal by a charity or any of the charity trustees of a charity against an
       order under subsection (1)(vii) above appointing a receiver and manager
       in respect of the charity's property and affairs, or
  (b) an appeal by a person against an order under subsection (1A)(i) or (3)(a)
       above removing him from his office or employment.
(7B) Subsection (12) of section 18 of this Act shall apply to an order under this
section which establishes a scheme for the administration of a charity as it applies
to such an order under that section.'

(6) In subsection (8), for the words from the beginning to 'the suspension' there shall
be substituted 'The power of the Commissioners to make an order under subsection
(1)(i) above shall not be exercisable so as to suspend any person from the exercise of his
office or employment for a period of more than twelve months; but (without
prejudice to the generality of section 40(1) of this Act) any such order made in the case
of any person may make provision as respects the period of his suspension'.

(7) In subsection (9), after 'section' there shall be inserted 'otherwise than by virtue of
subsection (1) above'.

(8) After subsection (9) there shall be inserted –

'(9A) The Commissioners shall, at such intervals as they think fit, review any
order made by them under paragraph (i), or any of paragraphs (iii) to (vii), of
subsection (1) above; and, if on any such review it appears to them that it would be
appropriate to discharge the order in whole or in part, they shall so discharge it
(whether subject to any savings or other transitional provisions or not).'

(9) For subsection (10) there shall be substituted –

'(10) If any person contravenes an order under subsection (1)(iv), (v) or (vi)
above, he shall be guilty of an offence and liable on summary conviction to a fine
not exceeding the fifth level on the standard scale.

(10A) Subsection (10) above shall not be taken to preclude the bringing of proceedings for breach of trust against any charity trustee or trustee for a charity in respect of a contravention of an order under subsection (1)(iv) or (vi) above (whether proceedings in respect of the contravention are brought against him under subsection (10) above or not).'

(10) Section 20 of the 1960 Act, as amended by this section, and with the omission of repealed provisions, is set out in Schedule 1 to this Act.

9. Supplementary provisions relating to receiver and manager appointed for a charity

After section 20 of the 1960 Act there shall be inserted –

'20A. Supplementary provisions relating to receiver and manager appointed for a charity

(1) The Commissioners may under section 20(1)(vii) of this Act appoint to be receiver and manager in respect of the property and affairs of a charity such person (other than an officer or employee of theirs) as they think fit.

(2) Without prejudice to the generality of section 40(1) of this Act, any order made by the Commissioners under section 20(1)(vii) of this Act may make provision with respect to the functions to be discharged by the receiver and manager appointed by the order; and those functions shall be discharged by him under the supervision of the Commissioners.

(3) In connection with the discharge of those functions any such order may provide –
  (a) for the receiver and manager appointed by the order to have such powers and duties of the charity trustees of the charity concerned (whether arising under this Act or otherwise) as are specified in the order;
  (b) for any powers or duties exercisable or falling to be performed by the receiver and manager by virtue of paragraph (a) above to be exercisable or performed by him to the exclusion of those trustees.

(4) Where a person has been appointed receiver and manager by any such order –
  (a) section 24 of this Act shall apply to him and to his functions as a person so appointed as it applies to a charity trustee of the charity concerned and to his duties as such; and
  (b) the Commissioners may apply to the High Court for directions in relation to any particular matter arising in connection with the discharge of those functions.

(5) The High Court may on an application under subsection (4)(b) above –
  (a) give such directions, or
  (b) make such orders declaring the rights of any persons (whether before the court or not),
as it thinks just; and the costs of any such application shall be paid by the charity concerned.

(6) Regulations may make provision with respect to –

(a) the appointment and removal of persons appointed in accordance with this section;

(b) the remuneration of such persons out of the income of the charities concerned;

(c) the making of reports to the Commissioners by such persons.

(7) Regulations under subsection (6) above may, in particular, authorise the Commissioners –

(a) to require security for the due discharge of his functions to be given by a person so appointed;

(b) to determine the amount of such a person's remuneration;

(c) to disallow any amount of remuneration in such circumstances as are prescribed by the regulations.'

10. Additional powers exercisable by Commissioners in relation to charitable companies

(1) At the end of section 30 of the 1960 Act (charitable companies: winding up) there shall be added –

'(2) Where a charity may be so wound up by the High Court, such a petition may also be presented by the Commissioners if, at any time after they have instituted an inquiry under section 6 of this Act with respect to the charity, they are satisfied as mentioned in section 20(1)(a) or (b) of this Act.

(3) Where a charitable company is dissolved, the Commissioners may make an application under section 651 of the Companies Act 1985 (power of court to declare dissolution of company void) for an order to be made under that section with respect to the company; and for this purpose subsection (1) of that section shall have effect in relation to a charitable company as if the reference to the liquidator of the company included a reference to the Commissioners.

(4) Where a charitable company's name has been struck off the register of companies under section 652 of the Companies Act 1985 (power of registrar to strike defunct company off register), the Commissioners may make an application under section 653(2) of that Act (objection to striking off by person aggrieved) for an order restoring the company's name to that register; and for this purpose section 653(2) shall have effect in relation to a charitable company as if the reference to any such person aggrieved as is there mentioned included a reference to the Commissioners.

(5) The powers exercisable by the Commissioners by virtue of this section shall be exercisable by them of their own motion, but shall be exercisable only with the agreement of the Attorney General on each occasion.

(6) In this section 'charitable company' means a company which is a charity.'

(2) The existing provisions of section 30 of the 1960 Act (as amended by the Companies Act 1989) shall accordingly constitute subsection (1) of that section.

11. Report of inquiry held by Commissioners to be evidence in certain proceedings

After section 28 of the 1960 Act there shall be inserted –

'28A. Report of s 6 inquiry to be evidence in certain proceedings

(1) A copy of the report of the person conducting an inquiry under section 6 of this Act shall, if certified by the Commissioners to be a true copy, be admissible in any proceedings to which this section applies –
  (a) as evidence of any fact stated in the report; and
  (b) as evidence of the opinion of that person as to any matter referred to in it.

(2) This section applies to –
  (a) any legal proceedings instituted by the Commissioners under this Part of this Act; and
  (b) any legal proceedings instituted by the Attorney General in respect of a charity.

(3) A document purporting to be a certificate issued for the purposes of subsection (1) above shall be received in evidence and be deemed to be such a certificate, unless the contrary is proved.'

12. Supervision by Commissioners of certain Scottish charities

(1) The following provisions of the 1960 Act (as amended by this Act), namely –
  (a) sections 6 and 7,
  (b) section 20 (except subsection (1A)(ii)), and
  (c) section 20A,
shall have effect in relation to any recognised body which is managed or controlled wholly or mainly in or from England or Wales as they have effect in relation to a charity; and in paragraph 3(6) of Schedule 1 to that Act (constitution etc. of Commissioners) the reference to sections 6, 20 and 20A of the Act includes a reference to those sections as applied by this subsection.

(2) Where –
  (a) a recognised body is managed or controlled wholly or mainly in or from Scotland, but
  (b) any person in England and Wales holds any property on behalf of the body or of any person concerned in its management or control,
then, if the Commissioners are satisfied as to the matters mentioned in subsection (3), they may make an order requiring the person holding the property not to part with it without their approval.

(3) The matters referred to in subsection (2) are –
  (a) that there has been any misconduct or mismanagement in the administration of the body; and
  (b) that it is necessary or desirable to make an order under that subsection for the purpose of protecting the property of the body or securing a proper application of such property for the purposes of the body;
and the reference in that subsection to the Commissioners being satisfied as to those matters is a reference to their being so satisfied on the basis of such information as may be supplied to them by the Lord Advocate.

(4) Where –
  (a) any person in England and Wales holds any property on behalf of a

recognised body or of any person concerned in the management or
control of such a body, and

(b) the Commissioners are satisfied (whether on the basis of such information as may be supplied to them by the Lord Advocate or otherwise) –

(i) that there has been any misconduct or mismanagement in the administration of the body, and

(ii) that it is necessary or desirable to make an order under this subsection
for the purpose of protecting the property of the body or securing a
proper application of such property for the purposes of the body,

the Commissioners may by order vest the property in such recognised body or charity
as is specified in the order in accordance with subsection (5), or require any persons in
whom the property is vested to transfer it to any such body or charity, or appoint any
person to transfer the property to any such body or charity.

(5) The Commissioners may specify in an order under subsection (4) such other
recognised body or such charity as they consider appropriate, being a body or charity
whose purposes are, in the opinion of the Commissioners, as similar in character to
those of the body referred to in paragraph (a) of that subsection as is reasonably
practicable; but the Commissioners shall not so specify any body or charity unless
they have received –

(a) from the persons concerned in the management or control of the body, or

(b) from the charity trustees of the charity,

as the case may be, written confirmation that they are willing to accept the property.

(6) In this section 'recognised body' has the same meaning as in Part I of the Law
Reform (Miscellaneous Provisions) (Scotland) (Act 1990 (Scottish charities).

Powers with respect to administration of charities

13. Commissioners' concurrent jurisdiction with High Court for certain purposes

(1) Section 18 of the 1960 Act (Commissioners' concurrent jurisdiction with High
Court for certain purposes) shall be amended as follows.

(2) At the end of subsection (4) there shall be added '; or

(c) in the case of a charity other than an exempt charity, on the
application of the Attorney General.'

(3) For subsection (5) there shall be substituted –

'(5) In the case of a charity which is not an exempt charity and whose income
from all sources does not in aggregate exceed £500 a year, the Commissioners
may exercise their jurisdiction under this section on the application –

(a) of any one or more of the charity trustees; or

(b) of any person interested in the charity; or

(c) of any two or more inhabitants of the area of the charity, if it is a local
charity.'

(4) In subsection (6), for the words from 'the Commissioners may' to '(5) above:'
there shall be substituted 'and the Commissioners have given the charity trustees an

opportunity to make representations to them, the Commissioners may proceed as if an application for a scheme had been made by the charity:'.

(5) After subsection (6) there shall be inserted –

'(6A) Where –
  (a) a charity cannot apply to the Commissioners for a scheme by reason of any vacancy among the charity trustees or the absence or incapacity of any of them, but
  (b) such an application is made by such number of the charity trustees as the Commissioners consider appropriate in the circumstances of the case,
the Commissioners may nevertheless proceed as if the application were an application made by the charity.'

(6) At the end of the section there shall be added –

'(13) If he thinks it expedient to do so –
  (a) in consequence of changes in the value of money, or
  (b) with a view to increasing the number of charities in respect of which the Commissioners may exercise their jurisdiction under this section in accordance with subsection (5) above,
the Secretary of State may by order amend that subsection by substituting a different sum for the sum for the time being specified there.
(14) Any such order shall be made by statutory instrument subject to annulment in pursuance of a resolution of either House of Parliament.'

14. Trust corporations appointed by Commissioners under 1960 Act

(1) After section 21 of the 1960 Act there shall be inserted –

'21A. Application of provisions to trust corporations appointed under ss 18 or 20

In the definition of 'trust corporation' contained in the following provisions, namely –
  (a) section 117(xxx) of the Settled Land Act 1925,
  (b) section 68(18) of the Trustee Act 1925,
  (c) section 205(xxviii) of the Law of Property Act 1925,
  (d) section 55(xxvi) of the Administration of Estates Act 1925, and
  (e) section 128 of the Supreme Court Act 1981,
the reference to a corporation appointed by the court in any particular case to be a trustee includes a reference to a corporation appointed by the Commissioners under this Act to be a trustee.'

(2) The amendment made by subsection (1) above shall be deemed always to have had effect; but in the section 21A inserted by that subsection the reference to section 128 of the Supreme Court Act 1981 shall, in relation to any time before 1st January 1982, be construed as a reference to section 175(1) of the Supreme Court of Judicature (Consolidation) Act 1925.

15. Application of property cy-près

(1) Section 14 of the 1960 Act (application cy-près of gifts of donors unknown or disclaiming) shall be amended as follows.

(2) In subsection (1) –
  (a) for 'after such advertisements and inquiries as are reasonable, cannot' there shall be substituted 'after –
    (i) the prescribed advertisements and inquiries have been published and made, and
    (ii) the prescribed period beginning with the publication of those advertisements has expired,
    cannot'; and
  (b) for 'written disclaimer' there shall be inserted 'disclaimer in the prescribed form'.

(3) After subsection (1) there shall be inserted –

'(1A) Where the prescribed advertisements and inquiries have been published and made by or on behalf of trustees with respect to any such property, the trustees shall not be liable to any person in respect of the property if no claim by him to be interested in it is received by them before the expiry of the period mentioned in subsection (1)(a)(ii) above.'

(4) In subsection (4)(b), for 'twelve' there shall be substituted 'six'.

(5) After subsection (4) there shall be inserted –

'(4A) Where –
    (a) any sum is, in accordance with any such directions, set aside for meeting any such claims, but
    (b) the aggregate amount of any such claims actually made exceeds the relevant amount,
then, if the Commissioners so direct, each of the donors in question shall be entitled only to such proportion of the relevant amount as the amount of his claim bears to the aggregate amount referred to in paragraph (b) above; and for this purpose 'the relevant amount' means the amount of the sum so set aside after deduction of any expenses properly incurred by the charity trustees in connection with claims relating to the donors' gifts.'

(6) After subsection (5) there shall be inserted –

'5(A) In this section 'prescribed' means prescribed by regulations made by the Commissioners; and such regulations may, as respects the advertisements which are to be published for the purposes of subsection (1)(a) above, make provision as to the form and content of such advertisements as well as the manner in which they are to be published.
(5B) Any regulations made by the Commissioners under this section shall be published by the Commissioners in such manner as they think fit.'

16. Common deposit funds

After section 22 of the 1960 Act there shall be inserted –

'22A. Schemes to establish common deposit funds

(1) The court or the Commissioners may by order make and bring into effect schemes (in this section referred to as 'common deposit schemes') for the establishment of common deposit funds under trusts which provide –
  (a) for sums to be deposited by or on behalf of a charity participating in the scheme and invested under the control of trustees appointed to manage the fund; and
  (b) for any such charity to be entitled (subject to the provisions of the scheme) to repayment of any sums so desposited and to interest thereon at a rate determined under the scheme.

(2) Subject to subsection (3) below, the following provisions of section 22 of this Act, namely –
  (a) subsections (2) to (4), and
  (b) subsections (7) to (11),
shall have effect in relation to common deposit schemes and common deposit funds as they have effect in relation to common investment schemes and common investment funds.

(3) In its application in accordance with subsection (2) above, subsection (4) of that section shall have effect with the substitution for paragraphs (b) and (c) of the following paragraphs –
  '(b) for regulating as to time, amount or otherwise the right to repayment of sums deposited in the fund;
  (c) for authorising a part of the income for any year to be credited to a reserve account maintained for the purpose of counteracting any losses accruing to the fund, and generally for regulating the manner in which the rate of interest on deposits is to be determined from time to time;'.'

17 Power of Commissioners to authorise certain ex gratia payments etc by charities

After section 23 of the 1960 Act there shall be inserted –

'23A. Power to authorise certain ex gratia payments etc

(1) Subject to subsection (3) below, the Commissioners may by order exercise the same power as is exercisable by the Attorney General to authorise the charity trustees of a charity –
  (a) to make any application of property of the charity, or
  (b) to waive to any extent, on behalf of the charity, its entitlement to receive any property,
in a case where the charity trustees –
        (i) (apart from this section) have no power to do so, but
        (ii) in all the circumstances regard themselves as being under a moral obligation to do so.

(2) The power conferred on the Commissioners by subsection (1) above shall be exercisable by them under the supervision of, and in accordance with such directions as may be given by, the Attorney General; and any such directions may in particular require the Commissioners, in such circumstances as are specified in the directions –

(a) to refrain from exercising that power; or

(b) to consult the Attorney General before exercising it.

(3) Where –

   (a) an application is made to the Commissioners for them to exercise that power in a case where they are not precluded from doing so by any such directions, but

   (b) they consider that it would nevertheless be desirable for the application to be entertained by the Attorney General rather than by them,

they shall refer the application to the Attorney General.

(4) It is hereby declared that where, in the case of any application made to them as mentioned in subsection (3)(a) above, the Commissioners determine the application by refusing to authorise charity trustees to take any action falling within subsection (1)(a) or (b) above, that refusal shall not preclude the Attorney General, on an application subsequently made to him by the trustees, from authorising the trustees to take that action.'

18. Dormant bank accounts of charities

(1) Where the Commissioners –

   (a) are informed by a relevant institution –

      (i) that it holds one or more accounts in the name of or on behalf of a particular charity ('the relevant charity'), and

      (ii) that the account, or (if it so holds two or more accounts) each of the accounts, is dormant, and

   (b) are unable, after making reasonable inquiries, to locate that charity or any of its trustees,

they may give a direction under subsection (2).

(2) A direction under this subsection is a direction which –

   (a) requires the institution concerned to transfer the amount, or (as the case may be) the aggregate amount, standing to the credit of the relevant charity in the account or accounts in question to such other charity as is specified in the direction in accordance with subsection (3); or

   (b) requires the institution concerned to transfer to each of two or more other charities so specified in the direction such part of that amount or aggregate amount as is there specified in relation to that charity.

(3) The Commissioners may specify in a direction under subsection (2) such other charity or charities as they consider appropriate, having regard, in a case where the purposes of the relevant charity are known to them, to those purposes and to the purposes of the other charity or charities; but the Commissioners shall not so specify any charity unless they have received from the charity trustees written confirmation that those trustees are willing to accept the amount proposed to be transferred to the charity.

(4) Any amount received by a charity by virtue of this section shall be received by the charity on terms that –

   (a) it shall be held and applied by the charity for the purposes of the charity, but

   (b) it shall, as property of the charity, nevertheless be subject to any restrictions on expenditure to which it was subject as property of the relevant charity.

(5) Where –
  (a) the Commissioners have been informed as mentioned in subsection (1)(a) by
      any relevant institution, and
  (b) before any transfer is made by the institution in pursuance of a direction under
      subsection (2), the institution has, by reason of any circumstances, cause to
      believe that the account, or (as the case may be) any of the accounts, held by it
      in the name of or on behalf of the relevant charity is no longer dormant.
the institution shall forthwith notify those circumstances in writing to the Commissioners; and, if it appears to the Commissioners that the account or accounts in
question is or are no longer dormant, they shall revoke any direction under subsection
(2) which has previously been given by them to the institution with respect to the
relevant charity.

(6) The receipt of any charity trustees or trustee for a charity in respect of any amount
received from a relevant institution by virtue of this section shall be a complete
discharge of the institution in respect of that amount.

(7) No obligation as to secrecy or other restriction on disclosure (however imposed)
shall preclude a relevant institution from disclosing any information to the Commissioners for the purpose of enabling them to discharge their functions under this
section.

(8) For the purposes of this section –
  (a) an account is dormant if no transaction, other than –
      (i)   a transaction consisting in a payment into the account, or
      (ii) a transaction which the institution holding the account has itself caused to
            be effected,
      has been effected in relation to the account within the period of five years
      immediately preceding the date when the Commissioners are informed as
      mentioned in paragraph (a) of subsection (1);
  (b) a 'relevant institution' means –
      (i)   the Bank of England;
      (ii) an institution which is authorised by the Bank of England to operate a
            deposit-taking business under Part I of the Banking Act 1987;
      (iii) a building society which is authorised by the Building Societies Commis-
            sion under section 9 of the Building Socities Act 1986 to raise money
            from its members; or
      (iv) such other institution mentioned in Schedule 2 to the Banking Act 1987 as
            the Secretary of State may prescribe by regulations; and
  (c) references to the transfer of any amount to a charity are references to its
      transfer –
      (i)   to the charity trustees, or
      (ii) to any trustee for the charity,
      as the charity trustees may determine (and any reference to any amount
      received by a charity shall be construed accordingly).

(9) For the purpose of determining the matters in respect of which any of the powers
conferred by section 6 or 7 of the 1960 Act (power of Commissioners to institute
inquiries or obtain information) may be exercised it shall be assumed that the
Commissioners have no functions under this section in relation to accounts to which
this subsection applies (with the result that, for example, a relevant institution shall
not, in connection with the functions of the Commissioners under this section, be

required under section 6(3)(a) of that Act to furnish any statements, or answer any questions or inquiries, with respect to any such accounts held by the institution).

This subsection applies to accounts which are dormant accounts by virtue of subsection (8)(a) above but would not be such accounts if sub-paragraph (i) of that provision were omitted.

(10) Subsection (1) shall not apply to any account held in the name of or on behalf of an exempt charity.

Charity accounts

19. Duty to keep accounting records

(1) The charity trustees of a charity shall ensure that accounting records are kept in respect of the charity which are sufficient to show and explain all the charity's transactions, and which are such as to –
  (a) disclose at any time, with reasonable accuracy, the financial position of the charity at that time, and
  (b) enable the trustees to ensure that, where any statements of accounts are prepared by them under section 20(1), those statements of accounts comply with the requirements of regulations under that provision.

(2) The accounting records shall in particular contain –
  (a) entries showing from day to day all sums of money received and expended by the charity, and the matters in respect of which the receipt and expenditure takes place; and
  (b) a record of the assets and liabilities of the charity.

(3) The charity trustees of a charity shall preserve any accounting records made for the purposes of this section in respect of the charity for at least six years from the end of the financial year of the charity in which they are made.

(4) Where a charity ceases to exist within the period of six years mentioned in subsection (3) as it applies to any accounting records, the obligation to preserve those records in accordance with that subsection shall continue to be discharged by the last charity trustees of the charity, unless the Commissioners consent in writing to the records being destroyed or otherwise disposed of.

(5) Nothing in this section applies to a charity which is a company.

20. Annual statements of accounts

(1) The charity trustees of a charity shall (subject to subsection (3)) prepare in respect of each financial year of the charity a statement of accounts complying with such requirements as to its form and contents as may be prescribed by regulations made by the Secretary of State.

(2) Without prejudice to the generality of subsection (1), regulations under that subsection may make provision –
  (a) for any such statement to be prepared in accordance with such methods and principles as are specified or referred to in the regulations;
  (b) as to any information to be provided by way of notes to the accounts;

and regulations under that subsection may also make provision for determining the financial years of a charity for the purposes of this Part and any regulations made under it.

(3) Where a charity's gross income in any financial year does not exceed £25,000, the charity trustees may, in respect of that year, elect to prepare the following, namely –
  (a) a receipts and payments account, and
  (b) a statement of assets and liabilities,
instead of a statement of accounts under subsection (1).

(4) The charity trustees of a charity shall preserve –
  (a) any statement of accounts prepared by them under subsection (1), or
  (b) any account and statement prepared by them under subsection (3),
for at least six years from the end of the financial year to which any such statement relates or (as the case may be) to which any such account and statement relate.

(5) Subsection (4) of section 19 shall apply in relation to the preservation of any such statement or account and statement as it applies in relation to the preservation of any accounting records (the references to subsection (3) of that section being read as references to subsection (4) above).

(6) The Secretary of State may by order amend subsection (3) above by substituting a different sum for the sum for the time being specified there.

(7) Nothing in this section applies to a charity which is a company.

21. Annual audit or examination of charity accounts

(1) Subsection (2) applies to a financial year of a charity ('the relevant year') if the charity's gross income or total expenditure in any of the following, namely –
  (a) the relevant year,
  (b) the financial year of the charity immediately preceding the relevant year (if any), and
  (c) the financial year of the charity immediately preceding the year specified in paragraph (b) (if any),
exceeds £100,000.

(2) If this subsection applies to a financial year of a charity, the accounts of the charity for that year shall be audited by a person who –
  (a) is, in accordance with section 25 of the Companies Act 1989 (eligibility for appointment), eligible for appointment as a company auditor, or
  (b) is a member of a body for the time being specified in regulations under section 22 below and is under the rules of that body eligible for appointment as auditor of the charity.

(3) If subsection (2) does not apply to a financial year of a charity, then (subject to subsection (4)) the accounts of the charity for that year shall, at the election of the charity trustees, either –
  (a) be examined by an independent examiner, that is to say an independent person who is reasonably believed by the trustees to have the requisite ability and practical experience to carry out a competent examination of the accounts, or
  (b) be audited by such a person as is mentioned in subsection (2).

(4) Where it appears to the Commissioners –
- (a) that subsection (2), or (as the case may be) subsection (3), has not been complied with in relation to a financial year of a charity within ten months from the end of that year, or
- (b) that, although subsection (2) does not apply to a financial year of a charity, it would nevertheless be desirable for the accounts of the charity for that year to be audited by such a person as is mentioned in that subsection,

the Commissioners may by order require the accounts of the charity for that year to be audited by such a person as is mentioned in that subsection.

(5) If the Commissioners make an order under subsection (4) with respect to a charity, then unless –
- (a) the order is made by virtue of paragraph (b) of that subsection, and
- (b) the charity trustees themselves appoint an auditor in accordance wtih the order,

the auditor shall be a person appointed by the Commissioners.

(6) The expenses of any audit carried out by an auditor appointed by the Commissioners under subsection (5), including the auditor's remuneration, shall be recoverable by the Commissioners –
- (a) from the charity trustees of the charity concerned, who shall be personally liable, jointly and severally, for those expenses; or
- (b) to the extent that it appears to the Commissioners not to be practical to seek recovery of those expenses in accordance with paragraph (a), from the funds of the charity.

(7) The Commissioners may –
- (a) give guidance to charity trustees in connection with the selection of a person for appointment as an independent examiner;
- (b) give such directions as they think appropriate with respect to the carrying out of an examination in pursuance of subsection (3)(a);

and any such guidance or directions may either be of general application or apply to a particular charity only.

(8) The Secretary of State may by order amend subsection (1) by substituting a different sum for the sum for the time being specified there.

(9) Nothing in this section applies to a charity which is a company; but section 8(3) to (6) of the 1960 Act (power of Commissioners to require condition and accounts of charity to be investigated and audited) shall continue to apply to such a charity.

22. Supplementary provisions relating to audits etc

(1) The Secretary of State may by regulations make provision –
- (a) specifying one or more bodies for the purposes of section 21(2)(b);
- (b) with respect to the duties of an auditor carrying out an audit under section 21, including provision with respect to the making by him of a report on –
  - (i) the statement of accounts prepared for the financial year in question under section 20(1), or
  - (ii) the account and statement so prepared under section 20(3), as the case may be;
- (c) with respect to the making by an independent examiner of a report in respect of an examination carried out by him under section 21;

(d) conferring on such an auditor or on an independent examiner a right of access with respect to books, documents and other records (however kept) which relate to the charity concerned;

(e) entitling such an auditor or an independent examiner to require, in the case of a charity, information and explanations from past or present charity trustees or trustees for the charity, or from past or present officers or employees of the charity;

(f) enabling the Commissioners, in circumstances specified in the regulations, to dispense with the requirements of section 21(2) or (3) in the case of a particular charity or in the case of any particular financial year of a charity.

(2) If any person fails to afford an auditor or an independent examiner any facility to which he is entitled by virtue of subsection (1)(d) or (e), the Commissioners may by order give –

(a) to that person, or

(b) to the charity trustees for the time being of the charity concerned,

such directions as the Commissioners think appropriate for securing that the default is made good.

(3) Section 727 of the Companies Act 1985 (power of court to grant relief in certain cases) shall have effect in relation to an auditor or independent examiner appointed by a charity in pursuance of section 21 above as it has effect in relation to a person employed as auditor by a company within the meaning of that Act.

23. Annual reports

(1) The charity trustees of a charity shall prepare in respect of each financial year of the charity an annual report containing –

(a) such a report by the trustees on the activities of the charity during that year, and

(b) such other information relating to the charity or to its trustees or officers,

as may be prescribed by regulations made by the Secretary of State.

(2) Without prejudice to the generality of subsection (1), regulations under that subsection may make provision –

(a) for any such report as is mentioned in paragraph (a) of that subsection to be prepared in accordance with such principles as are specified or referred to in the regulations;

(b) enabling the Commissioners to dispense with any requirement prescribed by virtue of subsection (1)(b) in the case of a particular charity or a particular class of charities, or in the case of a particular financial year of a charity or of any class of charities.

(3) The annual report required to be prepared under this section in respect of any financial year of a charity shall be transmitted to the Commissioners by the charity trustees –

(a) within ten months from the end of that year, or

(b) within such longer period as the Commissioners may for any special reason allow in the case of that report.

(4) Subject to subsection (5), any such annual report shall have attached to it the statement of accounts prepared for the financial year in question under section 20(1) or

(as the case may be) the account and statement so prepared under section 20(3), together with –

   (a) where the accounts of the charity for that year have been audited under section 21, a copy of the report made by the auditor on that statement of accounts or (as the case may be) on that account and statement;

   (b) where the accounts of the charity for that year have been examined under section 21, a copy of the report made by the independent examiner in respect of the examination carried out by him under that section.

(5) Subsection (4) does not apply to a charity which is a company, and any annual report transmitted by the charity trustees of such a charity under subsection (3) shall instead have attached to it a copy of the charity's annual accounts prepared for the financial year in question under Part VII of the Companies Act 1985, together with a copy of the auditors' report on those accounts.

(6) Any annual report transmitted to the Commissioners under subsection (3), together with the documents attached to it, shall be kept by the Commissioners for such period as they think fit.

24. Special provision as respects accounts and annual reports of exempt and other excepted charities

(1) Nothing in sections 19 to 23 applies to any exempt charity; but section 32(1) and (2) of the 1960 Act (general obligation to keep accounts) shall continue to apply to any such charity.

(2) Nothing in sections 21 to 23 applies to any charity which –

   (a) falls within section 4(4)(c) of the 1960 Act (certain charities with an annual income not exceeding £1,000), and

   (b) is not registered.

(3) Except in accordance with subsection (6) below, nothing in section 23 applies to any charity (other than an exempt charity or a charity which falls within section 4(4)(c) of the 1960 Act) which –

   (a) is excepted by section 4(4) of that Act (charities not required to be registered), and

   (b) is not registered.

(4) If requested to do so by the Commissioners, the charity trustees of any such charity as is mentioned in subsection (3) above shall prepare an annual report in respect of such financial year of the charity as is specified in the Commissioners' request.

(5) Any report prepared under subsection (4) above shall contain –

   (a) such a report by the charity trustees on the activities of the charity during the year in question, and

   (b) such other information relating to the charity or to its trustees or officers,

as may be prescribed by regulations made under section 23(1) in relation to annual reports prepared under that provision.

(6) Subsections (3) to (6) of section 23 shall apply to any report required to be prepared under subsection (4) above as if it were an annual report required to be prepared under subsection (1) of that section.

(7) Any reference in this section to a charity which falls within section 4(4)(c) of the 1960 Act includes a reference to a charity which falls within that provision but is also excepted from registration by section 4(4)(b) of that Act (charities excepted by order or regulations).

25. Public inspection of annual reports etc

(1) Any annual report or other document kept by the Commissioners in pursuance of section 23(6) shall be open to public inspection at all reasonable times –

    (a) during the period for which it is so kept; or

    (b) if the Commissioners so determine, during such lesser period as they may specify.

(2) Section 9 of the 1960 Act (supply by Commissioners of copies of documents open to public inspection) shall have effect as if the reference to that Act included a reference to subsection (1) above.

(3) Where any person –

    (a) requests the charity trustees of a charity in writing to provide him with a copy of the charity's most recent accounts, and

    (b) pays them such reasonable fee (if any) as they may require in respect of the costs of complying with the request,

those trustees shall comply with the request within the period of two months beginning with the date on which it is made.

(4) In subsection (3) the reference to a charity's most recent accounts is –

    (a) in the case of a charity other than one falling within any of paragraphs (b) to (d) below, a reference to the statement of accounts or account and statement prepared in pursuance of section 20(1) or (3) in respect of the last financial year of the charity the accounts for which have been audited or examined under section 21;

    (b) in the case of such a charity as is mentioned in section 24(2), a reference to the statement of accounts or account and statement prepared in pursuance of section 20(1) or (3) in respect of the last financial year of the charity in respect of which a statement of accounts or account and statement has or have been so prepared;

    (c) in the case of a charity which is a company, a reference to the annual accounts of the company most recently audited under Part VII of the Companies Act 1985; and

    (d) in the case of an exempt charity, a reference to the accounts of the charity most recently audited in pursuance of any statutory or other requirement or, if its accounts are not required to be audited, the accounts most recently prepared in respect of the charity.

26. Annual returns by registered charities

(1) Every registered charity shall prepare in respect of each of its financial years an annual return in such form, and containing such information, as may be prescribed by regulations made by the Commissioners.

(2) Any such return shall be transmitted to the Commissioners by the date by which the charity trustees are, by virtue of section 23(3), required to transmit to them the annual report required to be prepared in respect of the financial year in question.

(3) The Commissioners may dispense with the requirements of subsection (1) in the case of a particular charity or a particular class of charities, or in the case of a particular financial year of a charity or of any class of charities.

27. Offences

Any person who, without reasonable excuse, is persistently in default in relation to any requirement imposed –
  (a) by section 23(3) (taken with section 23(4) or (5), as the case may require), or
  (b) by section 25(3) or 26(2),
shall be guilty of an offence and liable on summary conviction to a fine not exceeding the fourth level on the standard scale.

Charity proceedings

28. Power of Commissioners to bring proceedings with respect to charities

After section 26 of the 1960 Act there shall be inserted –

'26A. Power of Commissioners to bring proceedings with respect to charities

(1) Subject to subsection (2) below, the Commissioners may exercise the same powers with respect to –
  (a) the taking of legal proceedings with reference to charities or the property or affairs of charities, or
  (b) the compromise of claims with a view to avoiding or ending such proceedings,
as are exercisable by the Attorney General acting ex officio.

(2) Subsection (1) above does not apply to the power of the Attorney General under section 30(1) of this Act to present a petition for the winding up of a charity.

(3) The practice and procedure to be followed in relation to any proceedings taken by the Commissioners under subsection (1) above shall be the same in all respects (and in particular as regards costs) as if they were proceedings taken by the Attorney General acting ex officio.

(4) No rule of law or practice shall be taken to require the Attorney General to be a party to any such proceedings.

(5) The powers exercisable by the Commissioners by virtue of this section shall be exercisable by them of their own motion, but shall be exercisable only with the agreement of the Attorney General on each occasion.'

Charity property

29. Divestment of charity property held by official custodian for charities

(1) The official custodian shall, in accordance with this section, divest himself of all property to which this subsection applies.

(2) Subsection (1) applies to any property held by the official custodian in his capacity as such, with the exception of –

(a) any land; and

(b) any property (other than land) which is vested in him by virtue of an order of the Commissioners under section 20 of the 1960 Act (power to act for protection of charities).

(3) Where property to which subsection (1) applies is held by the official custodian in trust for particular charities, he shall (subject to subsection (7)) divest himself of that property in such manner as the Commissioners may direct.

(4) Without prejudice to the generality of subsection (3), directions given by the Commissioners under that subsection may make different provision in relation to different property held by the official custodian or in relation to different classes or descriptions of property held by him, including (in particular) –

(a) provision designed to secure that the divestment required by subsection (1) is effected in stages or by means of transfers or other disposals taking place at different times;

(b) provision requiring the official custodian to transfer any specified investments, or any specified class or description of investments, held by him in trust for a charity –

    (i) to the charity trustees or any trustee for the charity, or

    (ii) to a person nominated by the charity trustees to hold any such investments in trust for the charity;

(c) provision requiring the official custodian to sell or call in any specified investments, or any specified class or description of investments, so held by him and to pay any proceeds of sale or other money accruing therefrom –

    (i) to the charity trustees or any trustee for the charity, or

    (ii) into any bank account kept in its name.

(5) The charity trustees of a charity may, in the case of any property falling to be transferred by the official custodian in accordance with a direction under subsection (3), nominate a person to hold any such property in trust for the charity; but a person shall not be so nominated unless –

(a) if an individual, he resides in England and Wales; or

(b) if a body corporate, it has a place of business there.

(6) Directions under subsection (3) shall, in the case of any property vested in the official custodian by virtue of section 22(6) of the 1960 Act (common investment funds), provide for any such property to be transferred –

(a) to the trustees appointed to manage the common investment fund concerned; or

(b) to any person nominated by those trustees who is authorised by or under the common investment scheme concerned to hold that fund or any part of it.

(7) Where the official custodian –
   (a) holds any relevant property in trust for a charity, but
   (b) after making reasonable inquiries is unable to locate the charity or any of its trustees,

he shall –
   (i) unless the relevant property is money, sell the property and hold the proceeds of sale pending the giving by the Commissioners of a direction under subsection (8);
   (ii) if the relevant property is money, hold it pending the giving of any such direction;

and for this purpose 'relevant property' means any property to which subsection (1) applies or any proceeds of sale or other money accruing to the official custodian in consequence of a direction under subsection (3).

(8) Where subsection (7) applies in relation to a charity ('the dormant charity'), the Commissioners may direct the official custodian –
   (a) to pay such amount as is held by him in accordance with that subsection to such other charity as is specified in the direction in accordance with subsection (9), or
   (b) to pay to each of two or more other charities so specified in the direction such part of that amount as is there specified in relation to that charity.

(9) The Commisioners may specify in a direction under subsection (8) such charity or charities as they consider appropriate, being in each case a charity whose purposes are, in the opinion of the Commissioners, as similar in character to those of the dormant charity as is reasonably practicable; but the Commissioners shall not so specify any charity unless they have received from the charity trustees written confirmation that they are willing to accept the amount proposed to be paid to the charity.

(10) Any amount received by a charity by virtue of subsection (8) shall be received by the charity on terms that –
   (a) it shall be held and applied by the charity for the purposes of the charity, but
   (b) it shall, as property of the charity, nevertheless be subject to any restrictions on expenditure to which it, or (as the case may be) the property which it represents, was subject as property of the dormant charity.

(11) At such time as the Commissioners are satisfied that the official custodian has divested himself of all property held by him in trust for particular charities, all remaining funds held by him as official custodian shall be paid by him into the Consolidated Fund.

(12) Nothing in subsection (11) applies in relation to any property held by the official custodian which falls within subsection (2)(a) or (b).

(13) In this section 'land' does not include any interest in land by way of mortgage or other security.

30. Provisions supplementary to s 29

(1) Any directions of the Commissioners under section 29 above shall have effect notwithstanding anything –
   (a) in the trusts of a charity, or
   (b) in section 17(1) of the 1960 Act (supplementary provisions as to property vested in official custodian).

(2) Subject to subsection (3), any provision –
    (a) of the trusts of a charity, or
    (b) of any directions given by an order of the Commissioners made in connection with a transaction requiring the sanction of an order under section 29(1) of the 1960 Act (restrictions on dealing with charity property),
shall cease to have effect if and to the extent that it requires or authorises personal property of the charity to be transferred to or held by the official custodian; and for this purpose 'personal property' extends to any mortgage or other real security, but does not include any interest in land other than such an interest by way of mortgage or other security.

(3) Subsection (2) does not apply to –
    (a) any provision of an order made under section 20 of the 1960 Act (power to act for protection of charities); or
    (b) any provision of any other order, or of any scheme, of the Commissioners if the provision requires trustees of a charity to make payments into an account maintained by the official custodian with a view to the accumulation of a sum as capital of the charity (whether or not by way of recoupment of a sum expended out of the charity's permanent endowment);
but any such provision as is mentioned in paragraph (b) shall have effect as if, instead of requiring the trustees to make such payments into an account maintained by the official custodian, it required the trustees to make such payments into an account maintained by them or by any other person (apart from the official custodian) who is either a trustee for the charity or a person nominated by them to hold such payments in trust for the charity.

(4) The disposal of any property by the official custodian in accordance with section 29 above shall operate to discharge him from his trusteeship of that property.

(5) Where any instrument issued by the official custodian in connection with any such disposal contains a printed reproduction of his official seal, that instrument shall have the same effect as if it were duly sealed with his official seal.

31. Divestment in the case of land subject to Reverter of Sites Act 1987

(1) Where –
    (a) any land is vested in the official custodian in trust for a charity, and
    (b) it appears to the Commissioners that section 1 of the 1987 Act (right of reverter replaced by trust for sale) will, or is likely to, operate in relation to the land at a particular time or in particular circumstances,
the jurisdiction which, under section 18 of the 1960 Act (Commissioners' concurrent jurisdiction with High Court for certain purposes), is exercisable by the Commissioners for the purpose of discharging a trustee for a charity may, at any time before section 1 of the 1987 Act operates in relation to the land, be exercised by them of their own motion for the purpose of –
    (i) making an order discharging the official custodian from his trusteeship of the land, and
    (ii) making such vesting orders and giving such directions as appear to them to be necessary or expedient in consequence.

(2) Where –
    (a) section 1 of the 1987 Act has operated in relation to any land which,

immediately before the time when that section so operated, was vested in the official custodian in trust for a charity, and

(b) the land remains vested in him but on the trust arising under that section,

the court or the Commissioners (of their own motion) may –

    (i) make an order discharging the official custodian from his trusteeship of the land, and

    (ii) (subject to the following provisions of this section) make such vesting orders and give such directions as appear to it or them to be necessary or expedient in consequence.

(3) Where any order discharging the official custodian from his trusteeship of any land –

    (a) is made by the court under section 16(3) of the 1960 Act (discharge of official custodian), or by the Commissioners under section 18 of that Act, on the grounds that section 1 of the 1987 Act will, or is likely to, operate in relation to the land, or

    (b) is made by the court or the Commissioners under subsection (2) above,

the persons in whom the land is to be vested on the discharge of the official custodian shall be the relevant charity trustees (as defined in subsection (4) below), unless the court or (as the case may be) the Commissioners is or are satisfied that it would be appropriate for it to be vested in some other persons.

(4) In subsection (3) above 'the relevant charity trustees' means –

    (a) in relation to an order made as mentioned in paragraph (a) of that subsection, the charity trustees of the charity in trust for which the land is vested in the official custodian immediately before the time when the order takes effect, or

    (b) in relation to an order made under subsection (2) above, the charity trustees of the charity in trust for which the land was vested in the official custodian immediately before the time when section 1 of the 1987 Act operated in relation to the land.

(5) Where –

    (a) section 1 of the 1987 Act has operated in relation to any such land as is mentioned in subsection (2)(a) above, and

    (b) the land remains vested in the official custodian as mentioned in subsection (2)(b) above,

then (subject to subsection (6)), all the powers, duties and liabilities that would, apart from this section, be those of the official custodian as trustee for sale of the land shall instead be those of the charity trustees of the charity concerned; and those trustees shall have power in his name and on his behalf to execute and do all assurances and things which they could properly execute or do in their own name and on their own behalf if the land were vested in them.

(6) Subsection (5) shall not be taken to require or authorise those trustees to sell the land at a time when it remains vested in the official custodian.

(7) Where –

    (a) the official custodian has been discharged from his trusteeship of any land by an order under subsection (2), and

    (b) the land has, in accordance with subsection (3), been vested in the charity trustees concerned or (as the case may be) in any persons other than those trustees, the land shall be held by those trustees, or (as the case may be) by those persons, as trustees for sale on the terms of the trust arising under section 1 of the 1987 Act.

(8) The official custodian shall not be liable to any person in respect of any loss or misapplication of any land vested in him in accordance with that section unless it is occasioned by or through any wilful neglect or default of his or of any person acting for him; but the Consolidated Fund shall be liable to make good to any person any sums for which the official custodian may be liable by reason of any such neglect or default.

(9) In this section –
    (a) 'the 1987 Act' means the Reverter of Sites Act 1987; and
    (b) any reference to section 1 of the 1987 Act operating in relation to any land is a reference to a trust for sale arising in relation to the land under that section.

32. Restrictions on dispositions of charity land

(1) Subject to the following provisions of this section and section 37, no land held by or in trust for a charity shall be sold, leased or otherwise disposed of without an order of the court or of the Commissioners.

(2) Subsection (1) above shall not apply to a disposition of such land if –
    (a) the disposition is made to a person who is not –
        (i) a connected person (as defined in Schedule 2 to this Act), or
        (ii) a trustee for, or nominee of, a connected person; and
    (b) the requirements of subsection (3) or (5) below have been complied with in relation to it.

(3) Except where the proposed disposition is the granting of such a lease as is mentioned in subsection (5), the charity trustees must, before entering into an agreement for the sale, or (as the case may be) for a lease or other disposition, of the land –
    (a) obtain and consider a written report on the proposed disposition from a qualified surveyor instructed by the trustees and acting exclusively for the charity;
    (b) advertise the proposed disposition for such period and in such manner as the surveyor has advised in his report (unless he has there advised that it would not be in the best interests of the charity to advertise the proposed disposition); and
    (c) decide that they are satisfied, having considered the surveyor's report, that the terms on which the disposition is proposed to be made are the best that can reasonably be obtained for the charity.

(4) For the purposes of subsection (3) a person is a qualified surveyor if –
    (a) he is a fellow or professional associate of the Royal Institution of Chartered Surveyors or of the Incorporated Society of Valuers and Auctioneers or satisfies such other requirement or requirements as may be prescribed by regulations made by the Secretary of State; and
    (b) he is reasonably believed by the charity trustees to have ability in, and experience of, the valuation of land of the particular kind, and in the particular area, in question;
and any report prepared for the purposes of that subsection shall contain such

information, and deal with such matters, as may be prescribed by regulations so made.

(5) Where the proposed disposition is the granting of a lease for a term ending not more than seven years after it is granted (other than one granted wholly or partly in consideration of a fine), the charity trustees must, before entering into an agreement for the lease –

(a) obtain and consider the advice on the proposed disposition of a person who is reasonably believed by the trustees to have the requisite ability and practical experience to provide them with competent advice on the proposed disposition; and

(b) decide that they are satisfied, having considered that person's advice, that the terms on which the disposition is proposed to be made are the best that can reasonably be obtained for the charity.

(6) Where –

(a) any land is held by or in trust for a charity, and

(b) the trusts on which it is so held stipulate that it is to be used for the purposes, or any particular purposes, of the charity,

then (subject to subsections (7) and (8) and without prejudice to the operation of the preceding provisions of this section), the land shall not be sold, leased or otherwise disposed of unless the charity trustees have previously –

(i) given public notice of the proposed disposition, inviting representations to be made to them within a time specified in the notice, being not less than one month from the date of the notice; and

(ii) taken into consideration any representations made to them within that time about the proposed disposition.

(7) Subsection (6) shall not apply to any such disposition of land as is there mentioned if –

(a) the disposition is to be effected with a view to acquiring by way of replacement other property which is to be held on the trusts referred to in paragraph (b) of that subsection; or

(b) the disposition is the granting of a lease for a term ending not more than two years after it is granted (other than one granted wholly or partly in consideration of a fine).

(8) The Commissioners may direct –

(a) that subsection (6) shall not apply to dispositions of land held by or in trust for a charity or class of charities (whether generally or only in the case of a specified class of dispositions or land, or otherwise as may be provided in the direction), or

(b) that that subsection shall not apply to a particular disposition of land held by or in trust for a charity,

if, on an application made to them in writing by or on behalf of the charity or charities in question, the Commissioners are satisfied that it would be in the interests of the charity or charities for them to give the direction.

(9) The restrictions on disposition imposed by this section apply notwithstanding anything in the trusts of a charity; but nothing in this section applies –

(a) to any disposition for which general or special authority is expressly given (without the authority being made subject to the sanction of an order of the court) by any statutory provision contained in or having effect under an Act of Parliament or by any scheme legally established; or

    (b) to any disposition of land held by or in trust for a charity which –

        (i) is made to another charity otherwise than for the best price that can reasonably be obtained, and

        (ii) is authorised to be so made by the trusts of the first-mentioned charity; or

    (c) to the granting, by or on behalf of a charity and in accordance with its trusts, of a lease to any beneficiary under those trusts where the lease –

        (i) is granted otherwise than for the best rent that can reasonably be obtained; and

        (ii) is intended to enable the demised premises to be occupied for the purposes, or any particular purposes, of the charity.

(10) Nothing in this section applies –

    (a) to any disposition of land held by or in trust for an exempt charity;

    (b) to any disposition of land by way of mortgage or other security; or

    (c) to any disposition of an advowson.

(11) In this section 'land' means land in England or Wales.

33. Supplementary provisions relating to dispositions of charity land

(1) Any of the following instruments, namely –

    (a) any contract for the sale, or for a lease or other disposition, of land which is held by or in trust for a charity, and

    (b) any conveyance, transfer, lease or other instrument effecting a disposition of such land,

shall state –

        (i) that the land is held by or in trust for a charity,

        (ii) whether the charity is an exempt charity and whether the disposition is one falling within paragraph (a), (b) or (c) of subsection (9) of section 32, and

        (iii) if it is not an exempt charity and the disposition is not one falling within any of those paragraphs, that the land is land to which the restrictions on disposition imposed by that section apply.

(2) Where any land held by or in trust for a charity is sold, leased or otherwise disposed of by a disposition to which subsection (1) or (2) of section 32 applies, the charity trustees shall certify in the instrument by which the disposition is effected –

    (a) (where subsection (1) of that section applies) that the disposition has been sanctioned by an order of the court or of the Commissioners (as the case may be), or

    (b) (where subsection (2) of that section applies) that the charity trustees have power under the trusts of the charity to effect the disposition, and that they have complied with the provisions of that section so far as applicable to it.

(3) Where subsection (2) above has been complied with in relation to any disposition of land, then in favour of a person who (whether under the disposition or afterwards) acquires an interest in the land for money or money's worth, it shall be conclusively presumed that the facts were as stated in the certificate.

(4) Where –
  (a) any land held by or in trust for a charity is sold, leased or otherwise disposed of by a disposition to which subsection (1) or (2) of section 32 applies, but
  (b) subsection (2) above has not been complied with in relation to the disposition,
then in favour of a person who (whether under the disposition or afterwards) in good faith acquires an interest in the land for money or money's worth, the disposition shall be valid whether or not –
    (i) (where subsection (1) of that section applies) the disposition has been sanctioned by an order of the court or of the Commissioners, or
    (ii) (where subsection (2) of that section applies) the charity trustees have power under the trusts of the charity to effect the disposition and have complied with the provisions of that section so far as applicable to it.

(5) Any of the following instruments, namely –
  (a) any contract for the sale, or for a lease or other disposition, of land which will, as a result of the disposition, be held by or in trust for a charity, and
  (b) any conveyance, transfer, lease or other instrument effecting a disposition of such land,
shall state –
    (i) that the land will, as a result of the disposition, be held by or in trust for a charity,
    (ii) whether the charity is an exempt charity, and
    (iii) if it is not an exempt charity, that the restrictions on disposition imposed by section 32 will apply to the land (subject to subsection (9) of that section).

(6) In section 29(1) of the Settled Land Act 1925 (charitable and public trusts) –
  (a) the requirement for a conveyance of land held on charitable, ecclesiastical or public trusts to state that it is held on such trusts shall not apply to any instrument to which subsection (1) above applies; and
  (b) the requirement imposed on a purchaser, in the circumstances mentioned in section 29(1) of that Act, to see that any consents or orders requisite for authorising a transaction have been obtained shall not apply in relation to any disposition in relation to which subsection (2) above has been complied with;
and expressions used in this subsection which are also used in that Act have the same meaning as in that Act.

(7) Where –
  (a) the disposition to be effected by any such instrument as is mentioned in subsection (1)(b) or (5)(b) will be a registered disposition, or
  (b) any such instrument will on taking effect be an instrument to which section 123(1) of the Land Registration Act 1925 (compulsory registration of title) applies,
the statement which, by virtue of subsection (1) or (5), is to be contained in the instrument shall be in such form as may be prescribed.

(8) Where –
  (a) an application is duly made –
    (i) for registration of a disposition of registered land, or
    (ii) for registration of a person's title under a disposition of unregistered land, and
  (b) the instrument by which the disposition is effected contains a statement complying with subsections (5) and (7) above, and

(c) the charity by or in trust for which the land is held as a result of the disposition is not an exempt charity,

the registrar shall enter in the register, in respect of the land, a restriction in such form as may be prescribed.

(9) Where –
  (a) any such restriction is entered in the register in respect of any land, and
  (b) the charity by or in trust for which the land is held becomes an exempt charity,

the charity trustees shall apply to the registrar for the restriction to be withdrawn; and on receiving any application duly made under this subsection the registrar shall withdraw the restriction.

(10) Where –
  (a) any registered land is held by or in trust for an exempt charity and the charity ceases to be an exempt charity, or
  (b) any registered land becomes, as a result of a declaration of trust by the registered proprietor, land held in trust for a charity (other than an exempt charity),

the charity trustees shall apply to the registrar for such a restriction as is mentioned in subsection (8) to be entered in the register in respect of the land; and on receiving any application duly made under this subsection the registrar shall enter such a restriction in the register in respect of the land.

(11) In this section –
  (a) references to a disposition of land do not include references to –
    (i)   a disposition of land by way of mortgage or other security,
    (ii) an advowson, or
    (iii)ʼ any release of a rentcharge falling within section 37(1); and
  (b) 'land' means land in England or Wales;

and subsections (7) to (10) above shall be construed as one with the Land Registration Act 1925.

34. Restrictions on mortgaging charity land

(1) Subject to subsection (2), no mortgage of land held by or in trust for a charity shall be granted without an order of the court or of the Commissioners.

(2) Subsection (1) shall not apply to a mortgage of any such land by way of security for the repayment of a loan where the charity trustees have, before executing the mortgage, obtained and considered proper advice, given to them in writing, on the matters mentioned in subsection (3).

(3) Those matters are –
  (a) whether the proposed loan is necessary in order for the charity trustees to be able to pursue the particular course of action in connection with which the loan is sought by them;
  (b) whether the terms of the proposed loan are reasonable having regard to the status of the charity as a prospective borrower; and
  (c) the ability of the charity to repay on those terms the sum proposed to be borrowed.

(4) For the purposes of subsection (2) proper advice is the advice of a person –
  (a) who is reasonably believed by the charity trustees to be qualified by his ability

in and practical experience of financial matters; and
  (b) who has no financial interest in the making of the loan in question;
and such advice may constitute proper advice for those purposes notwithstanding that
the person giving it does so in the course of his employment as an officer or employee
of the charity or of the charity trustees.

(5) This section applies notwithstanding anything in the trusts of a charity; but
nothing in this section applies to any mortgage for which general or special authority
is given as mentioned in section 32(9)(a).

(6) In this section –
  'land' means land in England or Wales;
  'mortgage' includes a charge.

(7) Nothing in this section applies to an exempt charity.

35. Supplementary provisions relating to mortgaging of charity land

(1) Any mortgage of land held by or in trust for a charity shall state –
  (a) that the land is held by or in trust for a charity,
  (b) whether the charity is an exempt charity and whether the mortgage is one
       falling within subsection (5) of section 34, and
  (c) if it is not an exempt charity and the mortgage is not one falling within that
       subsection, that the mortgage is one to which the restrictions imposed by that
       section apply;
and where the mortgage will be a registered disposition any such statement shall be in
such form as may be prescribed.

(2) Where subsection (1) or (2) of section 34 applies to any mortgage of land held by or
in trust for a charity, the charity trustees shall certify in the mortgage –
  (a) (where subsection (1) of that section applies) that the mortage has been
       sanctioned by an order of the court or of the Commissioners (as the case may
       be), or
  (b) (where subsection (2) of that section applies) that the charity trustees have
       power under the trusts of the charity to grant the mortgage, and that they have
       obtained and considered such advice as is mentioned in that subsection.

(3) Where subsection (2) above has been complied with in relation to any mortgage,
then in favour of a person who (whether under the mortgage or afterwards) acquires
an interest in the land in question for money or money's worth, it shall be conclusively
presumed that the facts were as stated in the certificate.

(4) Where –
  (a) subsection (1) or (2) of section 34 applies to any mortgage of land held by or in
       trust for a charity, but
  (b) subsection (2) above has not been complied with in relation to the mortgage,
then in favour of a person who (whether under the mortgage or afterwards) in good
faith acquires an interest in the land for money or money's worth, the mortgage shall
be valid whether or not –
  (i)   (where subsection (1) of that section applies) the mortgage has been
        sanctioned by an order of the court or of the Commissioners, or
  (ii) (where subsection (2) of that section applies) the charity trustees have

power under the trusts of the charity to grant the mortgage and have obtained and considered such advice as is mentioned in that subsection.

(5) In section 29(1) of the Settled Land Act 1925 (charitable and public trusts) –

  (a) the requirement for a mortgage of land held on charitable, ecclesiastical or public trusts (as a 'conveyance' of such land for the purposes of that Act) to state that it is held on such trusts shall not apply to any mortgage to which subsection (1) above applies; and

  (b) the requirement imposed on a mortgagee (as a 'purchaser' for those purposes), in the circumstances mentioned in section 29(1) of that Act, to see that any consents or orders requisite for authorising a transaction have been obtained shall not apply in relation to any mortgage in relation to which subsection (2) above has been complied with;

and expressions used in this subsection which are also used in that Act have the same meaning as in that Act.

(6) In this section –
'mortgage' includes a charge, and 'mortgagee' shall be construed accordingly;
'land' means land in England or Wales;
'prescribed' and 'registered disposition' have the same meaning as in the Land Registration Act 1925.

36. Removal of requirements under statutory provisions for consent to dealings with charity land

(1) Any provision –

  (a) establishing or regulating a particular charity and contained in, or having effect under, any Act of Parliament, or

  (b) contained in the trusts of a charity,

shall cease to have effect if and to the extent that it provides for dispositions of, or other dealings with, land held by or in trust for the charity to require the consent of the Commissioners (whether signified by order or otherwise).

(2) Any provision of an order or scheme under the Education Act 1944 or the Education Act 1973 relating to a charity shall cease to have effect if and to the extent that it requires, in relation to any sale, lease or other disposition of land held by or in trust for the charity, approval by the Commissioners or the Secretary of State of the amount for which the land is to be sold, leased or otherwise disposed of.

(3) In this section 'land' means land in England or Wales.

37. Release of charity rentcharges

(1) Section 32(1) shall not apply to the release by a charity of a rentcharge which it is entitled to receive if the release is given in consideration of the payment of an amount which is not less than ten times the annual amount of the rentcharge.

(2) Where a charity which is entitled to receive a rentcharge releases it in consideration of the payment of an amount not exceeding £500, any costs incurred by the charity in connection with proving its title to the rentcharge shall be recoverable by the charity from the person or persons in whose favour the rentcharge is being released.

(3) Neither section 32(1) nor subsection (2) above applies where a rentcharge which a charity is entitled to receive is redeemed under sections 8 to 10 of the Rentcharges Act 1977.

(4) The Secretary of State may by order amend subsection (2) above by substituting a different sum for the sum for the time being specified there.

(5) Subsections (2) to (8) of section 27 of the 1960 Act (special procedure for redemption of charity rentcharges) shall cease to have effect.

Powers of investment

38. Relaxation of restrictions on wider-range investments

(1) The Secretary of State may by order made with the consent of the Treasury –
  (a) direct that, in the case of a trust fund consisting of property held by or in trust for a charity, any division of the fund in pursuance of section 2(1) of the Trustee Investments Act 1961 (trust funds to be divided so that wider-range and narrower-range investments are equal in value) shall be made so that the value of the wider-range part at the time of the division bears to the then value of the narrower-range part such proportion as is specified in the order;
  (b) provide that, in its application in relation to such a trust fund, that Act shall have effect subject to such modifications so specified as the Secretary of State considers appropriate in consequence of, or in connection with, any such direction.

(2) Where, before the coming into force of an order under this section, a trust fund consisting of property held by or in trust for a charity has already been divided in pursuance of section 2(1) of that Act, the fund may, notwithstanding anything in that provision, be again divided (once only) in pursuance of that provision during the continuance in force of the order.

(3) No order shall be made under this section unless a draft of the order has been laid before and approved by a resolution of each House of Parliament.

(4) Expressions used in this section which are also used in the Trustee Investments Act 1961 have the same meaning as in that Act.

(5) In the application of this section to Scotland, 'charity' means a recognised body within the meaning of section 1(7) of the Law Reform (Miscellaneous Provisions) (Scotland) Act 1990.

39. Extension of powers of investment

(1) The Secretary of State may by regulations made with the consent of the Treasury make, with respect to property held by or in trust for a charity, provision authorising a trustee to invest such property in any manner specified in the regulations, being a manner of investment not for the time being included in any Part of Schedule 1 to the Trustee Investments Act 1961.

(2) Regulations under this section may make such provision –
  (a) regulating the investment of property in any manner authorised by virtue of subsection (1), and

(b) with respect to the variation and retention of investments so made,
as the Secretary of State considers appropriate.

(3) Such regulations may, in particular, make provision –
    (a) imposing restrictions with respect to the proportion of the property held by or
    in trust for a charity which may be invested in any manner authorised by
    virtue of subsection (1), being either restrictions applying to investment in
    any such manner generally or restrictions applying to investment in any
    particular such manner;
    (b) imposing the like requirements with respect to the obtaining and considera-
    tion of advice as are imposed by any of the provisions of section 6 of the
    Trustee Investments Act 1961 (duty of trustees in choosing investments).

(4) Any power of investment conferred by any regulations under this section –
    (a) shall be in addition to, and not in derogation from, any power conferred
    otherwise than by such regulations; and
    (b) shall not be limited by the trusts of a charity (in so far as they are not contained
    in any Act or instrument made under an enactment) unless it is excluded by
    those trusts in express terms;
but any such power shall only be exercisable by a trustee in so far as a contrary
intention is not expressed in any Act or in any instrument made under an enactment
and relating to the powers of the trustee.

(5) No regulations shall be made under this section unless a draft of the regulations
has been laid before and approved by a resolution of each House of Parliament.

(6) In this section 'property' –
    (a) in England and Wales, means real or personal property of any description,
    including money and things in action, but does not include an interest in
    expectancy; and
    (b) in Scotland, means property of any description (whether heritable or move-
    able, corporeal or incorporeal) which is presently enjoyable, but does not
    include a future interest, whether vested or contingent;
and any reference to property held by or in trust for a charity is a reference to property
so held, whether it is for the time being in a state of investment or not.

(7) In the application of this section to Scotland, 'charity' means a recognised body
within the meaning of section 1(7) of the Law Reform (Miscellaneous Provisions)
(Scotland) Act 1990.

Charitable companies

40. Charitable companies: alteration of objects clause etc

For subsections (2) and (3) of section 30A of the 1960 Act (as amended by the
Companies Act 1989) there shall be substituted –

    '(2) Where a charity is a company, any alteration by it –
    (a) of the objects clause in its memorandum of association, or
    (b) of any other provision in its memorandum of association, or any provision in
    its articles of association, which is a provision directing or restricting the

manner in which property of the company may be used or applied,
is ineffective without the prior written consent of the Commissioners.

(3) Where a company has made any such alteration in accordance with subsection (2) above and –
(a) in connection with the alteration is required by virtue of –
   (i) section 6(1) of the Companies Act 1985 (delivery of documents following alteration of objects), or
   (ii) that provision as applied by section 17(3) of that Act (alteration of condition in memorandum which could have been contained in articles),
   to deliver to the registrar of companies a printed copy of its memorandum, as altered, or
(b) is required by virtue of section 380(1) of that Act (registration etc. of resolutions and agreements) to forward to the registrar a printed or other copy of the special resolution effecting the alteration,
the copy so delivered or forwarded by the company shall be accompanied by a copy of the Commissioners' consent.

(4) Section 6(3) of the Act (offences) shall apply to any default by a company in complying with subsection (3) above as it applies to any such default as is mentioned in that provision.'

41. Charitable companies: requirement of consent of Commissioners to certain acts

After section 30B of the 1960 Act (as amended by the Companies Act 1989) there shall be inserted –

'30BA. Charitable companies: requirement of consent of Commissioners to certain acts

(1) Where a company is a charity –
(a) any approval given by the company for the purposes of any of the provisions of the Companies Act 1985 specified in subsection (2) below, and
(b) any affirmation by it for the purposes of section 322(2)(c) of that Act (affirmation of voidable arrangements under which assets are acquired by or from a director or person connected with him),
is ineffective without the prior written consent of the Commissioners.

(2) The provisions of the Companies Act 1985 referred to in subsection (1)(a) above are –
(a) section 312 (payment to director in respect of loss of office or retirement);
(b) section 313(1) (payment to director in respect of loss of office or retirement made in connection with transfer of undertaking or property of company);
(c) section 319(3) (incorporation in director's service contract of term whereby his employment will or may continue for a period of more than 5 years);
(d) section 320(1) (arrangement whereby assets are acquired by or from director or person connected with him);

(e) section 337(3)(a) (provision of funds to meet certain expenses incurred by
       director).'

42. Charitable companies: name to appear on correspondence etc

The following section shall be inserted in the 1960 Act after the section 30BA inserted
by section 41 above –

'30BB. Charitable companies: name to appear on correspondence etc

Section 30(7) of the Companies Act 1985 (exemption from requirements relating
to publication of name etc.) shall not, in its application to any company which is a
charity, have the effect of exempting the company from the requirements of
section 349(1) of that Act (company's name to appear in its correspondence etc).'

Small charities

43. Small charities: power to transfer all property, modify objects etc

(1) This section applies to a charity if –
  (a) its gross income in its last financial year did not exceed £5,000, and
  (b) it does not hold any land on trusts which stipulate that the land is to be used for
         the purposes, or any particular purposes, of the charity,
and it is neither an exempt charity nor a charitable company.

(2) Subject to the following provisions of this section, the charity trustees of a charity
to which this section applies may resolve for the purposes of this section –
  (a) that all the property of the charity should be transferred to such other charity
         as is specified in the resolution, being either a registered charity or a charity
         which is not required to be registered;
  (b) that all the property of the charity should be divided, in such manner as is
         specified in the resolution, between such two or more other charities as are so
         specified, being in each case either a registered charity or a charity which is not
         required to be registered;
  (c) that the trusts of the charity should be modified by replacing all or any of the
         purposes of the charity with such other purposes, being in law charitable, as
         are specified in the resolution;
  (d) that any provision of the trusts of the charity –
    (i) relating to any of the powers exercisable by the charity trustees in the
           administration of the charity, or
    (ii) regulating the procedure to be followed in any respect in connection with
            its administration,
         should be modified in such manner as is specified in the resolution.

(3) Any resolution passed under subsection (2) must be passed by a majority of not
less than two-thirds of such charity trustees as vote on the resolution.

(4) The charity trustees of a charity to which this section applies ('the transferor
charity') shall not have power to pass a resolution under subsection (2)(a) or (b) unless
they are satisfied –
  (a) that the existing purposes of the transferor charity have ceased to be conducive

to a suitable and effective application of the charity's resources; and

(b) that the purposes of the charity or charities specified in the resolution are as similar in character to the purposes of the transferor charity as is reasonably practicable;

and before passing the resolution they must have received from the charity trustees of the charity, or (as the case may be) of each of the charities, specified in the resolution written confirmation that those trustees are willing to accept a transfer of property under this section.

(5) The charity trustees of any such charity shall not have power to pass a resolution under subsection (2)(c) unless they are satisfied –

(a) that the existing purposes of the charity (or, as the case may be, such of them as it is proposed to replace) have ceased to be conducive to a suitable and effective application of the charity's resources; and

(b) that the purposes specified in the resolution are as similar in character to those existing purposes as is practical in the circumstances.

(6) Where charity trustees have passed a resolution under subsection (2), they shall –

(a) give public notice of the resolution in such manner as they think reasonable in the circumstances; and

(b) send a copy of the resolution to the Commissioners, together with a statement of their reasons for passing it.

(7) The Commissioners may, when considering the resolution, require the charity trustees to provide additional information or explanation –

(a) as to the circumstances in and by reference to which they have determined to act under this section, or

(b) relating to their compliance with this section in connection with the resolution;

and the Commissioners shall take into account any representations made to them by persons appearing to them to be interested in the charity where those representations are made within the period of six weeks beginning with the date when the Commissioners receive a copy of the resolution by virtue of subsection (6)(b).

(8) Where the Commissioners have so received a copy of a resolution from any charity trustees and it appears to them that the trustees have complied with this section in connection with the resolution, the Commissioners shall, within the period of three months beginning with the date when they receive the copy of the resolution, notify the trustees in writing either –

(a) that the Commissioners concur with the resolution; or

(b) that they do not concur with it.

(9) Where the Commissioners so notify their concurrence with the resolution, then –

(a) if the resolution was passed under subsection (2)(a) or (b), the charity trustees shall arrange for all the property of the transferor charity to be transferred in accordance with the resolution and on terms that any property so transferred –

(i) shall be held and applied by the charity to which it is transferred ('the transferee charity') for the purposes of that charity, but

(ii) shall, as property of the transferee charity, nevertheless be subject to any restrictions on expenditure to which it is subject as property of the transferor charity,

and those trustees shall arrange for it to be so transferred by such date as may be specified in the notification; and

(b) if the resolution was passed under subsection (2)(c) or (d), the trusts of the charity shall be deemed, as from such date as may be specified in the notification, to have been modified in accordance with the terms of the resolution.

(10) For the purpose of enabling any property to be transferred to a charity under this section, the Commissioners shall have power, at the request of the charity trustees of that charity, to make orders vesting any property of the transferor charity –

(a) in the charity trustees of the first-mentioned charity or in any trustee for that charity, or

(b) in any other person nominated by those charity trustees to hold the property in trust for that charity.

(11) The Secretary of State may by order amend subsection (1) by substituting a different sum for the sum for the time being specified there.

(12) In this section –

(a) 'charitable company' means a charity which is a company or other body corporate; and

(b) references to the transfer of property to a charity are references to its transfer –

(i)   to the charity trustees, or

(ii) to any trustee for the charity, or

(iii) to a person nominated by the charity trustees to hold it in trust for the charity,

as the charity trustees may determine.

44. Small charities: power to spend capital

(1) This section applies to a charity if –

(a) it has a permanent endowment which does not consist of or comprise any land, and

(b) its gross income in its last financial year did not exceed £1,000,

and it is neither an exempt charity nor a charitable company.

(2) Where the charity trustees of a charity to which this section applies are of the opinion that the property of the charity is too small, in relation to its purposes, for any useful purpose to be achieved by the expenditure of income alone, they may resolve for the purposes of this section that the charity ought to be freed from the restrictions with respect to expenditure of capital to which its permanent endowment is subject.

(3) Any resolution passed under subsection (2) must be passed by a majority of not less than two-thirds of such charity trustees as vote on the resolution.

(4) Before passing such a resolution the charity trustees must consider whether any reasonable possibility exists of effecting a transfer or division of all the charity's property under section 43 (disregarding any such transfer or division as would, in their opinion, impose on the charity an unacceptable burden of costs).

(5) Where charity trustees have passed a resolution under subsection (2), they shall –

(a) give public notice of the resolution in such manner as they think reasonable in the circumstances; and

(b) send a copy of the resolution to the Commissioners, together with a statement of their reasons for passing it.

(6) The Commissioners may, when considering the resolution, require the charity trustees to provide additional information or explanation –

(a) as to the circumstances in and by reference to which they have determined to act under this section, or

(b) relating to their compliance with this section in connection with the resolution;

and the Commissioners shall take into account any representations made to them by persons appearing to them to be interested in the charity where those representations are made within the period of six weeks beginning with the date when the Commissioners receive a copy of the resolution by virtue of subsection (5)(b).

(7) Where the Commissioners have so received a copy of a resolution from any charity trustees and it appears to them that the trustees have complied with this section in connection with the resolution, the Commissioners shall, within the period of three months beginning with the date when they receive the copy of the resolution, notify the trustees in writing either –

(a) that the Commissioners concur with the resolution; or

(b) that they do not concur with it.

(8) Where the Commissioners so notify their concurrence with the resolution, the charity trustees shall have, as from such date as may be specified in the notification, power by virtue of this section to expend any property of the charity without regard to any such restrictions as are mentioned in subsection (2).

(9) The Secretary of State may by order amend subsection (1) by substituting a different sum for the time being specified there.

(10) In this section 'charitable company' means a charity which is a company or other body corporate.

Disqualification for acting as charity trustee

45. Persons disqualified for being trustees of a charity

(1) Subject to the following provisions of this section, a person shall be disqualified for being a charity trustee or trustee for a charity if –

(a) he has been convicted of any offence involving dishonesty or deception;

(b) he has been adjudged bankrupt or sequestration of his estate has been awarded and (in either case) he has not been discharged;

(c) he has made a composition or arrangement with, or granted a trust deed for, his creditors and has not been discharged in respect of it;

(d) he has been removed from the office of charity trustee or trustee for a charity by an order made –

(i) by the Commissioners under section 20(1A)(i) of the 1960 Act (power to act for protection of charities) or under section 20(1)(i) of that Act (as in force before the commencement of section 8 of this Act), or

(ii) by the High Court,

on the grounds of any misconduct or mismanagement in the administration of the charity for which he was responisble or to which he was privy, or which he by his conduct contributed to or facilitated;

(e) he has been removed, under section 7 of the Law Reform (Miscellaneous

Provisions) (Scotland) Act 1990 (powers of Court of Session to deal with management of charities), from being concerned in the management or control of any body;

(f) he is subject to a disqualification order under the Company Directors Disqualification Act 1986 or to an order made under section 429(2)(b) of the Insolvency Act 1986 (failure to pay under county court administration order).

(2) In subsection (1) –
(a) paragraph (a) applies whether the conviction occurred before or after the commencement of that subsection, but does not apply in relation to any conviction which is a spent conviction for the purposes of the Rehabilitation of Offenders Act 1974;
(b) paragraph (b) applies whether the adjudication of bankruptcy or the sequestration occurred before or after the commencement of that subsection;
(c) paragraph (c) applies whether the composition or arrangement was made, or the trust deed was granted, before or after the commencement of that subsection; and
(d) paragraphs (d) to (f) apply in relation to orders made and removals effected before or after the commencement of that subsection.

(3) Where (apart from this subsection) a person is disqualified under subsection (1)(b) for being a charity trustee or trustee for any charity which is a company, he shall not be so disqualified if leave has been granted under section 11 of the Company Directors Disqualification Act 1986 (undischarged bankrupts) for him to act as director of the charity; and similarly a person shall not be disqualified under subsection (1)(f) for being a charity trustee or trustee for such a charity if –
(a) in the case of a person subject to a disqualification order, leave under the order has been granted for him to act as director of the charity, or
(b) in the case of a person subject to an order under section 429(2)(b) of the Insolvency Act 1986, leave has been granted by the court which made the order for him to so act.

(4) The Commissioners may, on the application of any person disqualified under subsection (1), waive his disqualification either generally or in relation to a particular charity or a particular class of charities; but no such waiver may be granted in relation to any charity which is a company if –
(a) the person concerned is for the time being prohibited, by virtue of –
(i) a disqualification order under the Company Directors Disqualification Act 1986, or
(ii) section 11(1) or 12(2) of that Act (undischarged bankrupts; failure to pay under county court administration order),
from acting as director of the charity; and
(b) leave has not been granted for him to act as director of any other company.

(5) Without prejudice to the generality of section 13 of the Interpretation Act 1978 (anticipatory exercise of powers), the Commissioners may –
(a) at any time before the commencement of subsection (1) above, and
(b) on the application of a person who would be disqualified under that subsection as from that commencement,

grant that person a waiver under subsection (4) taking effect as from that commence-ment.

(6) Any waiver under subsection (4) shall be notified in writing to the person concerned.

(7) For the purposes of this section the Commissioners shall keep, in such manner as they think fit, a register of all persons who have been removed from office as mentioned in subsection (1)(d) either –

    (a) by an order of the Commissioners made before or after the commencement of subsection (1), or

    (b) by an order of the High Court made after the commencement of that subsection;

and, where any person is so removed from office by an order of the High Court, the court shall notify the Commissioners of his removal.

(8) The entries in the register kept under subsection (7) shall be available for public inspection in legible form at all reasonable times.

46. Person acting as charity trustee while disqualified

(1) Subject to subsection (2), any person who acts as a charity trustee or trustee for a charity while he is disqualified for being such a trustee by virtue of section 45 shall be guilty of an offence and liable –

    (a) on summary conviction, to imprisonment for a term not exceeding six months or to a fine not exceeding the statutory maximum, or both;

    (b) on conviction on indictment, to imprisonment for a term not exceeding two years or to a fine, or both.

(2) Subsection (1) shall not apply where –

    (a) the charity concerned is a company; and

    (b) the disqualified person is disqualified by virtue only of paragraph (b) or (f) of section 45(1).

(3) Any acts done as charity trustee or trustee for a charity by a person disqualified for being such a trustee by virtue of section 45 shall not be invalid by reason only of that disqualification.

(4) Where the Commissioners are satisfied –

    (a) that any person has acted as charity trustee or trustee for a charity (other than an exempt charity) while disqualified for being such a trustee by virtue of section 45, and

    (b) that, while so acting, he has received from the charity any sums by way of remuneration or expenses, or any benefit in kind, in connection with his acting as charity trustee or trustee for the charity,

they may by order direct him to repay to the charity the whole or part of any such sums, or (as the case may be) to pay to the charity the whole or part of the monetary value (as determined by them) of any such benefit.

(5) Subsection (4) does not apply to any sums received by way of remuneration or expenses in respect of any time when the person concerned was not disqualified for being a charity trustee or trustee for the charity.

47. Minor and consequential amendments of 1960 Act

The 1960 Act shall have effect subject to the amendments specified in Schedule 3 to this Act (which are either minor amendments or amendments consequential on the preceding provisions of this Part of this Act).

48. Amendment of Charitable Trustees Incorporation Act 1872

The Charitable Trustees Incorporation Act 1872 shall have effect subject to the amendments specified in Schedule 4 to this Act.

49. Amendment of Redundant Churches and Other Religious Buildings Act 1969

The Redundant Churches and Other Religious Buildings Act 1969 shall have effect subject to the amendments specified in Schedule 5 to this Act.

50. Contributions towards maintenance etc of almshouses

(1) Any provision in the trusts of an almshouse charity which relates to the payment by persons resident in the charity's almshouses of contributions towards the cost of maintaining those almshouses and essential services in them shall cease to have effect if and to the extent that it provides for the amount, or the maximum amount, of such contributions to be a sum specified, approved or authorised by the Commissioners.

(2) In subsection (1) –
'almshouse' means any premises maintained as an almshouse, whether they are called an almshouse or not; and
'almshouse charity' means a charity which is authorised under its trusts to maintain almshouses.

51. Fees and other amounts payable to Commissioners

(1) The Secretary of State may by regulations require the payment to the Commissioners of such fees as may be prescribed in respect of –
  (a) the discharge by the Commissioners of such functions under the enactments relating to charities as may be prescribed;
  (b) the inspection of the register of charities or of other material kept by them under those enactments, or the furnishing of copies of or extracts from documents so kept.

(2) Regulations under this section may –
  (a) confer, or provide for the conferring of, exemptions from liability to pay a prescribed fee;
  (b) provide for the remission or refunding of a prescribed fee (in whole or in part) in prescribed circumstances.

(3) A statutory instrument containing any regulations under this section which require the payment of a fee in respect of any matter for which no fee was previously

payable shall not be made unless a draft of the regulations has been laid before and approved by a resolution of each House of Parliament.

(4) The Commissioners may impose charges of such amounts as they consider reasonable in respect of the supply of any publications produced by them.

(5) Any fees and other payments received by the Commissioners by virtue of this section shall be paid into the Consolidated Fund.

(6) In this section 'prescribed' means prescribed by regulations under this section.

52. Disclosure of information to and by Commissioners

(1) Subject to subsection (2) and to any express restriction imposed by or under any other enactment, a body or person to whom this section applies may disclose to the Charity Commissioners any information received by that body or person under or for the purposes of any enactment, where the disclosure is made by the body or person for the purpose of enabling or assisting the Commissioners to discharge any of their functions.

(2) Subsection (1) shall not have effect in relation to the Commissioners of Customs and Excise or the Commissioners of Inland Revenue; but either of those bodies of Commissioners ('the relevant body') may disclose to the Charity Commissioners the following information, namely –
- (a) the name and address of any institution which has for any purpose been treated by the relevant body as established for charitable purposes;
- (b) information as to the purposes of an institution and the trusts under which it is established or regulated, where the disclosure is made by the relevant body in order to give or obtain assistance in determining whether the institution ought for any purpose to be treated as established for charitable purposes; and
- (c) information with respect to an institution which has for any purpose been treated as so established but which appears to the relevant body –
  - (i) to be, or to have been, carrying on activities which are not charitable, or
  - (ii) to be, or to have been, applying any of its funds for purposes which are not charitable.

(3) In subsection (2) any reference to an institution shall, in relation to the Commissioners of Inland Revenue, be construed as a reference to an institution in England and Wales.

(4) Subject to subsection (5), the Charity Commissioners may disclose to a body or person to whom this section applies any information received by them under or for the purposes of any enactment, where the disclosure is made by the Commissioners –
- (a) for any purpose connected with the discharge of their functions, and
- (b) for the purpose of enabling or assisting that body or person to discharge any of its or his functions.

(5) Where any information disclosed to the Charity Commissioners under subsection (1) or (2) is so disclosed subject to any express restriction on the disclosure of the information by the Commissioners, the Commissioners' power of disclosure under subsection (4) shall, in relation to the information, be exercisable by them subject to any such restriction.

(6) This section applies to the following bodies and persons –

    (a) any government department (including a Northern Ireland department);

    (b) any local authority;

    (c) any constable; and

    (d) any other body or person discharging functions of a public nature (including a body or person discharging regulatory functions in relation to any description of activities).

(7) In subsection (6)(d) the reference to any such body or person as is there mentioned shall, in relation to a disclosure by the Charity Commissioners under subsection (4), be construed as including a reference to any such body or person in a country or territory outside the United Kingdom.

(8) Nothing in this section shall be construed as affecting any power of disclosure exercisable apart from this section.

(9) In this section 'enactment' includes an enactment comprised in subordinate legislation (within the meaning of the Interpretation Act 1978).

53. Data protection

An order under section 30 of the Data Protection Act 1984 (exemption from subject access provisions of data held for the purpose of discharging designated functions in connection with the regulation of financial services etc) may designate for the purposes of that section, as if they were functions conferred by or under such an enactment as is there mentioned, any functions of the Commissioners appearing to the Secretary of State to be –

    (a) connected with the protection of charities against misconduct or mismanagement (whether by trustees or other persons) in their administration; or

    (b) connected with the protection of the property of charities from loss or misapplication or with the recovery of such property.

54. Supply of false or misleading information to Commissioners etc

(1) Any person who knowingly or recklessly provides the Commissioners with information which is false or misleading in a material particular shall be guilty of an offence if the information –

    (a) is provided in purported compliance with a requirement imposed by or under a relevant enactment; or

    (b) is provided otherwise than as mentioned in paragraph (a) but in circumstances in which the person providing the information intends, or could reasonably be expected to know, that it would be used by the Commissioners for the purpose of discharging their functions under a relevant enactment.

(2) Any person who wilfully alters, suppresses, conceals or destroys any document which he is or is liable to be required, by or under a relevant enactment, to produce to the Commissioners shall be guilty of an offence.

(3) Any person guilty of an offence under this section shall be liable –

    (a) on summary conviction, to a fine not exceeding the statutory maximum;

    (b) on conviction on indictment, to imprisonment for a term not exceeding two years or to a fine, or both.

(4) In this section –

    (a) 'relevant enactment' means this Act, the 1960 Act or the Charitable Trustees Incorporation Act 1872; and

    (b) references to the Commissioners include references to any person conducting an inquiry under section 6 of the 1960 Act (general power to institute inquiries).

55. Restriction on institution of proceedings for certain offences

(1) No proceedings for an offence to which this section applies shall be instituted except by or with the consent of the Director of Public Prosecutions.

(2) This section applies to any offence under –

    (a) section 3 above;

    (b) section 20(10) of the 1960 Act, as amended by section 8 above;

    (c) section 27 above;

    (d) section 46(1) above; or

    (e) section 54 above.

56. Enforcement of requirements by order of Commissioners, and other provisions as to orders made by them

(1) If a person fails to comply with any requirement imposed by or under –

    (a) this Part of this Act,

    (b) the 1960 Act, or

    (c) the 1872 Act,

then (subject to subsection (2)) the Commissioners may by order give him such directions as they consider appropriate for securing that the default is made good.

(2) Subsection (1) does not apply to any such requirement if –

    (a) a person who fails to comply with, or is persistently in default in relation to, the requirement is liable to any criminal penalty; or

    (b) the requirement is imposed –

        (i) by an order of the Commissioners to which section 41 of the 1960 Act (enforcement of orders as for contempt of High Court) applies (whether by virtue of subsection (3) below or otherwise), or

        (ii) by a direction of the Commissioners to which that section applies by virtue of section 57(2) below.

(3) Section 41 of the 1960 Act applies to any order made by the Commissioners under subsection (1) above or under any of the following provisions, namely –

    (a) section 12 above,

    (b) section 22(2) above,

    (c) section 46 above, and

    (d) section 12A of the 1872 Act,

as that section applies to any such order of the Commissioners as is mentioned in that section.

(4) Subject to subsection (5) below, section 40 of the 1960 Act (miscellaneous provisions as to orders of Commissioners) shall apply to any order made by the Commissioners under this Act or the 1872 Act as it applies to any order made by them under the 1960 Act (the second reference to this Act in subsection (3) of that section being read as a reference to this Act or the 1872 Act, as the case may require).

(5) Subsection (3) of that section does not apply by virtue of subsection (4) above to any order made by the Commissioners under section 72 below or under section 12A of the 1872 Act.

(6) In this section 'the 1872 Act' means the Charitable Trustees Incorporation Act 1872.

57. Directions of the Commissioners

(1) Any direction given by the Commissioners under any provision contained in this Part of this Act or in the 1960 Act –
  (a) may be varied or revoked by a further direction given under that provision; and
  (b) shall be given in writing.

(2) In the 1960 Act –
  (a) subsections (1), (2) and (4) of section 40 (miscellaneous provisions as to orders of Commissioners) shall apply to any such direction as they apply to an order made by the Commissioners under that Act; and
  (b) section 41 (enforcement of orders as for contempt of High Court) shall apply to any such direction as it applies to any such order of the Commissioners as is mentioned in that section.

(3) In subsection (1) the reference to the Commissioners includes, in relation to a direction under section 6(3) of the 1960 Act (general power to institute inquiries), a reference to any person conducting an inquiry under that section.

(4) Nothing in this section shall be read as applying to any directions contained in an order made by the Commissioners under section 56(1) above.

PART II

CONTROL OF FUND-RAISING FOR CHARITABLE INSTITUTIONS

Preliminary

58. Interpretation of Part II

(1) In this Part –
'charitable contributions', in relation to any representation made by any commercial participator or other person, means –
  (a) the whole or part of –
    (i)   the consideration given for goods or services sold or supplied by him, or
    (ii) any proceeds (other than such consideration) of a promotional venture undertaken by him, or
  (b) sums given by him by way of donation in connection with the sale or supply of any such goods or services (whether the amount of such sums is determined by reference to the value of any such goods or services or otherwise);
'charitable institution' means a charity or an institution (other than a charity) which is established for charitable, benevolent or philanthropic purposes;
'charity' means a charity within the meaning of the Charities Act 1960;
'commercial participator', in relation to any charitable institution, means any person who –

(a) carries on for gain a business other than a fund-raising business, but

(b) in the course of that business, engages in any promotional venture in the course of which it is represented that charitable contributions are to be given to or applied for the benefit of the institution;

'company' has the meaning given by section 46 of the Charities Act 1960 (as amended by the Companies Act 1989);

'the court' means the High Court or a county court;

'credit card' means a card which is a credit-token within the meaning of the Consumer Credit Act 1974;

'debit card' means a card the use of which by its holder to make a payment results in a current account of his at a bank, or at any other institution providing banking services, being debited with the payment;

'fund-raising business' means any business carried on for gain and wholly or primarily engaged in soliciting or otherwise procuring money or other property for charitable, benevolent or philanthropic purposes;

'institution' includes any trust or undertaking;

'professional fund-raiser' means –

(a) any person (apart from a charitable institution) who carries on a fund-raising business, or

(b) any other person (apart from a person excluded by virtue of subsection (2) or (3)) who for reward solicits money or other property for the benefit of a charitable institution, if he does so otherwise than in the course of any fund-raising venture undertaken by a person falling within paragraph (a) above;

'promotional venture' means any advertising or sales campaign or any other venture undertaken for promotional purposes;

'radio or television programme' includes any item included in a programme service within the meaning of the Broadcasting Act 1990.

(2) In subsection (1), paragraph (b) of the definition of 'professional fund-raiser' does not apply to any of the following, namely –

(a) any charitable institution or any company connected with any such institution;

(b) any officer or employee of any such institution or company, or any trustee of any such institution, acting (in each case) in his capacity as such;

(c) any person acting as a collector in respect of a public charitable collection (apart from a person who is to be treated as a promoter of such a collection by virtue of section 65(3));

(d) any person who in the course of a relevant programme, that is to say a radio or television programme in the course of which a fund-raising venture is undertaken by –

(i) a charitable institution, or

(ii) a company connected with such an institution,

makes any solicitation at the instance of that institution or company; or

(e) any commercial participator;

and for this purpose 'collector' and 'public charitable collection' have the same meaning as in Part III of this Act.

(3) In addition, paragraph (b) of the definition of 'professional fund-raiser' does not apply to a person if he does not receive –

(a) more than –

(i) £5 per day, or

(ii) £500 per year,

by way of remuneration in connection with soliciting money or other property for the benefit of the charitable institution referred to in that paragraph; or

(b) more than £500 by way of remuneration in connection with any fund-raising venture in the course of which he solicits money or other property for the benefit of that institution.

(4) In this Part any reference to charitable purposes, where occurring in the context of a reference to charitable, benevolent or philanthropic purposes, is a reference to charitable purposes whether or not the purposes are charitable within the meaning of any rule of law.

(5) For the purposes of this Part a company is connected with a charitable institution if –

(a) the institution, or

(b) the institution and one or more other charitable institutions, taken together,

is or are entitled (whether directly or through one or more nominees) to exercise, or control the exercise of, the whole of the voting power at any general meeting of the company.

(6) In this Part –

(a) 'represent' and 'solicit' mean respectively represent and solicit in any manner whatever, whether expressly or impliedly and whether done –

(i) by speaking directly to the person or persons to whom the representation or solicitation is addressed (whether when in his or their presence or not), or

(ii) by means of a statement published in any newspaper, film or radio or television programme,

or otherwise, and references to a representation or solicitation shall be construed accordingly; and

(b) any reference to soliciting or otherwise procuring money or other property is a reference to soliciting or otherwise procuring money or other property whether any consideration is, or is to be, given in return for the money or other property or not.

(7) Where –

(a) any solicitation of money or other property for the benefit of a charitable institution is made in accordance with arrangements between any person and that institution, and

(b) under those arrangements that person will be responsible for receiving on behalf of the institution money or other property given in response to the solicitation,

then (if he would not be so regarded apart from this subsection) that person shall be regarded for the purposes of this Part as soliciting money or other property for the benefit of the institution.

(8) Where any fund-raising venture is undertaken by a professional fund-raiser in the course of a radio or television programme, any solicitation which is made by a person in the course of the programme at the instance of the fund-raiser shall be regarded for the purposes of this Part as made by the fund-raiser and not by that person (and shall be so regarded whether or not the solicitation is made by that person for any reward).

(9) In this Part 'services' includes facilities, and in particular –
  (a) access to any premises or event;
  (b) membership of any organisation;
  (c) the provision of advertising space; and
  (d) the provision of any financial facilities;
and references to the supply of services shall be construed accordingly.

(10) The Secretary of State may by order amend subsection (3) by substituting a different sum for any sum for the time being specified there.

Control of fund-raising

59. Prohibition on professional fund-raiser etc raising funds for charitable institution without an agreement in prescribed form

(1) It shall be unlawful for a professional fund-raiser to solicit money or other property for the benefit of a charitable institution unless he does so in accordance with an agreement with the institution satisfying the prescribed requirements.

(2) It shall be unlawful for a commercial participator to represent that charitable contributions are to be given to or applied for the benefit of a charitable institution unless he does so in accordance with an agreement with the institution satisfying the prescribed requirements.

(3) Where on the application of a charitable institution the court is satisfied –
  (a) that any person has contravened or is contravening subsection (1) or (2) in relation to the institution, and
  (b) that, unless restrained, any such contravention is likely to continue or be repeated,
the court may grant an injunction restraining the contravention; and compliance with subsection (1) or (2) shall not be enforceable otherwise than in accordance with this subsection.

(4) Where –
  (a) a charitable institution makes any agreement with a professional fund-raiser or a commercial participator by virtue of which –
    (i) the professional fund-raiser is authorised to solicit money or other property for the benefit of the institution, or
    (ii) the commercial participator is authorised to represent that charitable contributions are to be given to or applied for the benefit of the institution,
    as the case may be, but
  (b) the agreement does not satisfy the prescribed requirements in any respect,
the agreement shall not be enforceable against the institution except to such extent (if any) as may be provided by an order of the court.

(5) A professional fund-raiser or commercial participator who is a party to such an agreement as is mentioned in subsection (4)(a) shall not be entitled to receive any amount by way of remuneration or expenses in respect of anything done by him in pursuance of the agreement unless –
  (a) he is so entitled under any provision of the agreement, and

    (b) either –
       (i) the agreement satisfies the prescribed requirements, or
       (ii) any such provision has effect by virtue of an order of the court under subsection (4).

(6) In this section 'the prescribed requirements' means such requirements as are prescribed by regulations made by virtue of section 64(2)(a).

60. Professional fund-raisers etc required to indicate institutions benefiting and arrangements for remuneration

(1) Where a professional fund-raiser solicits money or other property for the benefit of one or more particular charitable institutions, the solicitation shall be accompanied by a statement clearly indicating –
    (a) the name or names of the institution or institutions concerned;
    (b) if there is more than one institution concerned, the proportions in which the institutions are respectively to benefit; and
    (c) (in general terms) the method by which the fund-raiser's remuneration in connection with the appeal is to be determined.

(2) Where a professional fund-raiser solicits money or other property for charitable, benevolent or philanthropic purposes of any description (rather than for the benefit of one or more particular charitable institutions), the solicitation shall be accompanied by a statement clearly indicating –
    (a) the fact that he is soliciting money or other property for those purposes and not for the benefit of any particular charitable institution or institutions;
    (b) the method by which it is to be determined how the proceeds of the appeal are to be distributed between different charitable institutions; and
    (c) (in general terms) the method by which his remuneration in connection with the appeal is to be determined.

(3) Where any representation is made by a commercial participator to the effect that charitable contributions are to be given to or applied for the benefit of one or more particular charitable institutions, the representation shall be accompanied by a statement clearly indicating –
    (a) the name or names of the institution or institutions concerned;
    (b) if there is more than one institution concerned, the proportions in which the institutions are respectively to benefit; and
    (c) (in general terms) the method by which it is to be determined –
       (i) what proportion of the consideration given for goods or services sold or supplied by him, or of any other proceeds of a promotional venture undertaken by him, is to be given to or applied for the benefit of the institution or institutions concerned, or
       (ii) what sums by way of donations by him in connection with the sale or supply of any such goods or services are to be so given or applied,
    as the case may require.

(4) If any such solicitation or representation as is mentioned in any of subsections (1) to (3) is made –
    (a) in the course of a radio or television programme, and
    (b) in association with an announcement to the effect that payment may be made,

in response to the solicitation or representation, by means of a credit or debit
card,
the statement required by virtue of subsection (1), (2) or (3) (as the case may be) shall
include full details of the right to have refunded under section 61(1) any payment of
£50 or more which is so made.

(5) If any such solicitation or representation as is mentioned in any of subsections (1)
to (3) is made orally but is not made –
    (a) by speaking directly to the particular person or persons to whom it is
        addressed and in his or their presence, or
    (b) in the course of any radio or television programme,
the professional fund-raiser or commercial participator concerned shall, within seven
days of any payment of £50 or more being made to him in response to the solicitation
or representation, give to the person making the payment a written statement –
    (i) of the matters specified in paragraphs (a) to (c) of that subsection; and
    (ii) including full details of the right to cancel under section 61(2) an agree-
        ment made in response to the solicitation or representation, and the right
        to have refunded under section 61(2) or (3) any payment of £50 or more
        made in response thereto.

(6) In subsection (5) above the reference to the making of a payment is a reference to
the making of a payment of whatever nature and by whatever means, including a
payment made by means of a credit card or a debit card; and for the purposes of that
subsection –
    (a) where the person making any such payment makes it in person, it shall be
        regarded as made at the time when it is so made;
    (b) where the person making any such payment sends it by post, it shall be
        regarded as made at the time when it is posted; and
    (c) where the person making any such payment makes it by giving, by telephone
        or by means of any other telecommunication apparatus, authority for an
        account to be debited with the payment, it shall be regarded as made at the
        time when any such authority is given.

(7) Where any requirement of subsections (1) to (5) is not complied with in relation to
any solicitation or representation, the professional fund-raiser or commercial participator concerned shall be guilty of an offence and liable on summary conviction to a
fine not exceeding the fifth level on the standard scale.

(8) It shall be a defence for a person charged with any such offence to prove that he
took all reasonable precautions and exercised all due diligence to avoid the commission of the offence.

(9) Where the commission by any person of an offence under subsection (7) is due to
the act or default of some other person, that other person shall be guilty of the offence;
and a person may be charged with and convicted of the offence by virtue of this
subsection whether or not proceedings are taken against the first-mentioned person.

(10) In this section –
'the appeal', in relation to any solicitation by a professional fund-raiser, means the
    campaign or other fund-raising venture in the course of which the solicitation is
    made;
'telecommunication apparatus' has the same meaning as in the Telecommunications
    Act 1984.

61. Cancellation of payments and agreements made in response to appeals

(1) Where –
  (a) a person ('the donor'), in response to any such solicitation or representation as is mentioned in any of subsections (1) to (3) of section 60 which is made in the course of a radio or television programme, makes any payment of £50 or more to the relevant fund-raiser by means of a credit card or a debit card, but
  (b) before the end of the period of seven days beginning with the date of the solicitation or representation, the donor serves on the relevant fund-raiser a notice in writing which, however expressed, indicates the donor's intention to cancel the payment,
the donor shall (subject to subsection (4) below) be entitled to have the payment refunded to him forthwith by the relevant fund-raiser.

(2) Where –
  (a) a person ('the donor'), in response to any solicitation or representation falling within subsection (5) of section 60, enters into an agreement with the relevant fund-raiser under which the donor is, or may be, liable to make any payment or payments to the relevant fund-raiser, and the amount or aggregate amount which the donor is, or may be, liable to pay to him under the agreement is £50 or more, but
  (b) before the end of the period of seven days beginning with the date when he is given any such written statement as is referred to in that subsection, the donor serves on the relevant fund-raiser a notice in writing which, however expressed, indicates the donor's intention to cancel the agreement,
the notice shall operate, as from the time when it is so served, to cancel the agreement and any liability of any person other than the donor in connection with the making of any such payment or payments, and the donor shall (subject to subsection (4) below) be entitled to have any payment of £50 or more made by him under the agreement refunded to him forthwith by the relevant fund-raiser.

(3) Where, in response to any solicitation or representation falling within subsection (5) of section 60, a person ('the donor') –
  (a) makes any payment of £50 or more to the relevant fund-raiser, but
  (b) does not enter into any such agreement as is mentioned in subsection (2) above,
then, if before the end of the period of seven days beginning with the date when the donor is given any such written statement as is referred to in subsection (5) of that section, the donor serves on the relevant fund-raiser a notice in writing which, however expressed, indicates the donor's intention to cancel the payment, the donor shall (subject to subsection (4) below) be entitled to have the payment refunded to him forthwith by the relevant fund-raiser.

(4) The right of any person to have a payment refunded to him under any of subsections (1) to (3) above –
  (a) is a right to have refunded to him the amount of the payment less any administrative expenses reasonably incurred by the relevant fund-raiser in connection with –
    (i) the making of the refund, or
    (ii) (in the case of a refund under subsection (2)) dealing with the notice of cancellation served by that person; and

(b) shall, in the case of a payment for goods already received, be conditional upon restitution being made by him of the goods in question.

(5) Nothing in subsections (1) to (3) above has effect in relation to any payment made or to be made in respect of services which have been supplied at the time when the relevant notice is served.

(6) In this section any reference to the making of a payment is a reference to the making of a payment of whatever nature and (in the case of subsection (2) or (3)) a payment made by whatever means, including a payment made by means of a credit card or a debit card; and subsection (6) of section 60 shall have effect for determining when a payment is made for the purposes of this section as it has effect for determining when a payment is made for the purposes of subsection (5) of that section.

(7) In this section 'the relevant fund-raiser', in relation to any solicitation or representation, means the professional fund-raiser or commercial participator by whom it is made.

(8) The Secretary of State may by order –
  (a) amend any provision of this section by substituting a different sum for the sum for the time being specified there; and
  (b) make such consequential amendments in section 60 as he considers appropriate.

62. Right of charitable institution to prevent unauthorised fund-raising

(1) Where on the application of any charitable institution –
  (a) the court is satisfied that any person has done or is doing either of the following, namely –
    (i) soliciting money or other property for the benefit of the institution, or
    (ii) representing that charitable contributions are to be given to or applied for the benefit of the institution,
  and that, unless restrained, he is likely to do further acts of that nature, and
  (b) the court is also satisfied as to one or more of the matters specified in subsection (2),
then (subject to subsection (3)) the court may grant an injunction restraining the doing of any such acts.

(2) The matters referred to in subsection (1)(b) are –
  (a) that the person in question is using methods of fund-raising to which the institution objects;
  (b) that that person is not a fit and proper person to raise funds for the institution; and
  (c) where the conduct complained of is the making of such representations as are mentioned in subsection (1)(a)(ii), that the institution does not wish to be associated with the particular promotional or other fund-raising venture in which that person is engaged.

(3) The power to grant an injunction under subsection (1) shall not be exercisable on the application of a charitable institution unless the institution has, not less than 28 days before making the application, served on the person in question a notice in writing –
  (a) requesting him to cease forthwith –

    (i) soliciting money or other property for the benefit of the institution, or
    (ii) representing that charitable contributions are to be given to or applied for the benefit of the institution,
    as the case may be: and
  (b) stating that, if he does not comply with the notice, the institution will make an application under this section for an injunction.

(4) Where –
  (a) a charitable institution has served on any person a notice under subsection (3) ('the relevant notice') and that person has complied with the notice, but
  (b) that person has subsequently begun to carry on activities which are the same, or substantially the same, as those in respect of which the relevant notice was served,

the institution shall not, in connection with an application made by it under this section in respect of the activities carried on by that person, be required by virtue of that subsection to serve a further notice on him, if the application is made not more than 12 months after the date of service of the relevant notice.

(5) This section shall not have the effect of authorising a charitable institution to make an application under this section in respect of anything done by a professional fund-raiser or commercial participator in relation to the institution.

63. False statements relating to institutions which are not registered charities

(1) Where –
  (a) a person solicits money or other property for the benefit of an institution in association with a representation that the institution is a registered charity, and
  (b) the institution is not such a charity,

he shall be guilty of an offence and liable on summary conviction to a fine not exceeding the fifth level on the standard scale.

(2) In subsection (1) 'registered charity' means a charity which is for the time being registered in the register of charities kept under section 4 of the Charities Act 1960.

Supplementary

64. Regulations about fund-raising

(1) The Secretary of State may make such regulations as appear to him to be necessary or desirable for any purposes connected with any of the preceding provisions of this Part.

(2) Without prejudice to the generality of subsection (1), any such regulations may –
  (a) prescribe the form and content of –
    (i) agreements made for the purposes of section 59, and
    (ii) notices served under section 62(3);
  (b) require professional fund-raisers or commercial participators who are parties to such agreements with charitable institutions to make available to the

institutions books, documents or other records (however kept) which relate to the institutions;

(c) specify the manner in which money or other property acquired by professional fund-raisers or commercial participators for the benefit of, or otherwise falling to be given to or applied by such persons for the benefit of, charitable institutions is to be transmitted to such institutions;

(d) provide for any provisions of section 60 or 61 having effect in relation to solicitations or representations made in the course of radio or television programmes to have effect, subject to any modifications specified in the regulations, in relation to solicitations or representations made in the course of such programmes –

(i) by charitable institutions, or

(ii) by companies connected with such institutions,

and, in that connection, provide for any other provisions of this Part to have effect for the purposes of the regulations subject to any modifications so specified;

(e) make other provision regulating the raising of funds for charitable, benevolent or philanthropic purposes (whether by professional fund-raisers or commercial participators or otherwise).

(3) In subsection (2)(c) the reference to such money or other property as is there mentioned includes a reference to money or other property which, in the case of a professional fund-raiser or commercial participator –

(a) has been acquired by him otherwise than in accordance with an agreement with a charitable institution, but

(b) by reason of any solicitation or representation in consequence of which it has been acquired, is held by him on trust for such an institution.

(4) Regulations under this section may provide that any failure to comply with a specified provision of the regulations shall be an offence punishable on summary conviction by a fine not exceeding the second level on the standard scale.

PART III

PUBLIC CHARITABLE COLLECTIONS

Preliminary

65. **Interpretation of Part III**

(1) In this Part –

(a) 'public charitable collection' means (subject to subsection (2)) a charitable appeal which is made –

(i) in any public place, or

(ii) by means of visits from house to house; and

(b) 'charitable appeal' means an appeal to members of the public to give money or other property (whether for consideration or otherwise) which is made in association with a representation that the whole or any part of its proceeds is to be applied for charitable, benevolent or philanthropic purposes.

(2) Subsection (1)(a) does not apply to a charitable appeal which –

(a) is made in the course of a public meeting; or

(b) is made –
    (i) on land within a churchyard or burial ground contiguous or adjacent to a place of public worship, or
    (ii) on other land occupied for the purposes of a place of public worship and contiguous or adjacent to it,
    being (in each case) land which is enclosed or substantially enclosed (whether by any wall or building or otherwise); or
(c) is an appeal to members of the public to give money or other property by placing it in an unattended receptacle;
and for the purposes of paragraph (c) above a receptacle is unattended if it is not in the possession or custody of a person acting as a collector.

(3) In this Part, in relation to a public charitable collection –
(a) 'promoter' means a person who (whether alone or with others and whether for remuneration or otherwise) organises or controls the conduct of the charitable appeal in question, and associated expressions shall be construed accordingly; and
(b) 'collector' means any person by whom that appeal is made (whether made by him alone or with others and whether made by him for remuneration or otherwise);
but where no person acts in the manner mentioned in paragraph (a) above in respect of a public charitable collection, any person who acts as a collector in respect of it shall for the purposes of this Part be treated as a promoter of it as well.

(4) In this Part –
'local authority' means the council of a district or of a London borough, the Common Council of the City of London, or the Council of the Isles of Scilly; and
'proceeds', in relation to a public charitable collection, means all money or other property given (whether for consideration or otherwise) in response to the charitable appeal in question.

(5) In this Part any reference to charitable purposes, where occurring in the context of a reference to charitable, benevolent or philanthropic purposes, is a reference to charitable purposes whether or not the purposes are charitable within the meaning of any rule of law.

(6) The functions exercisable under this Part by a local authority shall be exercisable –
(a) as respects the Inner Temple, by its Sub-Treasurer, and
(b) as respects the Middle Temple, by its Under Treasurer;
and references in this Part to a local authority or to the area of a local authority shall be construed accordingly.

(7) It is hereby declared that an appeal to members of the public (other than one falling within subsection (2)) is a public charitable collection for the purposes of this Part if –
(a) it consists in or includes the making of an offer to sell goods or to supply services, or the exposing of goods for sale, to members of the public, and
(b) it is made as mentioned in sub-paragraph (i) or (ii) of subsection (1)(a) and in association with a representation that the whole or any part of its proceeds is to be applied for charitable, benevolent or philanthropic purposes.
This subsection shall not be taken as prejudicing the generality of subsection (1)(b).

(8) In this section –
'house' includes any part of a building constituting a separate dwelling;

'public place', in relation to a charitable appeal, means –
  (a) any highway, and
  (b) (subject to subsection (9)) any other place to which, at any time when the appeal is made, members of the public have or are permitted to have access and which either –
    (i) is not within a building, or
    (ii) if within a building, is a public area within any station, airport or shopping precinct or any other similar public area.

(9) In subsection (8), paragraph (b) of the definition of 'public place' does not apply to –
  (a) any place to which members of the public are permitted to have access only if any payment or ticket required as a condition of access has been made or purchased; or
  (b) any place to which members of the public are permitted to have access only by virtue of permission given for the purposes of the appeal in question.

Prohibition on conducting unauthorised collections

66. Prohibition on conducting public charitable collections without authorisation

(1) No public charitable collection shall be conducted in the area of any local authority except in accordance with –
  (a) a permit issued by the authority under section 68; or
  (b) an order made by the Charity Commissioners under section 72.

(2) Where a public charitable collection is conducted in contravention of subsection (1), any promoter of that collection shall be guilty of an offence and liable on summary conviction to a fine not exceeding the fourth level on the standard scale.

Permits

67. Applications for permits to conduct public charitable collections

(1) An application for a permit to conduct a public charitablecollection in the area of a local authority shall be made to the authority by the person or persons proposing to promote that collection.

(2) Any such application –
  (a) shall specify the period for which it is desired that the permit, if issued, should have effect, being a period not exceeding 12 months; and
  (b) shall contain such information as may be prescribed by regulations under section 73.

(3) Any such application –
  (a) shall be made at least one month before the relevant day or before such later date as the local authority may in the case of that application allow, but
  (b) shall not be made more than six months before the relevant day;
and for this purpose 'the relevant day' means the day on which the collection is to be conducted or, where it is to be conducted on more than one day, the first of those days.

(4) Before determining any application duly made to them under this section, a local authority shall consult the chief officer of police for the police area which comprises or includes their area and may make such other inquiries as they think fit.

68. Determination of applications and issue of permits

(1) Where an application for a permit is duly made to a local authority under section 67 in respect of a public charitable collection, the authority shall either –
    (a) issue a permit in respect of the collection, or
    (b) refuse the application on one or more of the grounds specified in section 69, and, where they issue such a permit, it shall (subject to section 70) have effect for the period specified in the application in accordance with section 67(2)(a).

(2) A local authority may, at the time of issuing a permit under this section, attach to it such conditions as they think fit, having regard to the local circumstances of the collection; but the authority shall secure that the terms of any such conditions are consistent with the provisions of any regulations under section 73.

(3) Without prejudice to the generality of subsection (2), a local authority may attach conditions –
    (a) specifying the day of the week, date, time or frequency of the collection;
    (b) specifying the locality or localities within their area in which the collection may be conducted;
    (c) regulating the manner in which the collection is to be conducted.

(4) Where a local authority –
    (a) refuse to issue a permit, or
    (b) attach any condition to a permit under subsection (2),
they shall serve on the applicant written notice of their decision to do so and of the reasons for their decision; and that notice shall also state the right of appeal conferred by section 71(1) or (as the case may be) section 71(2), and the time within which such an appeal must be brought.

69. Refusal of permits

(1) A local authority may refuse to issue a permit to conduct a public charitable collection on any of the following grounds, namely –
    (a) that it appears to them that the collection would cause undue inconvenience to members of the public by reason of –
        (i)   the day of the week or date on which,
        (ii) the time at which,
        (iii) the frequency with which, or
        (iv) the locality or localities in which,
        it is proposed to be conducted;
    (b) that the collection is proposed to be conducted on a day on which another public charitable collection is already authorised (whether under section 68 or otherwise) to be conducted in the authority's area, or on the day falling immediately before, or immediately after, any such day;
    (c) that it appears to them that the amount likely to be applied for charitable, benevolent or philanthropic purposes in consequence of the collection would

be inadequate, having regard to the likely amount of the proceeds of the collection;

(d) that it appears to them that the applicant or any other person would be likely to receive an excessive amount by way of remuneration in connection with the collection;

(e) that the applicant has been convicted –
  (i) of an offence under section 5 of the 1916 Act, under the 1939 Act, under section 119 of the 1982 Act or regulations made under it, or under this Part or regulations made under section 73 below, or
  (ii) of any offence involving dishonesty or of a kind the commission of which would in their opinion be likely to be facilitated by the issuing to him of a permit under section 68 above;

(f) where the applicant is a person other than a charitable, benevolent or philanthropic institution for whose benefit the collection is proposed to be conducted, that they are not satisfied that the applicant is authorised (whether by any such institution or by any person acting on behalf of any such institution) to promote the collection; or

(g) that it appears to them that the applicant, in promoting any other collection authorised under this Part or under section 119 of the 1982 Act, failed to exercise due diligence –
  (i) to secure that persons authorised by him to act as collectors for the purposes of the collection were fit and proper persons;
  (ii) to secure that such persons complied with the provisions of regulations under section 73 below or (as the case may be) section 119 of the 1982 Act; or
  (iii) to prevent badges or certificates of authority being obtained by persons other than those he had so authorised.

(2) A local authority shall not, however, refuse to issue such a permit on the ground mentioned in subsection (1)(b) if it appears to them –
  (a) that the collection would be conducted only in one location, which is on land to which members of the public would have access only by virtue of the express or implied permission of the occupier of the land; and
  (b) that the occupier of the land consents to the collection being conducted there; and for this purpose 'the occupier', in relation to unoccupied land, means the person entitled to occupy it.

(3) In subsection (1) –
  (a) in the case of a collection in relation to which there is more than one applicant, any reference to the applicant shall be construed as a reference to any of the applicants; and
  (b) (subject to subsection (4)) the reference in paragraph (g)(iii) to badges or certificates of authority is a reference to badges or certificates of authority in a form prescribed by regulations under section 73 below or (as the case may be) under section 119 of the 1982 Act.

(4) Subsection (1)(g) applies to the conduct of the applicant (or any of the applicants) in relation to any public charitable collection authorised under regulations made under section 5 of the 1916 Act (collection of money or sale of articles in a street or other public place), or authorised under the 1939 Act (collection of money or other property by means of visits from house to house), as it applies to his conduct in relation to a

collection authorised under this Part, subject to the following modifications, namely –
- (a) in the case of a collection authorised under regulations made under the 1916 Act –
  - (i) the reference in sub-paragraph (ii) to regulations under section 73 below shall be construed as a reference to the regulations under which the collection in question was authorised, and
  - (ii) the reference in sub-paragraph (iii) to badges or certificates of authority shall be construed as a reference to any written authority provided to a collector pursuant to those regulations; and
- (b) in the case of a collection authorised under the 1939 Act –
  - (i) the reference in sub-paragraph (ii) to regulations under section 73 below shall be construed as a reference to regulations under section 4 of that Act, and
  - (ii) the reference in sub-paragraph (iii) to badges or certificates of authority shall be construed as a reference to badges or certificates of authority in a form prescribed by such regulations.

(5) In this section –
'the 1916 Act' means the Police, Factories, &c. (Miscellaneous Provisions) Act 1916;
'the 1939 Act' means the House to House Collections Act 1939; and
'the 1982 Act' means the Civic Government (Scotland) Act 1982.

70. **Withdrawal etc of permits**

(1) Where a local authority who have issued a permit under section 68 –
- (a) have reason to believe that there has been a change in the circumstances which prevailed at the time when they issued the permit, and are of the opinion that, if the application for the permit had been made in the new circumstances of the case, the permit would not have been issued by them, or
- (b) have reason to believe that any information furnished to them by the promoter (or, in the case of a collection in relation to which there is more than one promoter, by any of them) for the purposes of the application for the permit was false in a material particular,

then (subject to subsection (2)) they may –
- (i) withdraw the permit;
- (ii) attach any condition to the permit; or
- (iii) vary any existing condition of the permit.

(2) Any condition imposed by the local authority under subsection (1) (whether by attaching a new condition to the permit or by varying an existing condition) must be one that could have been attached to the permit under section 68(2) at the time when it was issued, assuming for this purpose –
- (a) that the new circumstances of the case had prevailed at that time, or
- (b) (in a case falling within paragraph (b) of subsection (1) above) that the authority had been aware of the true circumstances of the case at that time.

(3) Where a local authority who have issued a permit under section 68 have reason to believe that there has been or is likely to be a breach of any condition of it, or that a breach of such a condition is continuing, they may withdraw the permit.

(4) Where under this section a local authority withdraw, attach any condition to, or vary an existing condition of, a permit, they shall serve on the promoter written notice of their decision to do so and of the reasons for their decision; and that notice shall also state the right of appeal conferred by section 71(2) and the time within which such an appeal must be brought.

(5) Where a local authority so withdraw, attach any condition to, or vary an existing condition of, a permit, the permit shall nevertheless continue to have effect as if it had not been withdrawn or (as the case may be) as if the condition had not been attached or the variation had not been made –
  (a) until the time for bringing an appeal under section 71(2) has expired, or
  (b) if such an appeal is duly brought, until the determination or abandonment of the appeal.

71. Appeals

(1) A person who has duly applied to a local authority under section 67 for a permit to conduct a public charitable collection in the authority's area may appeal to a magistrates' court against a decision of the authority to refuse to issue a permit to him.

(2) A person to whom a permit has been issued under section 68 may appeal to a magistrates' court against –
  (a) a decision of the local authority under that section or section 70 to attach any condition to the permit; or
  (b) a decision of the local authority under section 70 to vary any condition so attached or to withdraw the permit.

(3) An appeal under subsection (1) or (2) shall be by way of complaint for an order, and the Magistrates' Courts Act 1980 shall apply to the proceedings; and references in this section to a magistrates' court are to a magistrates' court acting for the petty sessions area in which is situated the office or principal office of the local authority against whose decision the appeal is brought.

(4) Any such appeal shall be brought within 14 days of the date of service on the person in question of the relevant notice under section 68(4) or (as the case may be) section 70(4); and for the purposes of this subsection an appeal shall be taken to be brought when the complaint is made.

(5) An appeal against the decision of a magistrates' court on an appeal under subsection (1) or (2) may be brought to the Crown Court.

(6) On an appeal to a magistrates' court or the Crown Court under this section, the court may confirm, vary or reverse the local authority's decision and generally give such directions as it thinks fit, having regard to the provisions of this Part and of regulations under section 73.

(7) It shall be the duty of the local authority to comply with any directions given by the court under subsection (6); but the authority need not comply with any directions given by a magistrates' court –
  (a) until the time for bringing an appeal under subsection (5) has expired, or
  (b) if such an appeal is duly brought, until the determination or abandonment of the appeal.

72. Orders made by Charity Commissioners

(1) Where the Charity Commissioners are satisfied, on the application of any charity, that that charity proposes –
  (a) to promote public charitable collections –
      (i) throughout England and Wales, or
      (ii) throughout a substantial part of England and Wales,
      in connection with any charitable purposes pursued by the charity, or
  (b) to authorise other persons to promote public charitable collections as mentioned in paragraph (a),
the Commissioners may make an order under this subsection in respect of the charity.

(2) Such an order shall have the effect of authorising public charitable collections which –
  (a) are promoted by the charity in respect of which the order is made, or by persons authorised by the charity, and
  (b) are so promoted in connection with the charitable purposes mentioned in subsection (1),
to be conducted in such area or areas as may be specified in the order.

(3) An order under subsection (1) may –
  (a) include such conditions as the Commissioners think fit;
  (b) be expressed (without prejudice to paragraph (c)) to have effect without limit of time, or for a specified period only;
  (c) be revoked or varied by a further order of the Commissioners.

(4) Where the Commissioners, having made an order under subsection (1) in respect of a charity, make any further order revoking or varying that order, they shall serve on the charity written notice of their reasons for making the further order, unless it appears to them that the interests of the charity would not be prejudiced by the further order.

(5) In this section 'charity' and 'charitable purposes' have the same meaning as in the Charities Act 1960.

Supplementary

73. Regulations

(1) The Secretary of State may make regulations –
  (a) prescribing the information which is to be contained in applications made under section 67;
  (b) for the purpose of regulating the conduct of public charitable collections authorised under –
      (i) permits issued under section 68; or
      (ii) orders made by the Charity Commissioners under section 72.

(2) Regulations under subsection (1)(b) may, without prejudice to the generality of that provision, make provision –
  (a) about the keeping and publication of accounts;

(b) for the prevention of annoyance to members of the public;

(c) with respect to the use by collectors of badges and certificates of authority, or badges incorporating such certificates, and to other matters relating to such badges and certificates, including, in particular, provision –

(i) prescribing the form of such badges and certificates;

(ii) requiring a collector, on request, to permit his badge, or any certificate of authority held by him for the purposes of the collection, to be inspected by a constable or a duly authorised officer of a local authority, or by an occupier of any premises visited by him in the course of the collection;

(d) for prohibiting persons under a prescribed age from acting as collectors, and prohibiting others from causing them so to act.

(3) Regulations under this section may provide that any failure to comply with a specified provision of the regulations shall be an offence punishable on summary conviction by a fine not exceeding the second level on the standard scale.

74. Offences

(1) A person shall be guilty of an offence if, in connection with any charitable appeal, he displays or uses –

(a) a prescribed badge or a prescribed certificate of authority which is not for the time being held by him for the purposes of the appeal pursuant to regulations under section 73, or

(b) any badge or article, or any certificate or other document, so nearly resembling a prescribed badge or (as the case may be) a prescribed certificate of authority as to be likely to deceive a member of the public.

(2) A person guilty of an offence under subsection (1) shall be liable on summary conviction to a fine not exceeding the fourth level on the standard scale.

(3) Any person who, for the purposes of an application made under section 67, knowingly or recklessly furnishes any information which is false in a material particular shall be guilty of an offence and liable on summary conviction to a fine not exceeding the fourth level on the standard scale.

(4) In subsection (1) 'prescribed badge' and 'prescribed certificate of authority' mean respectively a badge and a certificate of authority in such form as may be prescribed by regulations under section 73.

PART IV

GENERAL

75. Offences by bodies corporate

Where any offence –

(a) under this Act or any regulations made under it, or

(b) under the Charities Act 1960,

is committed by a body corporate and is proved to have been committed with the consent or connivance of, or to be attributable to any neglect on the part of, any director, manager, secretary or other similar officer of the body corporate, or any person who was purporting to act in any such capacity, he as well as the body corporate shall be guilty of that offence and shall be liable to be proceeded against and punished accordingly.

In relation to a body corporate whose affairs are managed by its members, 'director' means a member of the body corporate.

76. Service of documents

(1) This section applies to –
  (a) any order or direction made or given by the Charity Commissioners under Part I of this Act;
  (b) any notice or other document required or authorised to be given or served under Part II of this Act; and
  (c) any notice required to be served under Part III of this Act.

(2) A document to which this section applies may be served on or given to a person (other than a body corporate) –
  (a) by delivering it to that person;
  (b) by leaving it at his last known address in the United Kingdom; or
  (c) by sending it by post to him at that address.

(3) A document to which this section applies may be served on or given to a body corporate by delivering it or sending it by post –
  (a) to the registered or principal office of the body in the United Kingdom, or
  (b) if it has no such office in the United Kingdom, to any place in the United Kingdom where it carries on business or conducts its activities (as the case may be).

(4) Any such document may also be served on or given to a person (including a body corporate) by sending it by post to that person at an address notified by that person for the purposes of this subsection to the person or persons by whom it is required or authorised to be served or given.

77. Regulations and orders

(1) Any regulations or order of the Secretary of State under this Act –
  (a) shall be made by statutory instrument; and
  (b) (subject to subsection (2)) shall be subject to annulment in pursuance of a resolution of either House of Parliament.

(2) Subsection (1)(b) does not apply –
  (a) to an order under section 38;
  (b) to any regulations under section 39;
  (c) to a statutory instrument to which section 51(3) applies; or
  (d) to an order under section 79(2).

(3) Any regulations or order of the Secretary of State under this Act may make –
  (a) different provision for different cases; and
  (b) such supplemental, incidental, consequential or transitional provision or savings as the Secretary of State considers appropriate.

(4) Before making any regulations under section 20, 22, 23, 64 or 73 the Secretary of State shall consult such persons or bodies of persons as he considers appropriate.

78. Minor and consequential amendments and repeals

(1) The enactments mentioned in Schedule 6 to this Act shall have effect subject to the amendments there specified (which are either minor amendments or amendments consequential on the provisions of this Act).

(2) The enactments mentioned in Schedule 7 to this Act (which include some that are already spent or are no longer of practical utility) are hereby repealed to the extent specified in the third column of that Schedule.

79. Short title, commencement and extent

(1) This Act may be cited as the Charities Act 1992.

(2) This Act shall come into force on such day as the Secretary of State may by order appoint; and different days may be so appointed for different provisions or for different purposes.

(3) Subject to subsections (4) to (6) below, this Act extends only to England and Wales.

(4) Section 52 and this section extend to the whole of the United Kingdom.

(5) Sections 38 and 39, and so much of section 77 as relates to those sections, extend to England and Wales and Scotland.

(6) The amendments in Schedule 6, and (subject to subsection (7)) the repeals in Schedule 7, have the same extent as the enactments to which they refer, and section 78 extends accordingly.,

(7) The repeal in Schedule 7 of the Police, Factories, &c. (Miscellaneous Provisions) Act 1916 does not extend to Northern Ireland.

SCHEDULES
SCHEDULE 1
Sections 2 and 8

SECTIONS 4 AND 20 OF THE CHARITIES ACT 1960, AS AMENDED

Section 4

4. The register of charities

(1) The Commissioners shall continue to keep a register of charities, which shall be kept by them in such manner as they think fit.

(2) There shall be entered in the register every charity not excepted by subsection (4) below; and a charity so excepted (other than one excepted by paragraph (a) of that subsection) may be entered in the register at the request of the charity, but (whether or not it was excepted at the time of registration) may at any time, and shall at the request of the charity, be removed from the register.

(2A) The register shall contain –
    (a) the name of every registered charity; and

(b) such other particulars of, and such other information relating to, every such charity as the Commissioners think fit.

(3) Any institution which no longer appears to the Commissioners to be a charity shall be removed from the register, with effect, where the removal is due to any change in its purposes or trusts, from the date of that change; and there shall also be removed from the register any charity which ceases to exist or does not operate.

(4) The following charities are not required to be registered, that is to say, –
(a) any charity comprised in the Second Schedule to this Act (in this Act referred to as an 'exempt charity');
(b) any charity which is excepted by order or regulations;
(c) any charity which has neither –
(i) any permanent endowment, nor
(ii) the use or occupation of any land,
and whose income from all sources does not in aggregate amount to more than £1,000 a year;
and no charity is required to be registered in respect of any registered place of worship.

(5) With any application for a charity to be registered there shall be supplied to the Commissioners copies of its trusts (or, if they are not set out in any extant document, particulars of them), and such other documents or information as may be prescribed or as the Commissioners may require for the purpose of the application.

(6) It shall be the duty –
(a) of the charity trustees of any charity which is not registered nor excepted from registration to apply for it to be registered, and to supply the documents and information required by subsection (5) above; and
(b) of the charity trustees (or last charity trustees) of any institution which is for the time being registered to notify the Commissioners if it ceases to exist, or if there is any change in its trusts, or in the particulars of it entered in the register, and to supply to the Commissioners particulars of any such change and copies of any new trusts or alterations of the trusts.

(7) The register (including the entries cancelled when institutions are removed from the register) shall be open to public inspection at all reasonable times; and copies (or particulars) of the trusts of any registered charity as supplied to the Commissioners under this section shall, so long as it remains on the register, be kept by them and be open to public inspection at all reasonable times, except in so far as regulations otherwise provide.

(7A) Where any information contained in the register is not in documentary form, subsection (7) above shall be construed as requiring the information to be available for public inspection in legible form at all reasonable times.

(7B) If the Commissioners so determine, that subsection shall not apply to any particular information contained in the register and specified in their determination.

(8) Nothing in the foregoing subsections shall require any person to supply the Commissioners with copies of schemes for the administration of a charity made otherwise than by the court, or to notify the Commissioners of any change made with respect to a registered charity by such a scheme, or require a person, if he refers the Commissioners to a document or copy already in the possession of the Commissioners, to supply a further copy of the document; but where by virtue of this

subsection a copy of any document need not be supplied to the Commissioners, a copy of it, if it relates to a registered charity, shall be open to inspection under subsection (7) above as if supplied to the Commissioners under this section.

(8A) If he thinks it expedient to do so –
    (a) in consequence of changes in the value of money, or
    (b) with a view to extending the scope of the exception provided for by subsection (4)(c) above,
the Secretary of State may by order amend subsection (4)(c) by substituting a different sum for the sum for the time being specified there.

(8B) Any such order shall be made by statutory instrument subject to annulment in pursuance of a resolution of either House of Parliament.

(9) In this section 'registered place of worship' means any land or building falling within section nine of the Places of Worship Registration Act, 1855, as amended by this Act (that is to say, the land and buildings which, if this Act had not been passed, would by virtue of that section as amended by subsequent enactments be partially exempted from the operation of the Charitable Trusts Act, 1853), and for the purposes of this subsection 'building' includes part of a building.

Section 20

20. Power to act for protection of charities

(1) Where, at any time after they have instituted an inquiry under section 6 of this Act with respect to any charity, the Commissioners are satisfied –
    (a) that there is or has been any misconduct or mismanagement in the administration of the charity; or
    (b) that it is necessary or desirable to act for the purpose of protecting the property of the charity or securing a proper application for the purposes of the charity of that property or of property coming to the charity;
the Commissioners may of their own motion do one or more of the following things, namely –
    (i)   by order suspend any trustee, charity trustee, officer, agent or employee of the charity from the exercise of his office or employment pending consideration being given to his removal (whether under this section or otherwise);
    (ii)   by order appoint such number of additional charity trustees as they consider necessary for the proper administration of the charity;
    (iii) by order vest any property held by or in trust for the charity in the official custodian for charities, or require the persons in whom any such property is vested to transfer it to him, or appoint any person to transfer any such property to him;
    (iv) order any person who holds any property on behalf of the charity, or of any trustee for it, not to part with the property without the approval of the Commissioners;
    (v)   order any debtor of the charity not to make any payment in or towards the discharge of his liability to the charity without the approval of the Commissioners;
    (vi) by order restrict (notwithstanding anything in the trusts of the charity)

the transactions which may be entered into, or the nature or amount of the payments which may be made, in the administration of the charity without the approval of the Commissioners;

(vii) by order appoint (in accordance with section 20A of this Act) a receiver and manager in respect of the property and affairs of the charity.

(1A) Where, at any time after they have instituted an inquiry under section 6 of this Act with respect to any charity, the Commissioners are satisfied –

(a) that there is or has been any misconduct or mismanagement in the administration of the charity; and

(b) that it is necessary or desirable to act for the purpose of protecting the property of the charity or securing a proper application for the purposes of the charity of that property or of property coming to the charity;

the Commissioners may of their own motion do either or both of the following things, namely –

(i) by order remove any trustee, charity trustee, officer, agent or employee of the charity who has been responsible for or privy to the misconduct or mismanagement or has by his conduct contributed to it or facilitated it;

(ii) by order establish a scheme for the administration of the charity.

(2) The references in subsection (1) or (1A) above to misconduct or mismanagement shall (notwithstanding anything in the trusts of the charity) extend to the employment for the remuneration or reward of persons acting in the affairs of the charity, or for other administrative purposes, of sums which are excessive in relation to the property which is or is likely to be applied or applicable for the purposes of the charity.

(3) The Commissioners may also remove a charity trustee by order made of their own motion –

(a) where, within the last five years, the trustee –
(i) having previously been adjudged bankrupt or had his estate sequestrated, has been discharged, or
(ii) having previously made a composition or arrangement with, or granted a trust deed for, his creditors, has been discharged in respect of it;

(aa) where the trustee is a corporation in liquidation;

(ab) where the trustee is incapable of acting by reason of mental disorder within the meaning of the Mental Health Act 1983;

(b) where the trustee has not acted, and will not declare his willingness or unwillingness to act;

(c) where the trustee is outside England and Wales or cannot be found or does not act, and his absence or failure to act impedes the proper administration of the charity.

(4) The Commissioners may by order of their own motion appoint a person to be a charity trustee –

(a) in place of a charity trustee removed by them under this section or otherwise;

(b) where there are no charity trustees, or where by reason of vacancies in their number or the absence or incapacity of any of their number the charity cannot apply for the appointment;

(c) where there is a single charity trustee, not being a corporation aggregate, and the Commissioners are of opinion that it is necessary to increase the number for the proper administration of the charity;

(d) where the Commissioners are of opinion that it is necessary for the proper administration of the charity to have an additional charity trustee, because one of the existing charity trustees who ought nevertheless to remain a charity trustee either cannot be found or does not act or is outside England and Wales.

(5) The powers of the Commissioners under this section to remove or appoint charity trustees of their own motion shall include power to make any such order with respect to the vesting in or transfer to the charity trustees of any property as the Commissioners could make on the removal or appointment of a charity trustee by them under section eighteen of this Act.

(6) Any order under this section for the removal or appointment of a charity trustee or trustee for a charity, or for the vesting or transfer of any property, shall be of the like effect as an order made under section eighteen of this Act.

(7) Subject to subsection (7A) below, subsections (10) and (11) of section 18 of this Act shall apply to orders under this section as they apply to orders under that section.

(7A) The requirement to obtain any such certificate or leave as is mentioned in the proviso to section 18(11) shall not apply to –
   (a) an appeal by a charity or any of the charity trustees of a charity against an order under subsection (1)(vii) above appointing a receiver and manager in respect of the charity's property and affairs, or
   (b) an appeal by a person against an order under subsection (1A)(i) or (3)(a) above removing him from his office or employment.

(7B) Subsection (12) of section 18 of this Act shall apply to an order under this section which establishes a scheme for the administration of a charity as it applies to such an order under that section.

(8) The power of the Commissioners to make an order under subsection (1)(i) above shall not be exercisable so as to suspend any person from the exercise of his office or employment for a period of more than twelve months; but (without prejudice to the generality of section 40(1) of this Act) any such order made in the case of any person may make provision as respects the period of his suspension for matters arising out of it, and in particular for enabling any person to execute any instrument in his name or otherwise act for him and, in the case of a charity trustee, for adjusting any rules governing the proceedings of the charity trustees to take account of the reduction in the number capable of acting.

(9) Before exercising any jurisdiction under this section otherwise than by virtue of subsection (1) above, the Commissioners shall give notice of their intention to do so to each of the charity trustees, except any that cannot be found or has no known address in the United Kingdom; and any such notice may be given by post and, if given by post, may be addressed to the recipient's last known address in the United Kingdom.

(9A) The Commissioners shall, at such intervals as they think fit, review any order made by them under paragraph (i), or any of paragraphs (iii) to (vii), of subsection (1) above; and, if on any such review it appears to them that it would be appropriate to discharge the order in whole or in part, they shall so discharge it (whether subject to any savings or other transitional provisions or not).

(10) If any person contravenes an order under subsection (1)(iv), (v) or (vi) above, he shall be guilty of an offence and liable on summary conviction to a fine not exceeding the fifth level on the standard scale.

(10A) Subsection (10) above shall not be taken to preclude the bringing of proceedings for breach of trust against any charity trustee or trustee for a charity in respect of a contravention of an order under subsection (1)(iv) or (vi) above (whether proceedings in respect of the contravention are brought against him under subsection (10) above or not).

(12) This section shall not apply to an exempt charity.

SCHEDULE 2

Section 32(2)

MEANING OF 'CONNECTED PERSON' FOR PURPOSES OF SECTION 32(2)

1. In section 32(2) 'connected person', in relation to a charity, means –
   (a) a charity trustee or trustee for the charity;
   (b) a person who is the donor of any land to the charity (whether the gift was made on or after the establishment of the charity);
   (c) a child, parent, grandchild, grandparent, brother or sister of any such trustee or donor;
   (d) an officer, agent or employee of the charity;
   (e) the spouse of any person falling within any of sub-paragraphs (a) to (d);
   (f) an institution which is controlled –
      (i) by any person falling within any of sub-paragraphs (a) to (e), or
      (ii) by two or more such persons taken together; or
   (g) a body corporate in which –
      (i) any connected person falling within any of sub-paragraphs (a) to (f) has a substantial interest, or
      (ii) two or more such persons, taken together, have a substantial interest.

2. (1) In paragraph 1(c) 'child' includes a stepchild and an illegitimate child.

(2) For the purposes of paragraph 1(e) a person living with another as that person's husband or wife shall be treated as that person's spouse.

3. For the purposes of paragraph 1(f) a person controls an institution if he is able to secure that the affairs of the institution are conducted in accordance with his wishes.

4. (1) For the purposes of paragraph 1(g) any such connected person as is there mentioned has a substantial interest in a body corporate if the person or institution in question –
   (a) is interested in shares comprised in the equity share capital of that body of a nominal value of more than one-fifth of that share capital, or
   (b) is entitled to exercise, or control the exercise of, more than one-fifth of the voting power at any general meeting of that body.

(2) The rules set out in Part I of Schedule 13 to the Companies Act 1985 (rules for interpretation of certain provisions of that Act) shall apply for the purposes of sub-paragraph (1) above as they apply for the purposes of section 346(4) of that Act ('connected persons' etc).

(3) In this paragraph 'equity share capital' and 'share' have the same meaning as in that Act.

SCHEDULE 3

Section 47

MINOR AND CONSEQUENTIAL AMENDMENTS OF CHARITIES ACT 1960

1. In section 1(2) (constitution etc. of Commissioners), for 'servants' substitute 'employees'.

2. In section 8 (receipt and audit of accounts of charities) –
  (a) omit subsections (1) and (2);
  (b) in subsection (3), for 'that the condition and accounts of a charity' substitute ', in the case of a charity which is a company, that the condition and accounts of the charity';
  (c) in subsection (4)(b), for 'servant' substitute 'employee';
  (d) in subsection (6), omit paragraph (a); and
  (e) omit subsection (7).

3. For section 9 substitute –

'9. Supply by Commissioners of copies of documents open to public inspection

The Commissioners shall, at the request of any person, furnish him with copies of, or extracts from, any document in their possession which is for the time being open to inspection under this Act.'

4. In section 16 (entrusting charity property to official custodian) –
  (a) for subsection (1) substitute –

'(1) The court may by order –
  (a) vest in the official custodian for charities any land or interest in land held by or in trust for a charity;
  (b) authorise or require the persons in whom any such land or interest is vested to transfer it to him; or
  (c) appoint any person to transfer any such land or interest to him;
and for this purpose 'interest in land' means any interest in land other than such an interest by way of mortgage or other security.'; and
  (b) omit subsection (2).

5. In section 17 (supplementary provisions as to property vested in official custodian) –
  (a) in subsection (2) –
    (i) at the beginning insert 'Subject to subsection (2A) below,'; and
    (ii) for the words from 'require him' onwards substitute 'execute or do in their own name and on their own behalf if the land or interest were vested in them.';
  (b) after that subsection insert –

'2(2A) If any land or interest in land is so vested in the official custodian for charities by virtue of an order under section 20 of this Act, the power conferred on the charity trustees by subsection (2) above shall not be exercisable by them in relation to any transaction affecting the land or interest, unless the transaction is authorised by order of the court or of the Commissioners.'; and

(c) in each of subsections (4) and (5), after '(2)' insert ', (2A)'.

6. In section 18(1)(b) (concurrent jurisdiction with High Court for certain purposes), for 'servant' substitute 'employee'.

7. In section 19(6) (further powers to make schemes or alter application of charitable property) –

(a) omit 'or the like reference from the Secretary of State'; and

(b) for 'or reference made with a view to a scheme,' substitute 'for a scheme, or in a case where they act by virtue of subsection (6) or (6A) of that section,'.

8. In section 21 (publicity for proceedings under sections 18 and 20 of the Act) –

(a) in subsection (2), after 'shall not apply' insert 'in the case of an order under section 20(1)(ii), or'; and

(b) in subsection (3), for 'servant' substitute 'employee'.

9. In section 22 (common investment schemes) –

(a) omit subsection (6); and

(b) in subsection (9), omit the words from ', and the' to 'endowment' (where last occurring).

10. In section 28 (authorisation by Commissioners of charity proceedings) –

(a) at the end of subsection (3) add '(other than those conferred by section 26A of this Act).'; and

(b) at the end of subsection (6) add ', or to the taking of proceedings by the Commissioners in accordance with section 26A of this Act.'

11. In section 30C(1) (charitable companies: status to appear on correspondence, etc) –

(a) in paragraph (c), omit 'by or'; and

(b) in paragraph (e), for 'its bills of parcels,' substitute 'bills rendered by it and in all its'.

12. Omit section 31 (protection of expression 'common good').

13. In section 32 (general obligation to keep accounts) –

(a) in subsection (2) –

(i) for 'seven' substitute 'six', and

(ii) for 'permit them to be' substitute 'consent in writing to their being'; and

(b) for subsection (3) substitute –

'(3) This section applies only to exempt charities.'

14. In section 34(2) (manner of executing documents), in paragraph (c), for 'and to the persons' onwards substitute 'the charity trustees from time to time of the charity and exercisable by such trustees.'

15. After section 40 insert –

'40A. Service of orders and directions under this Act

(1) This section applies to any order or direction made or given by the Commissioners under this Act.

(2) An order or direction to which this section applies may be served on a person (other than a body corporate) –
  (a) by delivering it to that person;
  (b) by leaving it at his last known address in the United Kingdom; or
  (c) by sending it by post to him at that address.

(3) An order or direction to which this section applies may be served on a body corporate by delivering it or sending it by post –
  (a) to the registered or principal office of the body in the United Kingdom, or
  (b) if it has no such office in the United Kingdom, to any place in the United Kingdom where it carries on business or conducts its activities (as the case may be).

(4) Any such order or direction may also be served on a person (including a body corporate) by sending it by post to that person at an address notified by that person to the Commissioners for the purposes of this subsection.

(5) In this section any reference to the Commissioners includes, in relation to a direction given under section 6(3) of this Act, a reference to any person conducting an inquiry under that section.'

16. In section 41 (enforcement of orders of Commissioners etc.), for paragraph (a) substitute –

'(a) to an order of the Commissioners under section 7(1) of this Act; or'.

17. In section 43 (regulations), after subsection (2) insert –

'(2A) Any regulations under this Act may make –
  (a) different provision for different cases;
  (b) such supplemental, incidental, consequential or transitional provision or savings as the person or persons making them considers or consider appropriate.'

18. In section 45 (construction of references to a charity etc.) –
  (a) in subsection (3) –
    (i) omit 'Subject to subsection (9) of section twenty-two of this Act,', and
    (ii) for 'so expended' substitute 'expended for the purposes of the charity'; and
  (b) in subsection (4), for the words from 'not having' to 'without' substitute 'whose income from all sources does not in aggregate amount to more than a specified amount shall be construed –
    (i) by reference to the gross revenues of the charity, or
    (ii) if the Commissioners so determine, by reference to the amount which they estimate to be the likely amount of those revenues,
    but without (in either case)'.

19. In section 46 (other definitions) –
  (a) in the definition of 'permanent endowment' omit ', subject to subsection (9) of section twenty-two of this Act,'; and
  (b) at the end add –

'(2) In this Act, except in so far as the context otherwise requires, 'document' includes information recorded in any form, and, in relation to information recorded otherwise than in legible form –

(a) any reference to its production shall be construed as a reference to the furnishing of a copy of it in legible form, and

(b) any reference to the furnishing of a copy of, or extract from, it shall accordingly be construed as a reference to the furnishing of a copy of, or extract from, it in legible form.';

and the existing provisions of section 46 (as amended by sub-paragraph (a) above) shall accordingly constitute subsection (1) of that section.

20. In each of sub-paragraphs (1) and (2) of paragraph 2 of Schedule 1 (appointment of assistant Commissioners etc.), for 'servants' substitute 'employees'.

21. (1) Paragraph 3 of Schedule 1 (procedure of Commissioners) shall be amended as follows.

(2) In sub-paragraph (4), for 'two shall be the quorum; and' substitute 'then –
   (a) if not more than four Commissioners hold office for the time being, the quorum shall be two Commissioners (of whom at least one must be a person having a qualification such as is mentioned in paragraph 1(2) above); and
   (b) if five Commissioners so hold office, the quorum shall be three Commissioners (of whom at least one must be a person having such a qualification); and'.

(3) At the end of the paragraph add –

'(6) It is hereby declared that the power of a commissioner or assistant commissioner to act for and in the name of the Commissioners in accordance with sub-paragraph (3) above may, in particular, be exercised in relation to functions of the Commissioners under sections 6, 20, 20A and 30 of this Act.'

22. In Schedule 2 (exempt charities), after paragraph (d) insert –
'(da) the National Gallery Trustees;
(db) the Tate Gallery Trustees;
(dc) the National Portrait Gallery;
(dd) the Wallace Collection Trustees;'.

SCHEDULE 4

Section 48

AMENDMENTS OF CHARITABLE TRUSTEES INCORPORATION ACT 1872

1. For section 1 of the Charitable Trustees Incorporation Act 1872 ('the 1872 Act') substitute –

'1. Incorporation of trustees of a charity

(1) Where –
   (a) the trustees of a charity, in accordance with section 3 of this Act, apply to the Commissioners for a certificate of incorporation of the trustees as a body corporate, and
   (b) the Commissioners consider that the incorporation of the trustees would be in the interests of the charity,

the Commissioners may grant such a certificate, subject to such conditions or directions as they think fit to insert in it.

(2) The Commissioners shall not, however, grant such a certificate in a case where the charity appears to them to be required to be registered in the register kept by them under section 4 of the Charities Act 1960 but is not so registered.

(3) On the grant of such a certificate –
(a) the trustees of the charity shall become a body corporate by such name as is specified in the certificate; and
(b) (without prejudice to the operation of section 5 of this Act) any relevant rights or liabilities of those trustees shall become rights or liabilities of that body.

(4) After their incorporation the trustees –
(a) may sue and be sued in their corporate name; and
(b) shall have the same powers, and be subject to the same restrictions and limitations, as respects the holding, acquisition and disposal of property for or in connection with the purposes of the charity as they had or were subject to while unincorporated;
and any relevant legal proceedings that might have been continued or commenced by or against the trustees may be continued or commenced by or against them in their corporate name.

(5) A body incorporated under this section need not have a common seal.

(6) In this section –
'relevant rights or liabilities' means rights or liabilities in connection with any property vesting in the body in question under section 2 of this Act; and
'relevant legal proceedings' means legal proceedings in connection with any such property.'

2. In section 2 (estate to vest in incorporated body), omit the words from '; and all' onwards.

3. For section 3 of the 1872 Act substitute –

'3. Applications for incorporation

(1) Every application to the Commissioners for a certificate of incorporation under this Act shall –
(a) be in writing and signed by the trustees of the charity concerned; and
(b) be accompanied by such documents or information as the Commissioners may require for the purpose of the application.

(2) The Commissioners may require –
(a) any statement contained in any such application, or
(b) any document or information supplied under subsection (1)(b) above,
to be verified in such manner as they may specify.'

4. In section 4 of the 1872 Act (nomination of trustees, etc), omit the words from '; and the appointment' onwards.

5. In section 5 of the 1872 Act (liability of trustees despite incorporation), omit the words from '; and nothing' onwards.

6. After section 6 of the 1872 Act insert –

'6A. Power of Commissioners to amend certificate of incorporation

(1) The Commissioners may amend a certificate of incorporation either on the application of the incorporated body to which it relates or of their own motion.

(2) Before making any such amendment of their own motion, the Commissioners shall by notice in writing –
> (a) inform the trustees of the relevant charity of their proposals, and
> (b) invite those trustees to make representations to them within a time specified in the notice, being not less than one month from the date of the notice.

(3) The Commissioners shall take into consideration any representations made by those trustees within the time so specified, and may then (without further notice) proceed with their proposals either without modification or with such modifications as appear to them to be desirable.

(4) The Commissioners may amend a certificate of incorporation either –
> (a) by making an order specifying the amendment; or
> (b) by issuing a new certificate of incorporation taking account of the amendment.'

7. In section 7 of the 1872 Act (Commissioners to keep record of applications for certificates etc and charge fees for inspection), omit the words from '; and there' onwards.

8. In section 8 of the 1872 Act (enforcement of orders and directions of Commissioners), for the words from 'shall also' onwards substitute 'section 41 of the Charities Act 1960 (enforcement of orders of Commissioners) shall apply to any trustee who fails to perform or observe any such condition or direction as it applies to a person guilty of disobedience to any such order of the Commissioners as is mentioned in that section.'

9. For section 12 of the 1872 Act substitute –

'12. Execution of documents by incorporated body

(1) This section has effect as respects the execution of documents by an incorporated body.

(2) If an incorporated body has a common seal, a document may be executed by the body by the affixing of its common seal.

(3) Whether or not it has a common seal, a document may be executed by an incorporated body either –
> (a) by being signed by a majority of the trustees of the relevant charity and expressed (in whatever form of words) to be executed by the body; or
> (b) by being executed in pursuance of an authority given under subsection (4) below.

(4) For the purposes of subsection (3)(b) above the trustees of the relevant charity in the case of an incorporated body may, subject to the trusts of the charity, confer on any two or more of their number –

(a) a general authority, or

(b) an authority limited in such manner as the trustees think fit,

to execute in the name and on behalf of the body documents for giving effect to transactions to which the body is a party.

(5) An authority under subsection (4) above –

    (a) shall suffice for any document if it is given in writing or by resolution of a meeting of the trustees of the relevant charity, notwithstanding the want of any formality that would be required in giving an authority apart from that subsection;

    (b) may be given so as to make the powers conferred exercisable by any of the trustees, or may be restricted to named persons or in any other way;

    (c) subject to any such restriction, and until it is revoked, shall, notwithstanding any change in the trustees of the relevant charity, have effect as a continuing authority given by the trustees from time to time of the charity and exercisable by such trustees.

(6) In any authority under subsection (4) above to execute a document in the name and on behalf of an incorporated body there shall, unless the contrary intention appears, be implied authority also to execute it for the body in the name and on behalf of the official custodian for charities or of any other person, in any case in which the trustees could do so.

(7) A document duly executed by an incorporated body which makes it clear on its face that it is intended by the person or persons making it to be a deed has effect, upon delivery, as a deed; and it shall be presumed, unless a contrary intention is proved, to be delivered upon its being so executed.

(8) In favour of a purchaser a document shall be deemed to have been duly executed by such a body if it purports to be signed –

    (a) by a majority of the trustees of the relevant charity, or

    (b) by such of the trustees of the relevant charity as are authorised by the trustees of that charity to execute it in the name and on behalf of the body,

and, where the document makes it clear on its face that it is intended by the person or persons making it to be a deed, it shall be deemed to have been delivered upon its being executed.

For this purpose 'purchaser' means a purchaser in good faith for valuable consideration and includes a lessee, mortgagee or other person who for valuable consideration acquires an interest in property.

12A. Power of Commissioners to dissolve incorporated body

(1) Where the Commissioners are satisfied –

    (a) that an incorporated body has no assets or does not operate, or

    (b) that the relevant charity in the case of an incorporated body has ceased to exist, or

    (c) that the institution previously constituting, or treated by them as constituting, any such charity has ceased to be, or (as the case may be) was not at the time of the body's incorporation, a charity, or

    (d) that the purposes of the relevant charity in the case of an incorporated body have been achieved so far as is possible or are in practice incapable of being achieved, they may of their own motion make an order dissolving the body as from such date as is specified in the order.

(2) Where the Commissioners are satisfied, on the application of the trustees of the relevant charity in the case of an incorporated body, that it would be in the interests of the charity for that body to be dissolved, the Commissioners may make an order dissolving the body as from such date as is specified in the order.

(3) Subject to subsection (4) below, an order made under this section with respect to an incorporated body shall have the effect of vesting in the trustees of the relevant charity, in trust for that charity, all property for the time being vested –
    (a) in the body, or
    (b) in any other person (apart from the official custodian for charities),
in trust for that charity.

(4) If the Commissioners so direct in the order –
    (a) all or any specified part of that property shall, instead of vesting in the trustees of the relevant charity, vest –
        (i) in a specified person as trustee for, or nominee of, that charity, or
        (ii) in such persons (other than the trustees of the relevant charity) as may be specified;
    (b) any specified investments, or any specified class or description of investments, held by any person in trust for the relevant charity shall be transferred –
        (i) to the trustees of that charity, or
        (ii) to any such person or persons as is or are mentioned in paragraph (a)(i) or (ii) above;
and for this purpose 'specified' means specified by the Commissioners in the order.

(5) Where an order to which this subsection applies is made with respect to an incorporated body –
    (a) any rights or liabilities of the body shall become rights or liabilities of the trustees of the relevant charity; and
    (b) any legal proceedings that might have been continued or commenced by or against the body may be continued or commenced by or against those trustees.

(6) Subsection (5) above applies to any order under this section by virtue of which –
    (a) any property vested as mentioned in subsection (3) above is vested –
    (i) in the trustees of the relevant charity, or
    (ii) in any person as trustee for, or nominee of, that charity; or
    (b) any investments held by any person in trust for the relevant charity are required to be transferred –
        (i) to the trustees of that charity, or
        (ii) to any person as trustee for, or nominee of, that charity.

(7) Any order made by the Commissioners under this section may be varied or revoked by a further order so made.'

10. For section 14 of the 1872 Act substitute –

'14. Interpretation

In this Act –
'charity' has the same meaning as in the Charities Act 1960;
'the Commissioners' means the Charity Commissioners;
'incorporated body' means a body incorporated under section 1 of this Act;
'the relevant charity', in relation to an incorporated body, means the charity the
   trustees of which have been incorporated as that body;
'the trustees', in relation to a charity, means the charity trustees within the
   meaning of the Charities Act 1960.'

11. Omit the Schedule (particulars to be supplied for the purposes of section 3 of the Act).

SCHEDULE 5

Section 49

AMENDMENTS OF REDUNDANT CHURCHES AND OTHER
RELIGIOUS BUILDINGS ACT 1969

1. For section 4 of the Redundant Churches and Other Religious Buildings Act 1969 ('the 1969 Act') substitute –

'4. Transfer of certain redundant places of public worship

(1) Subject to subsections (9) and (10) below, this section applies to any premises if –
   (a) the premises are held by or in trust for a charity ('the relevant charity'), and
   (b) the whole or part of the premises has been used as a place of public worship; but
   (c) the premises are not a church subject to the provisions of the Pastoral Measure 1983.

(2) If the court is satisfied, with respect to any premises to which this section applies ('the relevant premises') –
   (a) that those premises are no longer required (whether wholly or in part) for use as a place of public worship, and
   (b) that one of the following, namely –
      (i)   the Secretary of State,
      (ii) the Commission, or
      (iii) a prescribed charity,
      is or are willing to enter into an agreement to acquire those premises by way of gift or for a consideration other than full consideration, but
   (c) that it is not within the powers of the persons in whom those premises are vested to carry out such an agreement except by virtue of this section,
the court may, under its jurisdiction with respect to charities, establish a scheme for the making and carrying out of such an agreement.

(3) A scheme established under subsection (2) above may, if it appears to the court proper to do so, provide for the acquirer of the relevant premises also to acquire

(whether by gift or for a consideration other than full consideration or otherwise) –

    (a) any land held by or in trust for the relevant charity which is contiguous or adjacent to those premises; and

    (b) any objects which are or have been ordinarily kept on those premises.

(4) In subsections (2) and (3) above, in relation to the acquisition of the relevant premises or the acquisition of any land or object –

    (a) references to acquisition by the Secretary of State are references to acquisition by him under section 5 of the Historic Buildings and Ancient Monuments Act 1953 (acquisition by him of buildings of historic or architectural interest); and

    (b) references to acquisition by the Commission are references to acquisition by them under section 5A of that Act (acquisition by them of buildings of historic or architectural interest).

(5) A scheme established under subsection (2) above may also provide for conferring on the acquirer of the relevant premises –

    (a) such rights of way over any land held by or in trust for the relevant charity as appear to the court to be necessary –

        (i) for the purpose of the discharge of the acquirer's functions in relation to those premises or to any land acquired under the scheme, or

        (ii) for giving to the public reasonable access to those premises or to any such land, and

    (b) so far as is necessary for the purpose of the discharge of such functions or the giving of such access, any rights of way enjoyed by persons attending services at those premises.

(6) The Charity Commissioners may, on the application of the acquirer of the relevant premises, by order establish a scheme under section 18 of the Charities Act 1960 (Commissioners' concurrent jurisdiction with the High Court for certain purposes) making provision for the restoration of the relevant premises, or part of them, to use as a place of public worship.

(7) The Charity Commissioners may so establish any such scheme notwithstanding –

    (a) anything in subsection (4) of section 18 of that Act, or

    (b) that the relevant charity has ceased to exist;

and if the relevant charity has ceased to exist, any such scheme may provide for the constitution of a charity by or in trust for which the relevant premises are to be held on the restoration of those premises, or part of them, to use as a place of public worship.

(8) The Charity Commissioners shall have the same jurisdiction and powers in relation to the establishment of a scheme under subsection (2) above as they have under the provisions of section 18 of the Charities Act 1960 (except subsection (6)) in relation to the establishment of a scheme for the administration of a charity; and section 21 of that Act (publicity for proceedings under section 18, etc) shall accordingly have effect in relation to the establishment of a scheme under subsection (2) above as it has effect in relation to the establishment of a scheme for the administration of a charity.

(9) In relation to the Commission –

    (a) this section only applies to any premises falling within subsection (1) above

if they are situated in England, and
(b) references in this section to land are references only to land situated in England.

(10) In relation to a prescribed charity, this section only applies to any premises falling within subsection (1) above if they constitute either –
    (a) a listed building within the meaning of the Planning (Listed Buildings and Conservation Areas) Act 1990, or
    (b) a scheduled monument within the meaning of the Ancient Monuments and Archaeological Areas Act 1979.

(11) The Secretary of State may direct that any charity specified in the direction shall be a prescribed charity for the purposes of this section; and any direction under this subsection may be varied or revoked by a further direction given by the Secretary of State.

(12) References in this section to the acquirer of the relevant premises are references to the person or body acquiring those premises by virtue of a scheme established under subsection (2) above.

(13) In this section and section 5 below –
'the Commission' means the Historic Buildings and Monuments Commission for England;
'premises' includes a part of a building;
'prescribed charity' shall be construed by reference to subsection (11) above;
and sections 45 and 46 of the Charities Act 1960 (interpretation) shall have effect for the purposes of this section and section 5 below as they have effect for the purposes of that Act.'

2. For section 5 of the 1969 Act substitute –

'5. Trusts for repair etc of premises to continue after transfer under section 4

(1) Where any premises to which section 4 of this Act applies are acquired by the Secretary of State, the Commission or a prescribed charity in pursuance of that section, any property of a charity whose purposes include –
    (a) the repair and maintenance of those premises, or
    (b) the provision of objects for keeping on those premises, or
    (c) the maintenance of objects ordinarily kept there,
shall (subject to subsection (2) below) continue to be applicable for that purpose so long as the premises remain vested in the Secretary of State, the Commission or the prescribed charity, as the case may be.

(2) If so provided by the scheme under which the agreement for the acquisition of any such premises is made, subsection (1) above shall have effect in relation to the premises subject to and in accordance with any specified provisions of the scheme.

(3) Subsection (13) of section 4 of this Act has effect for the purposes of this section.'

SCHEDULE 6

MINOR AND CONSEQUENTIAL AMENDMENTS
CLERGY PENSIONS MEASURE 1961 (NO.3)

1. In section 33 (preservation of restrictions on certain transactions) –
   (a) for 'section twenty-nine of the Charities Act 1960' substitute 'section 32 of the Charities Act 1992'; and
   (b) for 'said Act' substitute 'Charities Act 1960'.

FINANCE ACT 1963 (C.25)

2. In section 65(2)(a) (miscellaneous exemptions), after '1960' insert 'or any common deposit scheme under section 22A of that Act'.

CATHEDRALS MEASURE 1963 (NO.2)

3. In section 20(2)(iii) (consents to disposal of land by cathedral bodies), for 'section twenty-nine of the Charities Act 1960' substitute 'section 32 of the Charities Act 1992'.

LEASEHOLD REFORM ACT 1967 (C.88)

4. In section 23(4) (grant of new tenancy), for 'section 29 of the Charities Act 1960' substitute 'section 32 of the Charities Act 1992'.

SHARING OF CHURCH BUILDINGS ACT 1969 (C.38)

5. In section 8(3) (shared buildings), for the words from the beginning to 'Commissioners)' substitute 'Section 32 of the Charities Act 1992 (restrictions on dispositions of charity land)'.

LOCAL GOVERNMENT ACT 1972 (C.70)

6. In section 131(3) (savings) –
   (a) for the words from 'section 29' to 'property)' substitute 'section 32 of the Charities Act 1992 (restrictions on disposition of charity land)'; and
   (b) for 'subsection (3)(a) of that section' substitute 'section 32(9)(a) of that Act'.

FIRE PRECAUTIONS (LOANS) ACT 1973 (C.11)

7. In section 1(7) (loans to meet certain expenditure), for the words from the beginning to 'property)' substitute 'Section 34 of the Charities Act 1992 (which restricts the charging of charity property)'.

THEATRES TRUST ACT 1976 (C.27)

8. In section 2(2)(d) (powers of trustees), for 'section 29 of the Charities Act 1960' substitute 'sections 32 and 34 of the Charities Act 1992'.

LOCAL GOVERNMENT (MISCELLANEOUS PROVISIONS) ACT 1982 (C.30)

9. In Schedule 4 (street trading), for paragraph 1(2)(j) substitute –

'(j) the doing of anything authorised by any permit or order under Part III of the Charities Act 1992.'

CIVIC GOVERNMENT (SCOTLAND) ACT 1982 (C.45)

10. In section 119(6)(d) (grounds for refusal of permission for public charitable collection in Scotland) –
  (a) after 'under', where secondly occurring, insert 'this section or'; and
  (b) after 'section', where secondly occurring, insert 'or under Part III of the Charities Act 1992 or regulations made under section 73 of that Act'.

COMPANIES ACT 1985 (C.6)

11. In each of the following provisions, namely –
  (a) section 209(1)(c) (interests to be disregarded for purposes of general disclosure provisions), and
  (b) paragraph 11(b) of Schedule 13 (interests to be disregarded for purposes of provisions relating to disclosure by directors etc),
after 'section 22' insert 'or 22A'.

HOUSING ACT 1985 (C.68)

12. For paragraph 12 of Schedule 1 substitute –

'12. A licence to occupy a dwelling-house is not a secure tenancy if –
  (a) the dwelling-house is an almshouse, and
  (b) the licence was granted by or on behalf of a charity which –
    (i) is authorised under its trusts to maintain the dwelling-house as an almshouse, and
    (ii) has no power under its trusts to grant a tenancy of the dwelling-house;
and in this paragraph 'almshouse' means any premises maintained as an almshouse, whether they are called an almshouse or not; and 'trusts', in relation to a charity, means the provisions establishing it as a charity and regulating its purposes and administration, whether those provisions take effect by way of trust or not.'

HOUSING ASSOCIATIONS ACT 1985 (C.69)

13. (1) In section 10(1) (excepted dispositions), for 'section 29 of the Charities Act 1960' substitute 'sections 32 and 34 of the Charities Act 1992'.

(2) In section 26(2) (accounting requirements), for the words from 'section 8' onwards substitute 'sections 19 to 23 of the Charities Act 1992 (charity accounts).'

(3) In section 35(2)(c) (power to transfer housing to local housing authority), for the words from 'section' to 'Commissioners)' substitute 'section 32 of the Charities Act 1992 (restrictions on dispositions of charity land)'.

FINANCIAL SERVICES ACT 1986 (C.60)

14. In section 45(1)(j) (miscellaneous exemptions), after 'section 22' insert 'or 22A'.

COAL INDUSTRY ACT 1987 (C.3)

15. In section 5 (power of Commissioners to make schemes relating to coal industry trusts), for subsection (8) substitute –

'(8) Sections 18(3), (8), (10) to (12), 19(1) to (5) and (7) and 21 of the Charities Act 1960 shall apply in relation to the powers of the Charity Commissioners and the making of schemes under this section as they apply in relation to their powers and the making of schemes under that Act; and sections 40(1) to (4), 40A and 42 of that Act shall apply to orders and decisions under this section as they apply to orders and decisions under that Act.

(8A) The Commissioners shall not proceed under section 19 of that Act (as applied by subsection (8) above) without the like application, and the like notice to the trustees of the trust in question, as would be required if they were proceeding under subsection (1) above; but on any application made with a view to a scheme under subsection (1) above the Commissioners may proceed under that subsection or under section 19 of that Act (as so applied) as appears to them appropriate.'

REVERTER OF SITES ACT 1987 (C.15)

16. In section 4(4) (supplementary provisions), after 'sections 40' insert ', 40A'.

INCOME AND CORPORATION TAXES ACT 1988 (C.1)

17. After paragraph 3 of Schedule 20 (charities: qualifying investments and loans) insert –

'3A. Any investment in a common deposit fund established under section 22A of the Charities Act 1960 or in any similar fund established for the exclusive benefit of charities by or under any enactment relating to any particular charities or class of charities.'

SCHEDULE 7

Section 78(2)

REPEALS

Chapter	Short title	Extent of repeal
1872 c.24.	Charitable Trustees Incorporation Act 1872.	In section 2, the words from '; and all' onwards. In section 4, the words from '; and the appointment' onwards. In section 5, the words from '; and nothing' onwards. In section 7, the words from '; and there' onwards. The Schedule.
1916 c.31.	Police, Factories, &c. (Miscellaneous Provisions) Act 1916.	The whole Act.
1939 c.44.	House to House Collections Act 1939.	The whole Act.

Chapter	Short title	Extent of repeal
1940 c.31.	War Charities Act 1940.	The whole Act.
1948 c.29.	National Assistance Act 1948.	Section 41.
1958 c.49.	Trading Representations (Disabled Persons) Act 1958.	Section 1(2)(b).
1959 c.72.	Mental Health Act 1959.	Section 8(3).
1960 c.58.	Charities Act 1960.	In section 4(6), the words from 'and any person' onwards. Section 6(6) and (9). Section 7(4). Section 8(1), (2), (6)(a) and (7). Section 16(2). In section 19(6), the words 'or the like reference from the Secretary of State'. In section 22, subsection (6) and, in subsection (9), the words from ', and the' to 'endowment' (where last occurring). Section 27. Section 29. In section 30C(1)(c), the words 'by or'. Section 31. Section 44. In section 45(3), the words 'Subject to subsection (9) of section twenty-two of this Act,'. In section 46, the words ', subject to subsection (9) of section twenty-two of this Act,'. In Schedule 1, in paragraph 1(3), the words 'Subject to sub-paragraph (6) below,'. In Schedule 6, the entry relating to the War Charities Act 1940.
1966 c.42.	Local Government Act 1966.	In Schedule 3, in column 1 of Part II, paragraph 20.
1968 c.60.	Theft Act 1968.	In Schedule 2, in Part III, the entry relating to the House to House Collections Act 1939.

Chapter	Short title	Extent of repeal
1970 c.42.	Local Authority Social Services Act 1970.	In Schedule 1, the entry relating to section 41 of the National Assistance Act 1948.
1972 c. 70.	Local Government Act 1972.	Section 210(8). In Schedule 29, paragraphs 22 and 23.
1983 c.41.	Health and Social Services and Social Security Adjudications Act 1983.	Section 30(3).
1983 c.47.	National Heritage Act 1983.	In Schedule 4, paragraphs 13 and 14.
1985 c.9.	Companies Consolidation (Consequential Provisions) Act 1985.	In Schedule 2, the entry relating to section 30(1) of the Charities Act 1960.
1985 c.20.	Charities Act 1985.	The whole Act.
1986 c.41.	Finance Act 1986.	Section 33.

APPENDIX 2

CHARITIES ACT 1960

(1960 c 58)

[NOTE: Italic type within the body of the Act indicates text replaced or repealed by the Charities Act 1992 as detailed in the annotations. It has been thought useful to preserve the text in force immediately before the commencement of the 1992 Act as well as setting out the new text.]

ARRANGEMENT OF SECTIONS

PART I
THE CENTRAL AUTHORITIES

PART II
PROVISIONS FOR INQUIRING INTO, MAKING KNOWN AND CO-ORDINATING CHARITABLE ACTIVITIES

Registration of charities

Powers of Commissioners and Minister to obtain information, etc

Powers of local authorities and of charity trustees

PART III
APPLICATION OF PROPERTY CY-PRÈS, AND ASSISTANCE AND SUPERVISION OF CHARITIES BY COURT AND CENTRAL AUTHORITIES

PART IV
MISCELLANEOUS PROVISIONS AS TO CHARITIES AND
THEIR AFFAIRS

PART V
SUPPLEMENTARY

An Act to replace with new provisions the Charitable Trusts Acts 1853 to 1939, and other enactments relating to charities, to repeal the mortmain Acts, to make further provision as to the powers exercisabe by or with respect to charities or with respect to gifts to charity, and for purposes connected therewith [29 July 1960]

PART 1

THE CENTRAL AUTHORITIES

1. The Charity Commissioners

(1) There shall continue to be a body of Charity Commissioners for England and Wales, and they shall have such functions as are conferred on them by this Act in addition to any functions under any other enactment not repealed by this Act.

(2) The provisions of the First Schedule to this Act shall have effect with respect to the constitution and proceedings of the Commissioners and other matters relating to the Commissioners and their officers and *servants*[1] [employees][1].

(3) The Commissioners shall (without prejudice to their specific powers and duties under other enactments) have the general function of promoting the effective use of charitable resources by encouraging the development of better methods of administration, by giving charity trustees information or advice on any matter affecting the charity and by investigating and checking abuses.

(4) It shall be the general object of the Commissioners so to act in the case of any charity (unless it is a matter of altering its purposes) as best to promote and make effective the work of the charity in meeting the needs designated by its trusts; but the Commissioners shall not themselves have power to act in the administration of a charity.

(5) The Commissioners shall, as soon as possible after the end of every year, make to the Secretary of State a report on their operations during that year, and he shall lay a copy of the report before each House of Parliament.

Amendment. [1]Word substituted: Charities Act 1992, s 47, Sch 3, para 1.

2. . . .[1]

Amendment. [1]Section repealed: Education Act 1973, s 1(1)(a), (3)–(5), Sch 1, para 1(2)–(7), Sch 2, Pt III, s 1(4), Sch 2, Pt II.

3. The official custodian for charities

(1) There shall be an 'official custodian for charities', whose function it shall be to act as trustee for charities in the cases provided for by this Act; and the official custodian for charities shall be by that name a corporation sole having perpetual succession and using an official seal, which shall be officially and judicially noticed.

(2) Such officer of the Commissioners as they may from time to time designate shall be the official custodian for charities.

(3) The official custodian for charities shall perform his duties in accordance with such general or special directions as may be given him by the Commissioners, and his expenses (except those re-imbursed to him or recovered by him as trustee for any charity) shall be defrayed by the Commissioners.

(4) Anything which is required to or may be done by, to or before the official custodian for charities may be done by, to or before any officer of the Commissioners generally or specially authorised by them to act for him during a vacancy in his office or otherwise.

(5) The official custodian for charities shall not be liable as trustee for any charity in respect of any loss or of the misapplication of any property, unless it is occasioned by or through the wilful neglect or default of the custodian or person acting for him; but the Consolidated Fund shall be liable to make good to a charity any sums for which the custodian may be liable by reason of any such neglect or default.

(6) The official custodian for charities shall keep such books of account and such records in relation thereto as may be directed by the Treasury, and shall prepare accounts in such form, in such manner and at such times as may be so directed.

(7) The accounts so prepared shall be examined and certified by the Comptroller and Auditor General, and the report to be made by the Commissioners to the Secretary of State for any year shall include a copy of the accounts so prepared for any period ending in or with the year, and of the certificate and report of the Comptroller and Auditor General with respect to those accounts.

(8) . . .[1]

Amendment. [1]Subsection repealed: Education Act 1973, s 1(4), (5), Sch 2, Pt III.

PART II

PROVISIONS FOR INQUIRING INTO, MAKING KNOWN AND CO-ORDINATING CHARITABLE ACTIVITIES

Registration of charities

4. Register of charities

(1) There shall be a register of charities which shall be established and maintained by the Commissioners and in which there shall be entered such particulars as the Commissioners may from time to time determine of any charity there registered.[2]

[(1) The Commissioners shall continue to keep a register of charities, which shall be kept by them in such manner as they think fit.][2]

(2) There shall be entered in the register every charity not excepted by subsection (4) below; and a charity so excepted [(other than one excepted by paragraph (a) of that subsection)][2] may be entered in the register at the request of the charity, but (whether or not it was excepted at the time of registration) may at any time, and shall at the request of the charity, be removed from the register.

[(2A) The register shall contain –
    (a) the name of every registered charity; and
    (b) such other particulars of, and such other information relating to, every such charity as the Commissioners think fit.][2]

(3) Any institution which no longer appears to the Commissioners to be a charity shall be removed from the register, with effect, where the removal is due to any change in its purposes or trusts, from the date of that change; and there shall also be removed from the register any charity which ceases to exist or does not operate.

(4) The following charities are not required to be registered, that is to say, –
   (a) any charity comprised in the Second Schedule to this Act (in this Act referred to as an 'exempt charity');
   (b) any charity which is excepted by order or regulations;
   (c) any charity having neither any permanent endowment, nor any income from property amounting to more than fifteen pounds a year, nor the use and occupation of any land;[2]
   [(c) any charity which has neither –
      (i) any permanent endowment, nor
      (ii) the use or occupation of any land,
      and whose income from all sources does not in aggregate amount to more than £1,000 a year;][2]
and no charity is required to be registered in respect of any registered place of worship.

(5) With any application for a charity to be registered there shall be supplied to the Commissioners copies of its trusts (or, if they are not set out in any extant document, particulars of them), and such other documents or information as may be prescribed or as the Commissioners may require for the purpose of the application.

(6) It shall be the duty –
   (a) of the charity trustees of any charity which is not registered nor excepted from registration to apply for it to be registered, and to supply the documents and information required by subsection (5) above; and
   (b) of the charity trustees (or last charity trustees) of any institution which is for the time being registered to notify the Commissioners if it ceases to exist, or if there is any change in its trusts, or in the particulars of it entered in the register, and to supply to the Commissioners particulars of any such change and copies of any new trusts or alterations of the trusts.
and any person who makes default in carrying out any of the duties imposed by this subsection may be required by order of the Commissioners to make good that default.[2]

(7) The register (including the entries cancelled when institutions are removed from the register) shall be open to public inspection at all reasonable times; and copies (or particulars) of the trusts of any registered charity as supplied to the Commissioners under this section shall, so long as it remains on the register, be kept by them and be open to public inspection at all reasonable times, except in so far as regulations otherwise provide.

[(7A) Where any information contained in the register is not in documentary form, subsection (7) above shall be construed as requiring the information to be available for public inspection in legible form at all reasonable times.

(7B) If the Commissioners so determine, that subsection shall not apply to any particular information contained in the register and specified in their determination.][2]

(8) Nothing in the foregoing subsections shall require any person to supply the Commissioners with copies of schemes for the administration of a charity made otherwise than by the court, or to notify the Commissioners of any change made with respect to a registered charity by such a scheme, or require a person, if he refers the

Commissioners to a document or copy already in the possession of the Commissioners . . .[1], to supply a further copy of the document; but where by virtue of this subsection a copy of any document need not be supplied to the Commissioners, a copy of it, if it relates to a registered charity, shall be open to inspection under subsection (7) above as if supplied to the Commissioners under this section.

[(8A) If he thinks it expedient to do so –
  (a) in consequence of changes in the value of money, or
  (b) with a view to extending the scope of the exception provided for by subsection (4)(c) above,
the Secretary of State may by order amend subsection (4)(c) by substituting a different sum for the sum for the time being specified there.

(8B) Any such order shall be made by statutory instrument subject to annulment in pursuance of a resolution of either House of Parliament.][2]

(9) In this section 'registered place of worship' means any land or building falling within section nine of the Places of Worship Registration Act 1855, as amended by this Act (that is to say, the land and buildings which, if this Act had not been passed, would by virtue of that section as amended by subsequent enactments be partially exempted from the operation of the Charitable Trusts Act 1853), and for the purposes of this subsection 'building' includes part of a building.

(10) . . .[1]

Amendments. [1]Words repealed: Education Act 1973, s 1(4), (5), Sch 2, Pt I, Pt III. [2]Words inserted, substituted or repealed: Charities Act 1992, s 2, s 78(2), Sch 7. The text of s 4 is also set out as amended in the Charities Act 1992, Sch 1.

---

5. Effect of, and claims and objections to, registration

(1) An institution shall for all purposes other than rectification of the register be conclusively presumed to be or have been a charity at any time when it is or was on the register of charities.

(2) Any person who is or may be affected by the registration of an institution as a charity may, on the ground that it is not a charity, object to its being entered by the Commissioners in the register, or apply to them for it to be removed from the register; and provision may be made by regulations as to the manner in which any such objection or application is to be made, prosecuted or dealt with.

(3) An appeal against any decision of the Commissioners to enter or not to enter an institution in the register of charities, or to remove or not to remove an institution from the register, may be brought in the High Court by the Attorney General, or by the persons who are or claim to be the charity trustees of the institution, or by any person whose objection or application under subsection (2) above is disallowed by the decision.

(4) If there is an appeal to the High Court against any decision of the Commissioners to enter an institution in the register, or not to remove an institution from the register, then until the Commissioners are satisfied whether the decision of the Commissioners is or is not to stand, the entry in the register shall be maintained, but shall be in suspense and marked to indicate that it is in suspense; and for the purposes of

subsection (1) above an institution shall be deemed not to be on the register during any period when the entry relating to it is in suspense under this subsection.

(5) Any question affecting the registration or removal from the register of an institution may, notwithstanding that it has been determined by a decision on appeal under subsection (3) above, be considered afresh by the Commissioners and shall not be concluded by that decision, if it appears to the Commissioners that there has been a change of circumstances or that the decision is inconsistent with a later judicial decision, whether given on such an appeal or not.

Powers of Commissioners and Minister to obtain information, etc

6. General power to institute inquiries

(1) The Commissioners may from time to time institute inquiries with regard to charities or a particular charity or class of charities, either generally or for particular purposes:
   Provided that no such inquiry shall extend to any exempt charity.

(2) The Commissioners may either conduct such an inquiry themselves or appoint a person to conduct it and make a report to them.

(3) For the purposes of any such inquiry the Commissioners *may by order, and a person appointed by them to conduct the inquiry may by precept, require*[3] [or a person appointed by them to conduct it, may direct][3] any person (subject to the provisions of this section) –
    (a) to furnish accounts and statements in writing with respect to any matter in question at the inquiry, being a matter on which he has or can reasonably obtain information, or to return answers in writing to any questions or inquiries addressed to him on any such matter, and to verify any such accounts, statements or answers by statutory declaration;
    (b) *to attend at a specified time and place and give evidence or produce documents in his custody or control which relate to any matter in question at the inquiry.*[3]
    [(b) to furnish copies of documents in his custody or under his control which relate to any matter in question at the inquiry, and to verify any such copies by statutory declaration;
    (c) to attend at a specified time and place and give evidence or produce any such documents.][3]

(4) For the purposes of any such inquiry evidence may be taken on oath, and the person conducting the inquiry may for that purpose administer oaths, or may instead of administering an oath require the person examined to make and subscribe a declaration of the truth of the matters about which he is examined.

(5) The Commissioners may pay to any person the necessary expenses of his attendance to give evidence or produce documents for the purpose of an inquiry under this section, and a person shall not be required in obedience to *an order or precept under paragraph (b)* [3][a direction under paragraph (c)][3] of subsection (3) above to go more than ten miles from his place of residence unless those expenses are paid or tendered to him.

(6) No person claiming to hold any property adversely to a charity, or freed or discharged from any charitable trust or charge, shall be required under this section to furnish any information or produce any document relating to that property or any trust or charge alleged to affect it.[3]

(7) Where the Commissioners propose to take any action in consequence of an inquiry under this section, they may publish the report of the person conducting the inquiry, or such other statement of the results of the inquiry as they think fit, in any manner calculated in their opinion to bring it to the attention of persons who may wish to make representations to them about the action to be taken.[3]

[(7) Where an inquiry has been held under this section, the Commissioners may either –
(a) cause the report of the person conducting the inquiry, or such other statement of the results of the inquiry as they think fit, to be printed and published, or
(b) publish any such report or statement in some other way which is calculated in their opinion to bring it to the attention of persons who may wish to make representations to them about the action to be taken.][3]

(8) The council of a county, . . .[1] county district . . .[1], the Common Council of the City of London and the council of a . . .[1] borough may contribute to the expenses of the Commissioners in connection with inquiries under this section into local charities in the council's area.

(9) If any person wilfully alters, suppresses, conceals or destroys any document which he may be required to produce under this section, he shall be liable on summary conviction to a fine not exceeding [level 3 on the standard scale][2], *or to imprisonment for a term not exceeding six months, or to both.*[3]

Amendments. [1]Words repealed: London Government Act 1963, s 93(1), Sch 18, Pt II and Local Government Act 1972, s 272(1), Sch 30. [2]Words substituted: Criminal Justice Act 1982, ss 38, 46. [3]Words substituted or repealed: Charities Act 1992, ss 6, 78(2), Sch 7.

7. Power to call for documents, and search records

(1) The Commissioners may by order require any person having in his possession or control any books, records, deeds or papers relating to a charity to furnish them with copies of or extracts from any of those documents or, unless the document forms part of the records or other documents of a court or of a public or local authority, require him to transmit the document itself to them for their inspection.[1]

[(1) The Commissioners may by order –
(a) require any person to furnish them with any information in his possession which relates to any charity and is relevant to the discharge of their functions or of the functions of the official custodian for charities;
(b) require any person who has in his custody or under his control any document which relates to any charity and is relevant to the discharge of their functions or of the functions of the official custodian for charities –
(i) to furnish them with a copy of or extract from the document, or
(ii) (unless the document forms part of the records or other documents of a court or of a public or local authority) to transmit the document itself to them for their inspection.][1]

(2) Any officer of the Commissioners, if so authorised by them, shall be entitled without payment to inspect and take copies of or extracts from the records or other documents of any court, or of any public registry or office of records, for any purpose connected with the discharge of the functions of the Commissioners or of the official custodian for charities.

(3) The Commissioners shall be entitled without payment to keep any copy or extract furnished to them under subsection (1) above; and where a document transmitted to them under that subsection for their inspection relates only to one or more charities and is not held by any person entitled as trustee or otherwise to the custody of it, the Commissioners may keep it or may deliver it to the charity trustees or to any other person who may be so entitled.

(4) No person claiming to hold any property adversely to a charity, or freed or discharged from any charitable trust or charge, shall be required under subsection (1) above to transmit to the Commissioners any document relating to that property or any trust or charge alleged to affect it, or to furnish any copy of or extract from any such document.[1]

(5) No person properly having the custody of documents relating only to an exempt charity shall be required under subsection (1) above to transmit to the Commissioners any of those documents, or to furnish any copy of or extract from any of them.

[(6) The rights conferred by subsection (2) above shall, in relation to information recorded otherwise than in legible form, include the right to require the information to be made available in legible form for inspection or for a copy or extract to be made of or from it.][1]

Amendments. [1]Words inserted, substituted or repealed: Charities Act 1992, s 7, s 78(2), Sch 7.

8. Receipt and audit of accounts of charities

(1) Statements of account giving the prescribed information about the affairs of a charity shall be transmitted to the Commissioners by the charity trustees on request; and, in the case of a charity having a permanent endowment, such a statement relating to the permanent endowment shall be transmitted yearly without any request, unless the charity is excepted by order or regulations.

(2) Any statement of account transmitted to the Commissioners in pursuance of subsection (1) above shall be kept by them for such period as they think fit; and during that period it shall be open to public inspection at all reasonable times.[2]

(3) The Commissioners may by order require *that the condition and accounts of a charity*[2] [in the case of a charity which is a company, that the condition and accounts of the charity][2] for such period as they think fit shall be investigated and audited by an auditor appointed by them, [being a person eligible for appointment as a company auditor under section 25 of the Companies Act 1989].[1]

(4) An auditor acting under subsection (3) above –
   (a) shall have a right of access to all books, accounts and documents relating to the charity which are in the possession or control of the charity trustees or to which the charity trustees have access;
   (b) shall be entitled to require from any charity trustee, past or present, and from any past or present officer or *servant*[2] [employee][2] of the charity such

information and explanation as he thinks necessary for the performance of his duties;

(c) shall at the conclusion or during the progress of the audit make such reports to the Commissioners about the audit or about the accounts or affairs of the charity as he thinks the case requires, and shall send a copy of any such report to the charity trustees.

(5) The expenses of any audit under subsection (3) above, including the remuneration of the auditor, shall be paid by the Commissioners.

(6) If any person –

(a) *fails to transmit to the Commissioners any statement of account required by subsection (1) above; or*[2]

(b) fails to afford an auditor any facility to which he is entitled under subsection (4) above;

the Commissioners may by order give to that person or to the charity trustees for the time being such directions as the Commissioners think appropriate for securing that the default is made good.

(7) *This section shall not apply to an exempt charity.*[2]

Amendments. [1]Words substituted: Companies Act 1989 (Eligibility for Appointment as Company Auditor) (Consequential Amendments) Regulations 1991, SI 1991/1997, reg 2, Schedule, para 7. [2]Words substituted or repealed: Charities Act 1992, s 47, Sch 3, para 2, s 78(2), Sch 7.

9. Exchange of information etc

(1) The Commissioners may furnish the Commissioners of Inland Revenue and other government departments and local authorities, and the Commissioners of Inland Revenue and other government departments and local authorities may furnish the Commissioners, with the names and addresses of institutions which have for any purpose been treated by the person furnishing the information as established for charitable purposes or, in order to give or obtain assistance in determining whether an institution ought to be treated as so established, with information as to the purposes of the institution and the trusts under which it is established or regulated.

(2) The Commissioners shall supply any person, on payment of such fee as they think reasonable, with copies of or extracts from any document in their possession which is for the time being open to public inspection under this Act.

[(3) Without prejudice to subsection (1) above, no obligation as to secrecy or other restriction upon the disclosure of information shall prevent the Commissioners of Inland Revenue from disclosing to the Commissioners information with respect to any institution which has for any purpose been treated as established for charitable purposes but which appears to the Commissioners of Inland Revenue to be or to have been carrying on activities which are not charitable or to be or to have been applying any of its funds for purposes which are not charitable.][1,2]

[9. Supply by Commissioners of copies of documents open to public inspection

The Commissioners shall, at the request of any person, furnish him with copies of, or extracts from, any document in their possession which is for the time being open to inspection under this Act.][2]

Amendments. [1]Subsection inserted: Finance Act 1986, s 33. [2]Section substituted: Charities Act 1992, s 47, Sch 3, para 3.

Powers of local authorities and of charity trustees

10. Local authority's index of local charities

(1) The council of a county or of a [district or London borough][1] may maintain an index of local charities or of any class of local charities in the council's area, and may publish information contained in the index, or summaries or extracts taken from it.

(2) A council proposing to establish or maintaining under this section an index of local charities or of any class of local charities shall, on request, be supplied by the Commissioners free of charge with copies of such entries in the register of charities as are relevant to the index or with particulars of any changes in the entries of which copies have been supplied before; and the Commissioners may arrange that they will without further request supply a council with particulars of any such changes.

(3) An index maintained under this section shall be open to public inspection at all reasonable times.

(4) A council may employ any voluntary organisation, . . .[1] as their agent for the purposes of this section, on such terms and within such limits (if any) or in such cases as they may agree; and for this purpose 'voluntary organisation' means any body of which the activities are carried on otherwise than for profit, not being a public or local authority.

(5) A joint board discharging any of a council's functions shall have the same powers under this section as the council as respects local charities in the council's area which are established for purposes similar or complementary to any services provided by the board.

(6), (7) . . .[1]

Amendments. [1]Words substituted or repealed: Local Government Act 1972, s 210(9), 10, 272(1), Sch 30.

11. Reviews of local charities by local authority

(1) The council of a county or of a [district or London borough][1] may, subject to the following provisions of this section, initiate, and carry out in co-operation with the charity trustees, a review of the working of any group of local charities with the same or similar purposes in the council's area, and may make to the Commissioners such report on the review and such recommendations arising from it as the council after consultation with the trustees think fit.

(2) A council having power to initiate reviews under this section may co-operate with other persons in any review by them of the working of local charities in the council's

area (with or without other charities), or may join with other persons in initiating and carrying out such a review.

(3) No review initiated by a council under this section shall extend to any charity without the consent of the charity trustees, nor to any ecclesiastical charity.

(4) No review initiated under this section by the council of a [district or London borough] [1]shall extend to the working in any county of a local charity established for purposes similar or complementary to any services provided by county councils, unless the review so extends with the consent of the council of that county . . .[1]

(5) Subsections (4) [and (5)][1] of the last foregoing section shall apply for the purposes of this section as they apply for the purposes of that.

Amendments. [1]Words substituted or repealed: Local Government Act 1972, ss 210(9)(b), (10), 272(1), Sch 30.

12. Co-operation between charities, and between charities and local authorities

(1) Any local council and any joint board discharging any functions of such a council may make, with any charity established for purposes similar or complementary to services provided by the council or board, arrangements for co-ordinating the activities of the council or board and those of the charity in the interests of persons who may benefit from those services or from the charity, and shall be at liberty to disclose to any such charity in the interests of those persons any information obtained in connection with the services provided by the council or board, whether or not arrangements have been made with the charity under this subsection.

In this subsection 'local council' means the council of a county, of a [London borough],[1] of a metropolitan borough, of a county district, . . .[1] or of a rural parish, and includes also the Common Council of the City of London and the Council of the Isles of Scilly.

(2) Charity trustees shall, notwithstanding anything in the trusts of the charity, have power by virtue of this subsection to do all or any of the following things, where it appears to them likely to promote or make more effective the work of the charity, and may defray the expense of so doing out of any income or moneys applicable as income of the charity, that is to say, –
   (a) they may co-operate in any review undertaken under the last foregoing section or otherwise of the working of charities or any class of charities;
   (b) they may make arrangements with an authority acting under subsection (1) above or with another charity for co-ordinating their activities and those of the authority or of the other charity;
   (c) they may publish information of other charities with a view to bringing them to the notice of those for whose benefit they are intended.

Amendments. [1]Words substituted or repealed: Local Government Act 1972, ss 210(9)(c), (10), 272(1), Sch 30.

PART III

APPLICATION OF PROPERTY CY-PRÈS, AND ASSISTANCE AND SUPERVISION OF CHARITIES BY COURT AND CENTRAL AUTHORITIES

Extended powers of court and variation of charters

13. Occasions for applying property cy-près

(1) Subject to subsection (2) below, the circumstances in which the original purposes of a charitable gift can be altered to allow the property given or part of it to be applied cy-près shall be as follows: –
  (a) where the original purposes, in whole or in part, –
    (i)   have been as far as may be fulfilled; or
    (ii) cannot be carried out, or not according to the directions given and to the spirit of the gift; or
  (b) where the original purposes provide a use for part only of the property available by virtue of the gift; or
  (c) where the property available by virtue of the gift and other property applicable for similar purposes can be more effectively used in conjunction, and to that end can suitably, regard being had to the spirit of the gift, be made applicable to common purposes; or
  (d) where the original purposes were laid down by reference to an area which then was but has since ceased to be a unit for some other purpose, or by reference to a class of persons or to an area which has for any reason since ceased to be suitable, regard being had to the spirit of the gift, or to be practical in administering the gift; or
  (e) where the original purposes, in whole or in part, have, since they were laid down, –
    (i)   been adequately provided for by other means; or
    (ii) ceased, as being useless or harmful to the community or for other reasons, to be in law charitable; or
    (iii) ceased in any other way to provide a suitable and effective method of using the property available by virtue of the gift, regard being had to the spirit of the gift.

(2) Subsection (1) above shall not affect the conditions which must be satisfied in order that property given for charitable purposes may be applied cy-près, except in so far as those conditions require a failure of the original purposes.

(3) References in the foregoing subsections to the original purposes of a gift shall be construed, where the application of the property given has been altered or regulated by a scheme or otherwise, as referring to the purposes for which the property is for the time being applicable.

(4) Without prejudice to the power to make schemes in circumstances falling within subsection (1) above, the court may by scheme made under the court's jurisdiction with respect to charities, in any case where the purposes for which the property is held are laid down by reference to any such area as is mentioned in the first column in the Third Schedule to this Act, provide for enlarging the area to any such area as is mentioned in the second column in the same entry in that Schedule.

(5) It is hereby declared that a trust for charitable purposes places a trustee under a duty, where the case permits and requires the property or some part of it to be applied cy-près, to secure its effective use for charity by taking steps to enable it to be so applied.

14. Application cy-près of gifts of donors unknown or disclaiming

(1) Property given for specific charitable purposes which fail shall be applicable cy-près as if given for charitable purposes generally, where it belongs –
- (a) to a donor who, *after such advertisements and inquiries as are reasonable, cannot*[1] [after –
  - (i) the prescribed advertisements and inquiries have been published and made, and
  - (ii) the prescribed period beginning with the publication of those advertisements has expired,
  cannot][1] be identified or cannot be found; or
- (b) to a donor who has executed a *written disclaimer*[1] [disclaimer in the prescribed form][1] of his right to have the property returned.

[(1A) Where the prescribed advertisements and inquiries have been published and made by or on behalf of trustees with respect to any such property, the trustees shall not be liable to any person in respect of the property if no claim by him to be interested in it is received by them before the expiry of the period mentioned in subsection (1)(a)(ii) above.][1]

(2) For the purposes of this section property shall be conclusively presumed (without any advertisement or inquiry) to belong to donors who cannot be identified, in so far as it consists –
- (a) of the proceeds of cash collections made by means of collecting boxes or by other means not adapted for distinguishing one gift from another; or
- (b) of the proceeds of any lottery, competition, entertainment, sale or similar money-raising activity, after allowing for property given to provide prizes or articles for sale or otherwise to enable the activity to be undertaken.

(3) The court may by order direct that property not falling within subsection (2) above shall for the purposes of this section be treated (without any advertisement or inquiry) as belonging to donors who cannot be identified, where it appears to the court either –
- (a) that it would be unreasonable, having regard to the amounts likely to be returned to the donors, to incur expense with a view to returning the property; or
- (b) that it would be unreasonable, having regard to the nature, circumstances and amount of the gifts, and to the lapse of time since the gifts were made, for the donors to expect the property to be returned.

(4) Where property is applied cy-près by virtue of this section, the donor shall be deemed to have parted with all his interest at the time when the gift was made; but where property is so applied as belonging to donors who cannot be identified or cannot be found, and is not so applied by virtue of subsection (2) or (3) above, –
- (a) the scheme shall specify the total amount of that property; and
- (b) the donor of any part of that amount shall be entitled, if he makes a claim not later than *twelve*[1] [six][1] months after the date on which the scheme is made, to

recover from the charity for which the property is applied a sum equal to that part, less any expenses properly incurred by the charity trustees after that date in connection with claims relating to his gift; and

(c) the scheme may include directions as to the provision to be made for meeting any such claim.

[(4A) Where –

(a) any sum is, in accordance with any such directions, set aside for meeting any such claims, but

(b) the aggregate amount of any such claims actually made exceeds the relevant amount,

then, if the Commissioners so direct, each of the donors in question shall be entitled only to such proportion of the relevant amount as the amount of his claim bears to the aggregate amount referred to in paragraph (b) above; and for this purpose 'the relevant amount' means the amount of the sum so set aside after deduction of any expenses properly incurred by the charity trustees in connection with claims relating to the donors' gifts.]¹

(5) For the purposes of this section, charitable purposes shall be deemed to 'fail' where any difficulty in applying property to those purposes makes that property or the part not applicable cy-près available to be returned to the donors.

[(5A) In this section 'prescribed' means prescribed by regulations made by the Commissioners; and such regulations may, as respects the advertisements which are to be published for the purposes of subsection (1)(a) above, make provision as to the form and content of such advertisements as well as the manner in which they are to be published.

(5B) Any regulations made by the Commissioners under this section shall be published by the Commissioners in such manner as they think fit.]¹

(6) In this section, except in so far as the context otherwise requires, references to a donor include persons claiming through or under the original donor, and references to property given include the property for the time being representing the property originally given or property derived from it.

(7) This section shall apply to property given for charitable purposes, notwithstanding that it was so given before the commencement of this Act.

Amendments. ¹Words inserted or substituted: Charities Act 1992, s 15.

15. Charities governed by charter, or by or under statute

(1) Where a Royal charter establishing or regulating a body corporate is amendable by the grant and acceptance of a further charter, a scheme relating to the body corporate or to the administration of property held by the body (including a scheme for the cy-près application of any such property) may be made by the court under the court's jurisdiction with respect to charities notwithstanding that the scheme cannot take effect without the alteration of the charter, but shall be so framed that the scheme, or such part of it as cannot take effect without the alteration of the charter, does not purport to come into operation unless or until Her Majesty thinks fit to amend the charter in such manner as will permit the scheme or that part of it to have effect.

(2) Where under the court's jurisdiction with respect to charities or the corresponding jurisdiction of a court in Northern Ireland, or under powers conferred by this Act or by any enactment relating to charities of the Parliament of Northern Ireland, a scheme is made with respect to a body corporate, and it appears to Her Majesty expedient, having regard to the scheme, to amend any Royal charter relating to that body, Her Majesty may, on the application of that body, amend the charter accordingly by Order in Council in any way in which the charter could be amended by the grant and acceptance of a further charter; and any such Order in Council may be revoked or varied in like manner as the charter it amends.

(3) The jurisdiction of the court with respect to charities shall not be excluded or restricted in the case of a charity of any description mentioned in the Fourth Schedule to this Act by the operation of the enactments or instruments there mentioned in relation to that description, and a scheme established for any such charity may modify or supersede in relation to it the provision made by any such enactment or instrument as if made by a scheme of the court, and may also make any such provision as is authorised by that Schedule.

Property vested in official custodian

16. Entrusting charity property to official custodian, and termination of trust

(1) The court may by order vest any property held by or in trust for a charity in the official custodian for charities, or authorise or require the persons in whom any such property is vested to transfer it to him, or appoint any person to transfrer any such property to him.[1]

[(1) The court may by order –
  (a) vest in the official custodian for charities any land or interest in land held by or in trust for a charity;
  (b) authorise or require the persons in whom any such land or interest is vested to transfer it to him; or
  (c) appoint any person to transfer any such land or interest to him;
and for this purpose 'interest in land' means any interest in land other than such an interest by way of mortgage or other security.][1]

(2) Where any personal property is held by or in trust for a charity, or is comprised in any testamentary gift to a charity, the property may with the agreement of the official custodian for charities be transferred to him; and his receipt for any such property comprised in a testamentary gift to a charity shall be a complete discharge of the personal representative.

In this subsection, the expression 'personal property' shall extend to any real security, but shall not include any interest in land otherwise than by way of security only.[1]

(3) Where property is vested in the official custodian for charities in trust for a charity, the court may make an order discharging him from the trusteeship as respects all or any of that property.

(4) Where the official custodian for charities is discharged from his trusteeship of any property, or the trusts on which he holds any property come to an end, the court may make such vesting orders and give such directions as may seem to the court to be necessary or expedient in consequence.

(5) No person shall be liable for any loss occasioned by his acting in conformity with an order under this section or by his giving effect to anything done in pursuance of such an order, or be excused from so doing by reason of the order having been in any respect improperly obtained; and no vesting or transfer of any property in pursuance of this section shall operate as a breach of a covenant or condition against alienation or give rise to a forfeiture.

Amendments. [1]Words substituted or repealed: Charities Act 1992, s 47, Sch 3, para 4, s 78(2), Sch 7.

---

17. Supplementary provisions as to property vested in official custodian

(1) Subject to the provisions of this Act, where property is vested in the official custodian for charities in trust for a charity, he shall not exercise any powers of management, but he shall as trustee of any property have all the same powers, duties and liabilities, and be entitled to the same rights and immunities, and be subject to the control and orders of the court, as a corporation appointed custodian trustee under section four of the Public Trustee Act 1906, except that he shall have no power to charge fees.

(2) [Subject to subsection (2A) below,][1] where any land or interest in land is vested in the official custodian for charities in trust for a charity, the charity trustees shall have power in his name and on his behalf to execute and do all assurances and things which they could properly *require him to execute or do* –
   (a) *for carrying out any transaction affecting the land or interest which is authorised by order of the court or of the Commissioners; or*
   (b) *for granting any lease for a term ending not more than twenty-two years after it is granted, not being a lease granted wholly or partly in consideration of a fine, or for accepting the surrender of a lease.*[1] [execute or do in their own name and on their own behalf if the land or interest were vested in them.][1]

[(2A) If any land or interest in land is so vested in the official custodian for charities by virtue of an order under section 20 of this Act, the power conferred on the charity trustees by subsection (2) above shall not be exercisable by them in relation to any transaction affecting the land or interest, unless the transaction is authorised by order of the court or of the Commissioners.][1]

(3) Where any land or interest in land is vested in the official custodian for charities in trust for a charity, the charity trustees shall have the like power to make obligations entered into by them binding on the land or interest as if it were vested in them; and any covenant, agreement or condition which is enforceable by or against the custodian by reason of the land or interest being vested in him shall be enforceable by or against the charity trustees as if the land or interest were vested in them.

(4) In relation to a corporate charity, subsections (2) [,(2A)][1] and (3) above shall apply with the substitution of references to the charity for references to the charity trustees.

(5) Subsections (2) [,(2A)][1] and (3) above shall not authorise any charity trustees or charity to impose any personal liability on the official custodian for charities.

(6) Where the official custodian for charities is entitled as trustee for a charity to the custody of securities or documents of title relating to the trust property, he may permit them to be in the possession or under the control of the charity trustees, without thereby incurring any liability.

Amendments. [1]Words inserted or substituted: Charities Act 1992, s 47, Sch 3, para 5.

Powers of Commissioners and Minister to make schemes, etc

18. Concurrent jurisdiction with High Court for certain purposes

(1) Subject to the provisions of this Act, the Commissioners may by order exercise the same jurisdiction and powers as are exercisable by the High Court in charity proceedings for the following purposes, that is to say: –
    (a) establishing a scheme for the administration of a charity;
    (b) appointing, discharging or removing a charity trustee or trustee for a charity, or removing an officer or *servant*[2] [employee][2];
    (c) vesting or transferring property, or requiring or entitling any person to call for or make any transfer of property or any payment.

(2) Where the court directs a scheme for the administration of a charity to be established, the court may by order refer the matter to the Commissioners for them to prepare or settle a scheme in accordance with such directions (if any) as the court sees fit to give, and any such order may provide for the scheme to be put into effect by order of the Commissioners as if prepared under subsection (1) above and without any further order of the court.

(3) The Commissioners shall not have jurisdiction under this section to try or determine the title at law or in equity to any property as between a charity or trustee for a charity and a person holding or claiming the property or an interest in it adversely to the charity, or to try or determine any question as to the existence or extent of any charge or trust.

(4) Subject to the following subsections, the Commissioners shall not exercise their jurisdiction under this section as respects any charity, except –
    (a) on the application of the charity; or
    (b) on an order of the court under subsection (2) above [; or
    (c) in the case of a charity other than an exempt charity, on the application of the Attorney General.][2]

(5) In the case of a charity not having any income from property amounting to more than fifty pounds a year, and not being an exempt charity, the Commissioners may exercise their jurisdiction under this section on the application –
    (a) of the Attorney General; or
    (b) of any one or more of the charity trustees, or of any person interested in the charity, or of any two or more inhabitants of the area of the charity, if it is a local charity.[2]

[(5) In the case of a charity which is not an exempt charity and whose income from all sources does not in aggregate exceed £500 a year, the Commissioners may exercise their jurisdiction under this section on the application –
    (a) of any one or more of the charity trustees; or

(b) of any person interested in the charity; or

(c) of any two or more inhabitants of the area of the charity, if it is a local charity.]²

(6) Where in the case of a charity, other than an exempt charity, the Commissioners are satisfied that the charity trustees ought in the interests of the charity to apply for a scheme, but have unreasonably refused or neglected to do so, *the Commissioners may apply to the Secretary of State for him to refer the case to them with a view to a scheme, and if, after giving the charity trustees an opportunity to make representations to him, the Secretary of State does so, the Commissioners may proceed accordingly without the application required by subsection (4) or (5) above:*² [and the Commissioners have given the charity trustees an opportunity to make representations to them, the Commissioners may proceed as if an application for a scheme had been made by the charity:]²

Provided that the Commissioners shall not have power in a case where they act by virtue of this subsection to alter the purposes of a charity, unless forty years have elapsed from the date of its foundation.

[(6A) Where –

(a) a charity cannot apply to the Commissioners for a scheme by reason of any vacancy among the charity trustees or the absence or incapacity of any of them, but

(b) such an application is made by such number of the charity trustees as the Commissioners consider appropriate in the circumstances of the case,

the Commissioners may nevertheless proceed as if the application were an application made by the charity.]²

(7) The Commissioners may on the application of any charity trustee or trustee for a charity exercise their jurisdiction under this section for the purpose of discharging him from his trusteeship.

(8) Before exercising any jurisdiction under this section otherwise than on an order of the court, the Commissioners shall give notice of their intention to do so to each of the charity trustees, except any that cannot be found or has no known address in the United Kingdom or who is party or privy to an application for the exercise of the jurisdiction; and any such notice may be given by post and, if given by post, may be addressed to the recipient's last known address in the United Kingdom.

(9) The Commissioners shall not exercise their jurisdiction under this section in any case (not referred to them by order of the court) which, by reason of its contentious character, or of any special question of law or of fact which it may involve, or for other reasons, the Commissioners may consider more fit to be adjudicated on by the court.

(10) An appeal against any order of the Commissioners under this section may be brought in the High Court by the Attorney General.

(11) An appeal against any order of the Commissioners under this section may also, at any time within the three months beginning with the day following that on which the order is published, be brought in the High Court by the charity or any of the charity trustees, or by any person removed from any office or employment by the order (unless he is removed with the concurrence of the charity trustees or with the approval of the special visitor, if any, of the charity):

Provided that no appeal shall be brought under this subsection except with a certificate of the Commissioners that it is a proper case for an appeal or with the leave of one of the judges of the High Court attached to the Chancery Division.

(12) Where an order of the Commissioners under this section establishes a scheme for the administration of a charity, any person interested in the charity shall have the like right of appeal under subsection (11) above as a charity trustee, and so also, in the case of a charity which is a local charity in any area, shall any two or more inhabitants of the area and the parish council of any rural parish comprising the area or any part of it . . .[1]

[(13) If he thinks it expedient to do so –
   (a) in consequence of changes in the value of money, or
   (b) with a view to increasing the number of charities in respect of which the Commissioners may exercise their jurisdiction under this section in accordance with subsection (5) above,
the Secretary of State may by order amend that subsection by substituting a different sum for the sum for the time being specified there.

(14) Any such order shall be made by statutory instrument subject to annulment in pursuance of a resolution of either House of Parliament.][2]

Amendments. [1]Words repealed: Local Government Act 1972, ss 210(9)(d), 10, 271(1), Sch 30. [2]Words inserted or substituted: Charities Act 1992, s 13, s 47, Sch 3, para 6.

---

19. Further powers to make schemes or alter application of charitable property

(1) Where it appears to the Commissioners that a scheme should be established for the administration of a charity, but also that it is necessary or desirable for the scheme to alter the provision made by an Act of Parliament establishing or regulating the charity or to make any other provision which goes or might go beyond the powers exercisable by them apart from this section, or that it is for any reason proper for the scheme to be subject to parliamentary review, then (subject to subsection (6) below) the Commissioners may settle a scheme accordingly with a view to its being given effect under this section.

(2) A scheme settled by the Commissioners under this section may be given effect by order of the Secretary of State made by a statutory instrument, and a draft of the statutory instrument shall be laid before Parliament.

(3) Without prejudice to the operation of section six of the Statutory Instruments Act 1946 in other cases, in the case of a scheme which goes beyond the powers exercisable apart from this section in altering a statutory provision contained in or having effect under any public general Act of Parliament, the order shall not be made unless the draft has been approved by resolution of each House of Parliament.

(4) Subject to subsection (5) below, any provision of a scheme brought into effect under this section may be modified or superseded by the court or the Commissioners

as if it were a scheme brought into effect by order of the Commissioners under section eighteen of this Act.

(5) Where subsection (3) above applies to a scheme, the order giving effect to it may direct that the scheme shall not be modified or superseded by a scheme brought into effect otherwise than under this section, and may also direct that that subsection shall apply to any scheme modifying or superseding the scheme to which the order gives effect.

(6) The Commissioners shall not proceed under this section without the like application *or the like reference from the Secretary of State*[2], and the like notice to the charity trustees, as would be required if they were proceeding (without an order of the court) under section eighteen of this Act; but on any application *or reference made with a view to a scheme,*[2] [for a scheme, or in a case where they act by virtue of subsection (6) or (6A) or that section,][2] the Commissioners may proceed under this section or that as appears to them appropriate.

(7) Notwithstanding anything in the trusts of a charity, no expenditure incurred in preparing or promoting a Bill in Parliament shall without the consent of the court or the Commissioners be defrayed out of any moneys applicable for the purposes of a charity:
    Provided that this subsection shall not apply in the case of an exempt charity.

(8) Where the Commissioners are satisfied –
    (a) that the whole of the income of a charity cannot in existing circumstances be effectively applied for the purposes of the charity; and
    (b) that, if those circumstances continue, a scheme might be made for applying the surplus cy-près; and
    (c) that it is for any reason not yet desirable to make such a scheme;
then the Commissioners may by order authorise the charity trustees at their discretion (but subject to any conditions imposed by the order) to apply any accrued or accruing income for any purposes for which it might be made applicable by such a scheme, and any application authorised by the order shall be deemed to be within the purposes of the charity:
    Provided that the order shall not extend to more than three hundred pounds out of income accrued before the date of the order, nor to income accruing more than three years after that date, nor to more than one hundred pounds out of the income accruing in any of those three years.

(9) . . .[1]

Amendments. [1]Words repealed: Education Act 1973, s 1(4), (5), Sch 2, Pt III. [2]Words substituted or repealed: Charities Act 1992, s 47, Sch 3, para 7, s 78(2), Sch 7.

---

20. Power to act for protection of charities

(1) Where the Commissioners are satisfied as the result of an inquiry instituted by them under section six of this Act –
    (a) that there has been in the administration of a charity any misconduct or mismanagement; and

(b) that it is necessary or desirable to act for the purpose of protecting the property of the charity or securing a proper application for the purposes of the charity of that property or of property coming to the charity;

then for that purpose the Commissioners may of their own motion do all or any of the following things: –

(i) they may by order remove any trustee, charity trustee, officer, agent or servant of the charity who has been responsible for or privy to the misconduct or mismanagement or has by his conduct contributed to it or facilitated it;

(ii) they may make any such order as is authorised by subsection (1) of section sixteen of this Act with respect to the vesting in or transfer to the official custodian for charities of property held by or in trust for the charity;

(iii) they may order any bank or other person who holds money or securities on behalf of the charity or of any trustee for it not to part with the money or securities without the approval of the Commissioners;

(iv) they may, notwithstanding anything in the trusts of the charity, by order restrict the transactions which may be entered into, or the nature or amount of the payments which may be made, in the administration of the charity without the approval of the Commissioners.⁴

[(1) Where, at any time after they have instituted an inquiry under section 6 of this Act with respect to any charity, the Commissioners are satisfied –

(a) that there is or has been any misconduct or mismanagement in the administration of the charity; or

(b) that it is necessary or desirable to act for the purpose of protecting the property of the charity or securing a proper application for the purposes of the charity of that property or of property coming to the charity;

the Commissioners may of their own motion do one or more of the following things, namely –

(i) by order suspend any trustee, charity trustee, officer, agent or employee of the charity from the exercise of his office or employment pending consideration being given to his removal (whether under this section or otherwise);

(ii) by order appoint such number of additional charity trustees as they consider necessary for the proper administration of the charity;

(iii) by order vest any property held by or in trust for the charity in the official custodian for charities, or require the persons in whom any such property is vested to transfer it to him, or appoint any person to transfer any such property to him;

(iv) order any person who holds any property on behalf of the charity, or of any trustee for it, not to part with the property without the approval of the Commissioners;

(v) order any debtor of the charity not to make any payment in or towards the discharge of his liability to the charity without the approval of the Commissioners;

(vi) by order restrict (notwithstanding anything in the trusts of the charity) the transactions which may be entered into, or the nature or amount of the payments which may be made, in the administration of the charity without the approval of the Commissioners;

(vii) by order appoint (in accordance with section 20A of this Act) a receiver and manager in respect of the property and affairs of the charity.

(1A) Where, at any time after they have instituted an inquiry under section 6 of this Act with respect to any charity, the Commissioners are satisfied –

    (a) that there is or has been any misconduct or mismanagement in the administration of the charity; and

    (b) that it is necessary or desirable to act for the purpose of protecting the property of the charity or securing a proper application for the puposes of the charity of that property or of property coming to the charity;

the Commissioners may of their own motion do either or both of the following things, namely –

    (i) by order remove any trustee, charity trustee, officer, agent or employee of the charity who has been responsible for or privy to the misconduct or mismanagement or has by his conduct contributed to it or facilitated it;

    (ii) by order establish a scheme for the administration of the charity.][4]

(2) The references in subsection (1) [or (1A)][4] above to misconduct or mismanagement shall (notwithstanding anything in the trusts of the charity) extend to the employment for the remuneration or reward of persons acting in the affairs of the charity, or for other administrative purposes, of sums which are excessive in relation to the property which is or is likely to be applied or applicable for the purposes of the charity.

(3) The Commissioners may also remove a charity trustee by order made of their own motion –

    (a) where the trustee . . .[1] is a bankrupt or a corporation in liquidation, or is incapable of acting by reason of mental disorder within the meaning of the Mental Health Act 1959;

    [(a) where, within the last five years, the trustee –

    (i) having previously been adjudged bankrupt or had his estate sequestrated, has been discharged, or

    (ii) having previously made a composition or arrangement with, or granted a trust deed for, his creditors, has been discharged in respect of it;

    (aa) where the trustee is a corporation in liquidation;

    (ab) where the trustee is incapable of acting by reason of mental disorder within the meaning of the Mental Health Act 1983;][4]

    (b) where the trustee has not acted, and will not declare his willingness or unwillingness to act;

    (c) where the trustee is outside England and Wales or cannot be found or does not act, and his absence or failure to act impedes the proper administration of the charity.

(4) The Commissioners may by order made of their own motion appoint a person to be a charity trustee –

    (a) in place of a charity trustee removed by them under this section or otherwise;

    (b) where there are no charity trustees, or where by reason of vacancies in their number or the absence or incapacity of any of their number the charity cannot apply for the appointment;

    (c) where there is a single charity trustee, not being a corporation aggregate, and the Commissioners are of opinion that it is necessary to increase the number for the proper administration of the charity;

    (d) where the Commissioners are of opinion that it is necessary for the proper administration of the charity to have an additional charity trustee, because one

11.5.2   The first paragraph should read:

'This exemption of charitable institutions is further extended by s 58(2)(a) of the 1992 Act to *any company connected with a charitable institution* provided that company is not carrying on a fund-raising business (see 11.6.1). If a company is connected with a charitable institution as defined in s 58(2)(a) but carries on a fund-raising business as defined in the first part of the definition of professional fund-raiser, that company can be a professional fund-raiser and subject to the controls set out in the Act even though it is connected with a charitable institution.'

Page 97

12.3.1 and 12.3.2   These paragraphs should be ignored and replaced by the following:

'12.3.1 The exclusion of companies connected with a charitable institution (see 11.5.2) from, in part, the definition of a professional fund-raiser does not extend to commercial participators. Therefore, a trading company owned by a charitable institution will fall within the definition of commercial participator.'

This is very much at odds with the discussions that took place on the Bill in its committee stage. At that point, it was generally believed that trading subsidiaries of charitable institutions would not be treated as commercial participators and would be outside the scope of Part 2 of the 1992 Act. It is possible that the government may address this in the regulations to be made under s 64(1) because the power under that section is extremely widely drawn – the Secretary of State 'may make such regulations as appear to him to be necessary or desirable for any purposes connected with any of' the provisions of Part 2.

The discussion in 12.3.1 and 12.3.2 was based on two premises. First, if the trading subsidiary was established as a fund-raising business it could not be a commercial participator. Secondly, since companies connected with a charitable institution are in part excluded from the definition of 'professional fund-raiser', it would be sufficient to establish the trading subsidiary as a fund-raising business in order to exclude that trading subsidiary from the scope of Part 2. However, this does not work. The exemption of a company connected with a charitable institution from the definition of professional fund-raiser does not extend to a company which carries on a fund-raising business (see 11.5.2, as amended). It only extends to a company connected with a charitable institution which, for reward, solicits money or other property for the benefit of a charitable institution which is done otherwise than in the course of a fund-raising venture.

The author apologises for any inconvenience.

of the existing charity trustees who ought nevertheless to remain a charity trustee either cannot be found or does not act or is outside England and Wales.

(5) The powers of the Commissioners under this section to remove or appoint charity trustees of their own motion shall include power to make any such order with respect to the vesting in or transfer to the charity trustees of any property as the Commissioners could make on the removal or appointment of a charity trustee by them under section eighteen of this Act.

(6) Any order under this section for the removal or appointment of a charity trustee or trustee for a charity, or for the vesting or transfer of any property, shall be of the like effect as an order made under section eighteen of this Act.

(7) Subsections (10) and (11) of section eighteen of this Act shall apply to orders under this section as they apply to orders under that, save that where the Commissioners have by order removed a trustee, charity trustee, officer, agent, or servant of a charity under the power conferred by subsection (1) of this section, an appeal against such an order may be brought by any person so removed without a certificate of the Commissioners and without the leave of one of the judges of the High Court attached to the Chancery Division.[4]

[(7) Subject to subsection (7A) below, subsections (10) and (11) of section 18 of this Act shall apply to orders under this section as they apply to orders under that section.

(7A) The requirement to obtain any such certificate or leave as is mentioned in the proviso to section 18(11) shall not apply to –
   (a) an appeal by a charity or any of the charity trustees of a charity against an order under subsection (1)(vii) above appointing a receiver and manager in respect of the charity's property and affairs, or
   (b) an appeal by a person against an order under subsection (1A)(i) or (3)(a) above removing him from his office or employment.

(7B) Subsection (12) of section 18 of this Act shall apply to an order under this section which establishes a scheme for the administration of a charity as it applies to such an order under that section.][4]

(8) *The power of the Commissioners under subsection (1) above to remove a trustee, charity trustee, officer, agent or servant of a charity shall include power to suspend him from the exercise of his office or employment pending the consideration of his removal (but not for a period longer than three months), and to make provision as respects the period of the suspension*[4] [The power of the Commissioners to make an order under subsection (1)(i) above shall not be exercisable so as to suspend any person from the exercise of his office or employment for a period of more than twelve months; but (without prejudice to the generality of section 40(1) of this Act) any such order made in the case of any person may make provision as respects the period of his suspension][4] for matters arising out of it, and in particular for enabling any person to execute any instrument in his name or otherwise act for him and, in the case of a charity trustee, for adjusting any rules governing the proceedings of the charity trustees to take account of the reduction in the number capable of acting.

(9) Before exercising any jurisdiction under this section, [otherwise than by virtue of subsection (1) above][4] the Commissioners shall give notice of their intention to do so to each of the charity trustees, except any that cannot be found or has no known address in the United Kingdom; and any such notice may be given by post and if given by post, may be addressed to the recipient's last known address in the United Kingdom.

[(9A) The Commissioners shall, at such intervals as they think fit, review any order made by them under paragraph (i), or any of paragraphs (iii) to (vii), of subsection (1) above; and, if on any such review it appears to them that it would be appropriate to discharge the order in whole or in part, they shall so discharge it (whether subject to any savings or other transitional provisions or not).]⁴

*(10) If any person contravenes an order under paragraph (iii) of subsection (1) above, he shall be liable on summary conviction to a fine not exceeding [level 3 on the standard scale]², or to imprisonment for a term not exceeding six months, or to both; but no proceedings for an offence punishable under this subsection shall be instituted except by or with the consent of the Commissioners.*⁴

[(10) If any person contravenes an order under subsection (1)(iv), (v) or (vi) above, he shall be guilty of an offence and liable on summary conviction to a fine not exceeding the fifth level on the standard scale.

(10A) Subsection (10) above shall not be taken to preclude the bringing of proceedings for breach of trust against any charity trustee or trustee for a charity in respect of a contravention of an order under subsection (1)(iv) or (vi) above (whether proceedings in respect of the contravention are brought against him under subsection (10) above or not).]⁴

(11) . . .³

(12) This section shall not apply to an exempt charity.

Amendments. ¹Words repealed: Criminal Law Act 1967, s 10(2), Sch 3, Pt III. ²Words substituted: Criminal Justice Act 1982, ss 38, 46. ³Subsection repealed: Education Act 1973, s 1(4), (5), Sch 2, Pt III. ⁴Words inserted, or substituted: Charities Act 1992, s 8. The text of s 20 is also set out as amended in the Charities Act 1992, Sch 1.

[20A. Supplementary provisions relating to receiver and manager appointed for a charity

(1) The Commissioners may under section 20(1)(vii) of this Act appoint to be receiver and manager in respect of the property and affairs of a charity such person (other than an officer or employee of theirs) as they think fit.

(2) Without prejudice to the generality of section 40(1) of this Act, any order made by the Commissioners under section 20(1)(vii) of this Act may make provision with respect to the functions to be discharged by the receiver and manager appointed by the order; and those functions shall be discharged by him under the supervision of the Commissioners.

(3) In connection with the discharge of those functions any such order may provide –
   (a) for the receiver and manager appointed by the order to have such powers and duties of the charity trustees of the charity concerned (whether arising under this Act or otherwise) as are specified in the order;
   (b) for any powers or duties exercisable or falling to be performed by the receiver and manager by virtue of paragraph (a) above to be exercisable or performed by him to the exclusion of those trustees.

(4) Where a person has been appointed receiver and manager by any such order –
   (a) section 24 of this Act shall apply to him and to his functions as a person so

appointed as it applies to a charity trustee of the charity concerned and to his duties as such; and

(b) the Commissioners may apply to the High Court for directions in relation to any particular matter arising in connection with the discharge of those functions.

(5) The High Court may on an application under subsection (4)(b) above –

(a) give such directions, or

(b) make such orders declaring the rights of any persons (whether before the court or not),

as it thinks just; and the costs of any such application shall be paid by the charity concerned.

(6) Regulations may make provision with respect to –

(a) the appointment and removal of persons appointed in accordance with this section;

(b) the remuneration of such persons out of the income of the charities concerned;

(c) the making of reports to the Commissioners by such persons.

(7) Regulations under subsection (6) above may, in particular, authorise the Commissioners –

(a) to require security for the due discharge of his functions to be given by a person so appointed;

(b) to determine the amount of such a person's remuneration;

(c) to disallow any amount of remuneration in such circumstances as are prescribed by the regulations.][4]

Amendment. [1]Section inserted: Charities Act 1992, s 9.

21. Publicity for proceedings under ss 18 and 20

(1) The Commissioners shall not make any order under this Act to establish a scheme for the administration of a charity, or submit such a scheme to the court or the Secretary of State for an order giving it effect, unless not less than one month previously there has been given public notice of their proposals, inviting representations to be made to them within a time specified in the notice, being not less than one month from the date of such notice, and, in the case of a scheme relating to a local charity in a rural parish (other than an ecclesiastical charity), a draft of the scheme has been communicated to the parish council or, in the case of a parish not having a parish council, to the chairman of the parish meeting.

(2) The Commissioners shall not make any order under this Act to appoint, discharge or remove a charity trustee or trustee for a charity (other than the official custodian for charities), unless not less than one month previously there has been given the like public notice as is required by subsection (1) above for an order establishing a scheme:

Provided that this subsection shall not apply [in the case of an order under section 20(1)(ii), or][1] in the case of an order discharging or removing a trustee if the Commissioners are of opinion that it is unnecessary and not in his interest to give publicity to the proposal to discharge or remove him.

(3) Before the Commissioners make an order under this Act to remove without his consent a charity trustee or trustee for a charity, or an officer, agent or *servant*[1]

[employee]¹ of a charity, the Commissioners shall, unless he cannot be found or has no known address in the United Kingdom, give him not less than one month's notice of their proposal inviting representations to be made to them within a time specified in the notice.

(4) Where notice is given of any proposals as required by subsections (1) to (3) above, the Commissioners shall take into consideration any representations made to them about the proposals within the time specified in the notice, and may (without further notice) proceed with the proposals either without modification or with such modifications as appear to them to be desirable.

(5) Where the Commissioners make an order which is subject to appeal under subsection (11) of section eighteen of this Act, the order shall be published either by giving public notice of it or by giving notice of it to all persons entitled to appeal against it under that subsection, as the Commissioners think fit.

(6) Where the Commissioners make an order under this Act to establish a scheme for the administration of a charity, a copy of the order shall, for not less than one month after the order is published, be available for public inspection at all reasonable times at the Commissioners' office and also at some convenient place in the area of the charity, if it is a local charity.

(7) Any notice to be given under this section of any proposals or order shall give such particulars of the proposals or order, or such directions for obtaining information about them, as the Commissioners think sufficient and appropriate, and any public notice shall be given in such manner as they think sufficient and appropriate.

(8) Any notice to be given under this section, other than a public notice, may be given by post and, if given by post, may be addressed to the recipient's last known address in the United Kingdom.

Amendment. ¹Words inserted or substituted: Charities Act 1992, s 47, Sch 3, para 8.

[21A. Application of provisions to trust corporations appointed under ss 18 or 20

In the definition of 'trust corporation' contained in the following provisions, namely –
  (a) section 117(xxx) of the Settled Land Act 1925,
  (b) section 68(18) of the Trustee Act 1925,
  (c) section 205(xxviii) of the Law of Property Act 1925,
  (d) section 55(xxvi) of the Administration of Estates Act 1925, and
  (e) section 128 of the Supreme Court Act 1981,
the reference to a corporation appointed by the court in any particular case to be a trustee includes a reference to a corporation appointed by the Commissioners under this Act to be a trustee.]¹

Amendment. ¹Section inserted: Charities Act 1992, s 14.

Establishment of common investment funds

22. Schemes to establish common investment funds

(1) The court or the Commissioners may by order make and bring into effect schemes (in this section referred to as 'common investment schemes') for the establishment of common investment funds under trusts which provide –

(a) for property transferred to the fund by or on behalf of a charity participating in the scheme to be invested under the control of trustees appointed to manage the fund; and

(b) for the participating charities to be entitled (subject to the provisions of the scheme) to the capital and income of the fund in shares determined by reference to the amount or value of the property transferred to it by or on behalf of each of them and to the value of the fund at the time of the transfers.

(2) The court or the Commissioners may make a common investment scheme on the application of any two or more charities.

(3) A common investment scheme may be made in terms admitting any charity to participate, or the scheme may restrict the right to participate in any manner.

(4) A common investment scheme may make provision for, and for all matters connected with, the establishment, investment, management and winding up of the common investment fund, and may in particular include provision –

(a) for remunerating persons appointed trustees to hold or manage the fund or any part of it, with or without provision authorising a person to receive the remuneration notwithstanding that he is also a charity trustee for a participating charity;

(b) for restricting the size of the fund, and for regulating as to time, amount or otherwise the right to transfer property to or withdraw it from the fund, and for enabling sums to be advanced out of the fund by way of loan to a participating charity pending the withdrawal of property from the fund by the charity;

(c) for enabling income to be withheld from distribution with a view to avoiding fluctuations in the amounts distributed, and generally for regulating distributions of income;

(d) for enabling moneys to be borrowed temporarily for the purpose of meeting payments to be made out of the fund;

(e) for enabling questions arising under the scheme as to the right of a charity to participate, or as to the rights of participating charities, or as to any other matter, to be conclusively determined by the decision of the trustees managing the fund or in any other manner;

(f) for regulating the accounts and information to be supplied to participating charities.

(5) A common investment scheme, in addition to the provision for property to be transferred to the fund on the basis that the charity shall be entitled to a share in the capital and income of the fund, may include provision for enabling sums to be deposited by or on behalf of a charity on the basis that (subject to the provisions of the scheme) the charity shall be entitled to repayment of the sums deposited and to interest thereon at a rate determined by or under the scheme; and where a scheme makes any such provision it shall also provide for excluding from the amount of capital and

income to be shared between charities participating otherwise than by way of deposit such amounts (not exceeding the amounts properly attributable to the making of deposits) as are from time to time reasonably required in respect of the liabilities of the fund for the repayment of deposits and for the interest on deposits, including amounts required by way of reserve.

(6) A common investment scheme may provide for the assets of the common investment fund or any of them to be vested in the official custodian for charities, and, if made by the Commissioners or if they consent, may also appoint him or authorise him to be appointed trustee to manage the fund or any part of it, and as managing trustee he shall, subject to section three of this Act, have the same powers, duties and liabilities as other managing trustees; but where a common investment scheme provides for the official custodian for charities to exercise any discretion with respect to the investment of the fund it shall make provision for him to be advised by a committee of persons who have special experience of investment and finance or of the administration of trusts, or who represent or are nominated by bodies having that experience.[3]

(7) Except in so far as a common investment scheme provides to the contrary, the rights under it of a participating charity shall not be capable of being assigned or charged, nor shall any trustee or other person concerned in the management of the common investment fund be required or entitled to take account of any trust or other equity affecting a participating charity or its property or rights.

(8) The powers of investment of every charity shall include power to participate in common investment schemes, unless the power is excluded by a provision specifically referring to common investment schemes in the trusts of the charity.

(9) A common investment fund shall be deemed for all purposes to be a charity, *and the assets of the fund shall be treated for the purposes of this Act as a permanent endowment, except that if the scheme establishing the fund admits to participation only charities not having a permanent endowment, the fund shall be treated as a charity not having a permanent endowment;*[3] and if the scheme admits only exempt charities, the fund shall be an exempt charity for the purposes of this Act.

(10) . . .[2]

(11) [Subsection (9)][2] above shall apply not only to common investment funds established under the powers of this section, but also to any similar fund established for the exclusive benefit of charities by or under any enactment relating to any particular charities or class of charity.

(12) . . .[1]

Amendments. [1]Words repealed: Education Act 1973, s 1(4), (5), Sch 2, Pt III. [2]Words substituted or repealed: Financial Services Act 1986, s 212 (2), (3), Sch 16, para 1, Sch 17, Pt I. [3]Words inserted or repealed: Charities Act 1992, s 47, Sch 3, para 9, s 78(2), Sch 7.

[22A. Schemes to establish common deposit funds

(1) The court or the Commissioners may by order make and bring into effect schemes (in this section referred to as 'common deposit schemes') for the establishment of common deposit funds under trusts which provide –
    (a) for sums to be deposited by or on behalf of a charity participating in the

scheme and invested under the control of trustees appointed to manage the fund; and

(b) for any such charity to be entitled (subject to the provisions of the scheme) to repayment of any sums so deposited and to interest thereon at a rate determined under the scheme.

(2) Subject to subsection (3) below, the following provisions of section 22 of this Act, namely –

(a) subsections (2) to (4), and
(b) subsections (7) to (11),

shall have effect in relation to common deposit schemes and common deposit funds as they have effect in relation to common investment schemes and common investment funds.

(3) In its application in accordance with subsection (2) above, subsection (4) of that section shall have effect with the substitution for paragraphs (b) and (c) of the following paragraphs –

'(b) for regulating as to time, amount or otherwise the right to repayment of sums deposited in the fund;
(c) for authorising a part of the income for any year to be credited to a reserve account maintained for the purpose of counteracting any losses accruing to the fund, and generally for regulating the manner in which the rate of interest on deposits is to be determined from time to time;'.][1]

Amendment. [1]Section inserted: Charities Act 1992, s 16.

Miscellaneous powers of Commissioners and Minister

23. Power to authorise dealings with charity property etc

(1) Subject to the provisions of this section, where it appears to the Commissioners that any action proposed or contemplated in the administration of a charity is expedient in the interests of the charity, they may by order sanction that action, whether or not it would otherwise be within the powers exercisable by the charity trustees in the administration of the charity; and anything done under the authority of such an order shall be deemed to be properly done in the exercise of those powers.

(2) An order under this section may be made so as to authorise a particular transaction, compromise or the like, or a particular application of property, or so as to give a more general authority, and (without prejudice to the generality of subsection (1) above) may authorise a charity to use common premises, or employ a common staff, or otherwise combine for any purpose of administration, with any other charity.

(3) An order under this section may give directions as to the manner in which any expenditure is to be borne and as to other matters connected with or arising out of the action thereby authorised; and where anything is done in pursuance of an authority given by any such order, any directions given in connection therewith shall be binding on the charity trustees for the time being as if contained in the trusts of the charity:

Provided that any such directions may on the application of the charity be modified or superseded by a further order.

(4) Without prejudice to the generality of subsection (3) above, the directions which may be given by an order under this section shall in particular include directions for meeting any expenditure out of a specified fund, for charging any expenditure to capital or to income, for requiring expenditure charged to capital to be recouped out of income within a specified period, for restricting the costs to be incurred at the expense of the charity, or for the investment of moneys arising from any transaction.

(5) An order under this section may authorise any act, notwithstanding that it is prohibited by any of the disabling Acts mentioned in subsection (6) below, or that the trusts of the charity provide for the act to be done by or under the authority of the court; but no such order shall authorise the doing of any act expressly prohibited by Act of Parliament other than the disabling Acts or by the trusts of the charity, or confer any authority in relation to a disused church as defined in that subsection, or shall extend or alter the purposes of the charity.

(6) The Acts referred to in subsection (5) above as the disabling Acts are the Ecclesiastical Leases Act 1571, the Ecclesiastical Leases Act 1572, the Ecclesiastical Leases Act 1575 and the Ecclesiastical Leases Act 1836; and in that subsection 'disused church' means a building which has been consecrated and of which the use or disposal is regulated, and can be further regulated, by a scheme having effect under the Union of Benefices Measures 1923 to 1952 or the Reorganisation Areas Measures 1944 and 1954, and extends to any land which under such a scheme is to be used or disposed of with a disused church, and for this purpose 'building' includes part of a building.

[23A. Power to authorise certain ex gratia payments etc

(1) Subject to subsection (3) below, the Commissioners may by order exercise the same power as is exercisable by the Attorney General to authorise the charity trustees of a charity –
  (a) to make any application of property of the charity, or
  (b) to waive to any extent, on behalf of the charity, its entitlement to receive any property,
in a case where the charity trustees –
    (i) (apart from this section) have no power to do so, but
    (ii) in all the circumstances regard themselves as being under a moral obligation to do so.

(2) The power conferred on the Commissioners by subsection (1) above shall be exercisable by them under the supervision of, and in accordance with such directions as may be given by, the Attorney General; and any such directions may in particular require the Commissioners, in such circumstances as are specified in the directions –
  (a) to refrain from exercising that power; or
  (b) to consult the Attorney General before exercising it.

(3) Where –
  (a) an application is made to the Commissioners for them to exercise that power in a case where they are not precluded from doing so by any such directions, but
  (b) they consider that it would nevertheless be desirable for the application to be entertained by the Attorney General rather than by them,
they shall refer the application to the Attorney General.

(4) It is hereby declared that where, in the case of any application made to them as mentioned in subsection (3)(a) above, the Commissioners determine the application by refusing to authorise charity trustees to take any action falling within subsection (1)(a) or (b) above, that refusal shall not preclude the Attorney General, on an application subsequently made to him by the trustees, from authorising the trustees to take that action.]¹

Amendment. ¹Section inserted: Charities Act 1992, s 17.

24. Power to advise charity trustees

(1) The Commissioners may on the written application of any charity trustee give him their opinion or advice on any matter affecting the performance of his duties as such.

(2) A charity trustee or trustee for a charity acting in accordance with the opinion or advice of the Commissioners given under this section with respect to the charity shall be deemed, as regards his responsibility for so acting, to have acted in accordance with his trust, unless, when he does so, either –
  (a) he knows or has reasonable cause to suspect that the opinion or advice was given in ignorance of material facts; or
  (b) the decision of the court has been obtained on the matter or proceedings are pending to obtain one.

25. Powers for preservation of charity documents

(1) The Commissioners may provide books in which any deed, will or other document relating to a charity may be enrolled.

(2) The Commissioners may accept for safe keeping any document of or relating to a charity, and the charity trustees or other persons having the custody of documents of or relating to a charity (including a charity which has ceased to exist) may with the consent of the Commissioners deposit them with the Commissioners for safe keeping, except in the case of documents required by some other enactment to be kept elsewhere.

(3) Where a document is enrolled by the Commissioners or is for the time being deposited with them under this section, evidence of its contents may be given by means of a copy certified by any officer of the Commissioners generally or specially authorised by them to act for this purpose; and a document purporting to be such a copy shall be received in evidence without proof of the official position, authority or handwriting of the person certifying it or of the original document being enrolled or deposited as aforesaid.

(4) Regulations may make provision for such documents deposited with the Commissioners under this section as may be prescribed to be destroyed or otherwise disposed of after such period or in such circumstances as may be prescribed.

(5) Subsections (3) and (4) above shall apply to any document transmitted to the Commissioners under section seven of this Act and kept by them under subsection (3) of that section, as if the document had been deposited with them for safe keeping under this section.

26. Power to order taxation of solicitor's bill

(1) The Commissioners may order that a solicitor's bill of costs for business done for a charity, or for charity trustees for a charity, shall be taxed, together with the costs of the taxation, by a taxing officer in such division of the High Court as may be specified in the order, or by the taxing officer of any other court having jurisdiction to order the taxation of the bill.

(2) On any order under this section for the taxation of a solicitor's bill the taxation shall proceed, and the taxing officer shall have the same powers and duties, and the costs of the taxation shall be borne, as if the order had been made, on the application of the person chargeable with the bill, by the court in which the costs are taxed.

(3) No order under this section for the taxation of a solicitor's bill shall be made after payment of the bill, unless the Commissioners are of opinion that it contains exorbitant charges; and no such order shall in any case be made where the solicitor's costs are not subject to taxation on an order of the High Court by reason either of an agreement as to his remuneration or of the lapse of time since payment of the bill.

[26A. Power of Commissioners to bring proceedings with respect to charities

(1) Subject to subsection (2) below, the Commissioners may exercise the same powers with respect to –
    (a) the taking of legal proceedings with reference to charities or the property or affairs of charities, or
    (b) the compromise of claims with a view to avoiding or ending such proceedings,
as are exercisable by the Attorney General acting ex officio.

(2) Subsection (1) above does not apply to the power of the Attorney General under section 30(1) of this Act to present a petition for the winding up of a charity.

(3) The practice and procedure to be followed in relation to any proceedings taken by the Commissioners under subsection (1) above shall be the same in all respects (and in particular as regards costs) as if they were proceedings taken by the Attorney General acting ex officio.

(4) No rule of law or practice shall be taken to require the Attorney General to be a party to any such proceedings.

(5) The powers exercisable by the Commissioners by virtue of this section shall be exercisable by them of their own motion, but shall be exercisable only with the agreement of the Attorney General on each occasion.][1]

Amendment. [1]Section inserted: Charities Act 1992, s 28.

27. *Powers for recovery or redemption of charity rentcharges*

(1) Where it appears to the Commissioners that a charity is entitled to receive a rentcharge issuing out of any land, or out of the rents, profits or other income of any land, they may take legal proceedings on behalf of the charity for recovering the rentcharge or compelling payment.

(2) Where a charity is entitled to receive a rentcharge issuing out of any land, the Commissioners may give to the estate owner in respect of the fee simple in the land (or, if the rentcharge is payable in respect of an estate for a term of years, then to the estate owner in respect of that estate) a notice to treat with the charity trustees for the redemption of the rentcharge.

(3) Where a notice to treat is given under subsection (2) above in respect of any land, and the rentcharge is still subsisting at the expiration of ten years from the date on which the notice is given, then (subject to the provisions of this section) the person who is then the estate owner in respect of the relevant estate in the land shall be liable to pay the redemption price to the charity or to the person entitled to receive it as trustee for the charity, and on payment or tender of the redemption price shall be entitled to a proper and effective release of the rentcharge (or, if he has so requested, a proper and effective transfer of it to a person nominated by him).

(4) For the purposes of subsection (3) above the redemption price for a rentcharge shall be such as may be determined in accordance with regulations made by the Treasury.

(5) Proceedings for the recovery of sums due under subsection (3) above may be taken by the Commissioners on behalf of the charity.

(6) Where an estate owner of land liable to a rentcharge has by law or by contract any right of indemnity or contribution in respect of the rentcharge against any person or property, then on his redeeming the rentcharge in accordance with subsection (3) above he shall have the like right of indemnity or contribution in respect of the redemption price.

(7) For the purposes of the Land Charges Act 1925 and of the Land Registration Act 1925 a notice to treat under this section shall be treated as a land charge affecting the estate of the estate owner to whom it is given, and those Acts shall apply to the notice to treat as they apply to an estate contract.

(8) Where an estate owner of land liable to a rentcharge pays it through an agent, a notice to treat under this section, if given to the agent on behalf of the estate owner, shall for the purposes of this section be deemed to be given to the estate owner, notwithstanding that the agent's authority from the estate owner does not extend to accepting the notice on his behalf.

(9) This section shall apply to any periodical payment other than rent incident to a reversion as it applies to a rentcharge.[1]

Amendment. [1]Section repealed: Charities Act 1992, s 78(2), Sch 7.

Miscellaneous

28. Taking of legal proceedings

(1) Charity proceedings may be taken with reference to a charity either by the charity, or by any of the charity trustees, or by any person interested in the charity, or by any two or more inhabitants of the area of the charity, if it is a local charity, but not by any other person.

(2) Subject to the following provisions of this section, no charity proceedings relating to a charity (other than an exempt charity) shall be entertained or proceeded with in any court unless the taking of the proceedings is authorised by order of the Commissioners.

(3) The Commissioners shall not, without special reasons, authorise the taking of charity proceedings where in their opinion the case can be dealt with by them under the powers of this Act [(other than those conferred by section 26A of this Act)][1].

(4) This section shall not require any order for the taking of proceedings in a pending cause or matter or for the bringing of any appeal.

(5) Where the foregoing provisions of this section require the taking of charity proceedings to be authorised by an order of the Commissioners, the proceedings may nevertheless be entertained or proceeded with if after the order had been applied for and refused leave to take the proceedings was obtained from one of the judges of the High Court attached to the Chancery Division.

(6) Nothing in the foregoing subsections shall apply to the taking of proceedings by the Attorney General, with or without a relator [, or to the taking of proceedings by the Commissioners in accordance with section 26A of this Act.][1]

(7) Where it appears to the Commissioners, on an application for an order under this section or otherwise, that it is desirable for legal proceedings to be taken with reference to any charity (other than an exempt charity) or its property or affairs, and for the proceedings to be taken by the Attorney General, the Commissioners shall so inform the Attorney General, and send him such statements and particulars as they think necessary to explain the matter.

(8) In this section 'charity proceedings' means proceedings in any court in England or Wales brought under the court's jurisdiction with respect to charities, or brought under the court's jurisdiction with respect to trusts in relation to the administration of a trust for charitable purposes.

(9) The Charities Procedure Act 1812 and so much of any local or private Act establishing or regulating a charity as relates to the persons by whom or the manner or form in which any charity proceedings may be brought shall cease to have effect.

Amendment. [1]Words added: Charities Act 1992, s 47, Sch 3, para 10.

[28A. Report of s 6 inquiry to be evidence in certain proceedings

(1) A copy of the report of the person conducting an inquiry under section 6 of this Act shall, if certified by the Commissioners to be a true copy, be admissible in any proceedings to which this section applies –
    (a) as evidence of any fact stated in the report; and
    (b) as evidence of the opinion of that person as to any matter referred to in it.

(2) This section applies to –
    (a) any legal proceedings instituted by the Commissioners under this Part of this Act; and
    (b) any legal proceedings instituted by the Attorney General in respect of a charity.

(3) A document purporting to be a certificate issued for the purposes of subsection (1) above shall be received in evidence and be deemed to be such a certificate, unless the contrary is proved.][1]

Amendment. [1]Section inserted: Charities Act 1992, s 11.

29. Restrictions on dealing with charity property

(1) Subject to the exceptions provided for by this section, no property forming part of the permanent endowment of a charity shall, without an order of the court or of the Commissioners, be mortgaged or charged by way of security for the repayment of money borrowed, nor, in the case of land in England or Wales, be sold, leased or otherwise disposed of.

(2) Subsection (1) above shall apply to any land which is held by or in trust for a charity and is or has at any time been occupied for the purposes of the charity, as it applies to land forming part of the permanent endowment of a charity; but a transaction for which the sanction of an order under subsection (1) above is required by virtue only of this subsection shall, notwithstanding that it is entered into without such an order, be valid in favour of a person who (then or afterwards) in good faith acquires an interest in or charge on the land for money or money's worth.

(3) This section shall apply notwithstanding anything in the trusts of a charity, but shall not require the sanction of an order –
- *(a) for any transaction for which general or special authority is expressly given (without the authority being made subject to the sanction of an order) by any statutory provision contained in or having effect under an Act of Parliament or by any scheme legally established; or*
- *(b) for the granting of a lease for a term ending not more than twenty-two years after it is granted, not being a lease granted wholly or partly in consideration of a fine; or*
- *(c) for any disposition of an advowson.*

(4) This section shall not apply to an exempt charity, nor to any charity which is excepted by order or regulations.[1]

Amendment. [1]Section repealed: Charities Act 1992: s 78(2), Sch 7.

[30. Charitable companies: winding up

[(1)][2] Where a charity may be wound up by the High Court under the Insolvency Act 1986, a petition for it to be wound up under that Act by any court in England or Wales having jurisdiction may be presented by the Attorney General, as well as by any person authorised by that Act.

[(2) Where a charity may be so wound up by the High Court, such a petition may also be presented by the Commissioners if, at any time after they have instituted an inquiry under section 6 of this Act with respect to the charity, they are satisfied as mentioned in section 20(1)(a) or (b) of this Act.

(3) Where a charitable company is dissolved, the Commissioners may make an application under section 651 of the Companies Act 1985 (power of court to declare dissolution of company void) for an order to be made under that section with respect to the company; and for this purpose subsection (1) of that section shall have effect in relation to a charitable company as if the reference to the liquidator of the company included a reference to the Commissioners.

(4) Where a charitable company's name has been struck off the register of companies under section 652 of the Companies Act 1985 (power of registrar to strike defunct company off register), the Commissioners may make an application under section 653(2) of that Act (objection to striking off by person aggrieved) for an order

restoring the company's name to that register; and for this purpose section 653(2) shall have effect in relation to a charitable company as if the reference to any such person aggrieved as is there mentioned included a reference to the Commissioners.

(5) The powers exercisable by the Commissioners by virtue of this section shall be exercisable by them of their own motion, but shall be exercisable only with the agreement of the Attorney General on each occasion.

(6) In this section 'charitable company' means a company which is a charity.][2]

30A. Charitable companies: alteration of objects clause

(1) Where a charity is a company or other body corporate having power to alter the instruments establishing or regulating it as a body corporate, no exercise of that power which has the effect of the body ceasing to be a charity shall be valid so as to affect the application of –

  (a) any property acquired under any disposition or agreement previously made otherwise than for full consideration in money or money's worth, or any property representing property so acquired,

  (b) any property representing income which has accrued before the alteration is made, or

  (c) the income from any such property as aforesaid.

(2) Where a charity is a company, any alteration by it of the objects clause in its memorandum of association is ineffective without the prior written consent of the Commissioners; and it shall deliver a copy of that consent to the registrar of companies under section 6(1)(a) or (b) of the Companies Act 1985 along with the printed copy of the memorandum as altered.

(3) Section 6(3) of that Act (offences) applies in relation to a default in complying with subsection (2) as regards the delivery of a copy of the Commissioners' consent.[2]

[(2) Where a charity is a company, any alteration by it –

  (a) of the objects clause in its memorandum of association, or

  (b) of any other provision in its memorandum of association, or any provision in its articles of association, which is a provision directing or restricting the manner in which property of the company may be used or applied,

is ineffective without the prior written consent of the Commissioners.

(3) Where a company has made any such alteration in accordance with subsection (2) above and –

  (a) in connection with the alteration is required by virtue of –

    (i)   section 6(1) of the Companies Act 1985 (delivery of documents following alteration of objects), or

    (ii)   that provision as applied by section 17(3) of that Act (alteration of condition in memorandum which could have been contained in articles), to deliver to the registrar of companies a printed copy of its memorandum, as altered, or

  (b) is required by virtue of section 380(1) of that Act (registration etc of resolutions and agreements) to forward to the registrar a printed or other copy of the special resolution effecting the alteration,

the copy so delivered or forwarded by the company shall be accompanied by a copy of the Commissioners' consent.

(4) Section 6(3) of that Act (offences) shall apply to any default by a company in complying with subsection (3) above as it applies to any such default as is mentioned in that provision.]²

30B. Charitable companies: invalidity of certain transactions

(1) Sections 35 and 35A of the Companies Act 1985 (capacity of company not limited by its memorandum; power of directors to bind company) do not apply to the acts of a company which is a charity except in favour of a person who –
  (a) gives full consideration in money or money's worth in relation to the act in question, and
  (b) does not know that the act is not permitted by the company's memorandum or, as the case may be, is beyond the powers of the directors,
or who does not know at the time the act is done that the company is a charity.

(2) However, where such a company purports to transfer or grant an interest in property, the fact that the act was not permitted by the company's memorandum or, as the case may be, that the directors in connection with the act exceeded any limitation on their powers under the company's constitution, does not affect the title of a person who subsequently acquires the property or any interest in it for full consideration without actual notice of any such circumstances affecting the validity of the company's Act.

(3) In any proceedings arising out of subsection (1) the burden of proving –
  (a) that a person knew that an act was not permitted by the company's memorandum or was beyond the powers of the directors, or
  (b) that a person knew that the company was a charity,
lies on the person making that allegation.

(4) Where a company is a charity, the ratification of an act under section 35(3) of the Companies Act 1985, or the ratification of a transaction to which section 322A of that Act applies (invalidity of certain transactions to which directors or their associates are parties), is ineffective without the prior written consent of the Commissioners.

[30BA. Charitable companies: requirement of consent of Commissioners to certain acts

(1) Where a company is a charity –
  (a) any approval given by the company for the purposes of any of the provisions of the Companies Act 1985 specified in subsection (2) below, and
  (b) any affirmation by it for the purposes of section 322(2)(c) of that Act (affirmation of voidable arrangements under which assets are acquired by or from a director or person connected with him),
is ineffective without the prior written consent of the Commissioners.

(2) The provisions of the Companies Act 1985 referred to in subsection (1)(a) above are –
  (a) section 312 (payment to director in respect of loss of office or retirement);
  (b) section 313(1) (payment to director in respect of loss of office or retirement made in connection with transfer of undertaking or property of company);
  (c) section 319(3) (incorporation in director's service contract of term whereby his employment will or may continue for a period of more than 5 years);

(d) section 320(1) (arrangement whereby assets are acquired by or from director or person connected with him);

(e) section 337(3)(a) (provision of funds to meet certain expenses incurred by director).][2]

[30BB. Charitable companies: name to appear on correspondence etc

Section 30(7) of the Companies Act 1985 (exemption from requirements relating to publication of name etc.) shall not, in its application to any company which is a charity, have the effect of exempting the company from the requirements of section 349(1) of that Act (company's name to appear in its correspondence etc).][2]

30C. Charitable companies: status to appear on correspondence etc

(1) Where a company is a charity and its name does not include the word 'charity' or the word 'charitable', the fact that the company is a charity shall be stated in English in legible characters –

(a) in all business letters of the company,

(b) in all its notices and other official publications,

(c) in all bills of exchange, promissory notes, endorsements, cheques and orders for money or goods purporting to be signed *by or*[2] on behalf of the company,

(d) in all conveyances purporting to be executed by the company, and

(e) in all *its bills of parcels*[2] [bills rendered by it and in all its][2] invoices, receipts and letters of credit.

(2) In subsection (1)(d) 'conveyance' means any instrument creating, transferring, varying or extinguishing an interest in land.

(3) Section 349(2) to (4) of the Companies Act 1985 (offences in connection with failure to include required particulars in business letters, &c) apply in relation to a contravention of subsection (1) above.][1]

Amendments. [1]Sections 30, 30A, 30B and 30C inserted and substituted: Companies Act 1989, s 111(1). [2]Words inserted, substituted and repealed: Charities Act 1992, ss 10, 40, 41, 42, 47, Sch 3, para 11, s 78(2), Sch 7.

31. Protection of expression 'common good'

(1) It shall not be lawful, without the consent of the Commissioners, to invite gifts in money or in kind to the funds of, or to any fund managed by, an institution which has the words 'common good' in its name, other than a body corporate established by Royal charter, or to any fund described in or in connection with the invitation by a name which includes the words 'common good' otherwise than as part of the name of such a body corporate.

(2) The words 'common good' shall not, without the consent of the Commissioners, be used in the name of any institution established in England or Wales, other than a body corporate established by Royal charter.

(3) Any person contravening subsection (1) or (2) of this section shall be guilty of an offence and liable on summary conviction to a fine not exceeding [level 3 of the standard scale].[1,2]

Amendments. [1]Words substituted: Criminal Justice Act 1982, ss 38, 46. [2]Section repealed: Charities Act 1992, s 47, Sch 3, para 12, s 78(2), Sch 7.

PART IV

MISCELLANEOUS PROVISIONS AS TO CHARITIES AND
THEIR AFFAIRS

32. General obligation to keep accounts

(1) Charity trustees shall keep proper books of account with respect to the affairs of
the charity, and charity trustees not required by or under the authority of any other
Act to prepare periodical statements of account shall prepare consecutive statements
of account consisting on each occasion of an income and expenditure account relating
to a period of not more than fifteen months and a balance sheet relating to the end of
that period.

(2) The books of account and statements of account relating to any charity shall be
preserved for a period of *seven* [2][six][2] years at least, unless the charity ceases to exist
and the Commissioners *permit them to be* [2][consent in writing to their being][2] destroyed
or otherwise disposed of.

*(3) The statements of account relating to a parochial charity in a rural parish, other than an
ecclesiastical charity, shall be sent annually to the parish council or, if there is no parish council,
to the chairman of the parish meeting, and shall be presented by the council or chairman at the
next parish meeting.*[2]

[(3) This section applies only to exempt charities.][2] . . .[1]

Amendments. [1]Words repealed: Local Government Act 1972, s 272(1), Sch 30. [2]Words
substituted: Charities Act 1992, s 47, Sch 3, para 13.

33. Manner of giving notice of charity meetings etc

(1) All notices which are required or authorised by the trusts of a charity to be given
to a charity trustee, member or subscriber may be sent by post, and, if sent by post,
may be addressed to any address given as his in the list of charity trustees, members or subscribers for the time being in use at the office or principal office of the
charity.

(2) Where any such notice required to be given as aforesaid is given by post, it shall be
deemed to have been given by the time at which the letter containing it would be
delivered in the ordinary course of post.

(3) No notice required to be given as aforesaid of any meeting or election need
be given to any charity trustee, member or subscriber, if in the list above mentioned
he has no address in the United Kingdom.

34. Manner of executing instruments

(1) Charity trustees may, subject to the trusts of the charity, confer on any of their
body (not being less than two in number) a general authority, or an authority limited
in such manner as the trustees think fit, to execute in the names and on behalf of the
trustees assurances or other deeds or instruments for giving effect to transactions to

which the trustees are a party; and any deed or instrument executed in pursuance of an authority so given shall be of the same effect as if executed by the whole body.

(2) An authority under subsection (1) above –
    (a) shall suffice for any deed or instrument if it is given in writing or by resolution of a meeting of the trustees, notwithstanding the want of any formality that would be required in giving an authority apart from that subsection;
    (b) may be given so as to make the powers conferred exercisable by any of the trustees, or may be restricted to named persons or in any other way;
    (c) subject to any such restriction, and until it is revoked, shall, notwithstanding any change in the charity trustees, have effect as a continuing authority given by *and to the persons who from time to time are of their body*[1] [the charity trustees from time to time of the charity and exercisable by such trustees].[1]

(3) In any authority under this section to execute a deed or instrument in the names and on behalf of charity trustees there shall, unless the contrary intention appears, be implied authority also to execute it from them in the name and on behalf of the official custodian for charities or of any other person, in any case in which the charity trustees could do so.

(4) Where a deed or instrument purports to be executed in pursuance of this section, then in favour of a person who (then or afterwards) in good faith acquires for money or money's worth an interest in or charge on property or the benefit of any covenant or agreement expressed to be entered into by the charity trustees, it shall be conclusively presumed to have been duly executed by virtue of this section.

(5) The powers conferred by this section shall be in addition to and not in derogation of any other powers.

Amendment. [1]Words substituted: Charities Act 1992, s 47, Sch 3, para 14.

35. Transfer and evidence of title to property vested in trustees

(1) Where, under the trusts of a charity, trustees of property held for the purposes of the charity may be appointed or discharged by resolution of a meeting of the charity trustees, members or other persons, a memorandum declaring a trustee to have been so appointed or discharged shall be sufficient evidence of that fact, if the memorandum is signed either at the meeting by the person presiding or in some other manner directed by the meeting, and is attested by two persons present at the meeting.

(2) A memorandum evidencing the appointment or discharge of a trustee under subsection (1) above, if executed as a deed, shall have the like operation under section forty of the Trustee Act 1925 (which relates to vesting declarations as respects trust property in deeds appointing or discharging trustees), as if the appointment or discharge were effected by the deed.

(3) For the purposes of this section, where a document purports to have been signed and attested as mentioned in subsection (1) above, then on proof (whether by evidence or as a matter of presumption) of the signature the document shall be presumed to have been so signed and attested, unless the contrary is shown.

(4) This section shall apply to a memorandum made at any time, except that subsection (2) shall apply only to those made after the commencement of this Act.

(5) This section shall apply in relation to any institution to which the Literary and Scientific Institutions Act 1854 applies, as it applies in relation to a charity.

(6) The Trustee Appointment Act 1850, the Trustee Appointment Act 1869, the Trustees Appointment Act 1890, and in so far as it applies any of those Acts the School Sites Act 1852, shall cease to have effect; but where, at the commencement of this Act, the provisions of those Acts providing for the appointment of trustees apply in relation to any land, those provisions shall have effect as if contained in the conveyance or other instrument declaring the trusts on which the land is then held.

36. Miscellaneous provisions as to evidence

(1) Where, in any proceedings to recover or compel payment of any rentcharge or other periodical payment claimed by or on behalf of a charity out of land or of the rent, profits or other income of land, otherwise than as rent incident to a reversion, it is shown that the rentcharge or other periodical payment has at any time been paid for twelve consecutive years to or for the benefit of the charity, that shall be prima facie evidence of the perpetual liability to it of the land or income, and no proof of its origin shall be necessary.

(2) In any proceedings, the following documents, that is to say, –
    (a) the printed copies of the reports of the Commissioners for enquiring concerning charities, 1818 to 1837, who were appointed under the Act 58 Geo 3 c 91 and subsequent Acts; and
    (b) the printed copies of the reports which were made for various counties and county boroughs to the Charity Commissioners by their assistant Commissioners and presented to the House of Commons as returns to orders of various dates beginning with the eighth day of December, eighteen hundred and ninety, and ending with the ninth day of September, nineteen hundred and nine;
shall be admissible as evidence of the documents and facts stated in them.

(3) Evidence of any order, certificate or other document issued by the Commissioners may be given by means of a copy retained by them, or taken from a copy so retained, and certified to be a true copy by any officer of the Commissioners generally or specially authorised by them to act for this purpose; and a document purporting to be such a copy shall be received in evidence without proof of the official position, authority or handwriting of the person certifying it.

37. Parochial charities

(1) Where trustees hold any property for the purposes of a public recreation ground, or of allotments (whether under inclosure Acts or otherwise), for the benefit of inhabitants of a rural parish having a parish council, or for other charitable purposes connected with such a rural parish, except for an ecclesiastical charity, they may with the approval of the Commissioners and with the consent of the parish council transfer the property to the parish council or to persons appointed by the parish council; and the council or their appointees shall hold the property on the same trusts and subject to the same conditions as the trustees did.

    This subsection shall apply to property held for any public purposes as it applies to property held for charitable purposes, . . .[1]

(2) Where the charity trustees of a parochial charity in a rural parish, not being an ecclesiastical charity nor a charity founded within the preceding forty years, do not include persons elected by the local government electors, ratepayers or inhabitants of the parish or appointed by the parish council or parish meeting, the parish council or parish meeting may appoint additional charity trustees, to such number as the Commissioners may allow; and if there is a sole charity trustee not elected or appointed as aforesaid of any such charity, the number of the charity trustees may, with the approval of the Commissioners, be increased to three of whom one may be nominated by the person holding the office of the sole trustee and one by the parish council or parish meeting.

. . .[1]

(3) Where, under the trusts of a charity other than an ecclesiastical charity, the inhabitants of a rural parish (whether in vestry or not) or a select vestry were formerly (in 1894) entitled to appoint charity trustees for, or trustees or beneficiaries of, the charity, then –

    (a) in a parish having a parish council, the appointment shall be made by the parish council or, in the case of beneficiaries, by persons appointed by the parish council; and

    (b) in a parish not having a parish council, the appointment shall be made by the parish meeting.

(4) Where overseers as such or, except in the case of an ecclesiastical charity, churchwardens as such were formerly (in 1894) charity trustees of or trustees for a parochial charity in a rural parish, either alone or jointly with other persons, then instead of the former overseer or churchwarden trustees there shall be trustees (to a number not greater than that of the former overseer, or churchwarden trustees) appointed by the parish council or, if there is no parish council, by the parish meeting.

(5) Where, outside the county of London, overseers of a parish as such were formerly (in 1927) charity trustees of or trustees for any charity, either alone or jointly with other persons, then instead of the former overseer trustees there shall be trustees (to a number not greater than that of the former overseer trustees) appointed –

    (a) where the parish is a rural parish, by the parish council or, if there is no parish council, by the parish meeting; and

. . .[1]

(6) Any appointment of a charity trustee or trustee for a charity which is made by virtue of this section shall be for a term of four years, but a retiring trustee shall be eligible for re-appointment:

  Provided that –

    (a) on an appointment under subsection (2), where no previous appointments have been made by virtue of that subsection or of the corresponding provision of the Local Government Act 1894, and more than one trustee is appointed, half of those appointed (or as nearly as may be) shall be appointed for a term of two years; and

    (b) an appointment made to fill a casual vacancy shall be for the remainder of the term of the previous appointment.

(7) This section shall not affect the trusteeship, control or management of any voluntary school within the meaning of the Education Act 1944 [or of any grant-maintained school][2].

(8) The provisions of this section shall not extend to the Isles of Scilly, and shall have effect subject to any order (including any future order) made under any enactment relating to local government with respect to local government areas or the powers of local authorities.

(9) In this section the expression 'formerly (in 1894)' relates to the period immediately before the passing of the Local Government Act 1894, and the expression 'formerly (in 1927)' to the period immediately before the first day of April, nineteen hundred and twenty-seven; and the word 'former' shall be construed accordingly.

Amendments. [1]Words repealed: Local Government Act 1972, s 272(1), Sch 30. [2]Words substituted: Education Reform Act 1988, s 237, Sch 12, Pt 1, para 9.

38. Repeal of law of mortmain

(1), (2) . . .[1]

(3) The repeal by this Act of the Mortmain and Charitable Uses Act 1891 shall have effect in relation to the wills of persons dying before the passing of this Act so as to abrogate any requirement to sell land then unsold, but not so as to enable effect to be given to a direction to lay out personal estate in land without an order under section eight of that Act or so as to affect the power to make such an order.

(4) Any reference in any enactment or document to a charity within the meaning, purview and interpretation of the Charitable Uses Act 1601 or of the preamble to it, shall be construed as a reference to a charity within the meaning which the word bears as a legal term according to the law of England and Wales.

(5) No repeal made by this Act shall affect any power to hold land in Northern Ireland without licence in mortmain; . . .[2]

Amendments. [1]Words repealed: Education Act 1973, s 1(4), Sch 2, Pt 1. [2]Words repealed: Northern Ireland Constitution Act 1973, s 41(1), Sch 6, Pt 1.

39. Repeal of obsolete enactments

(1) . . .[1]

(2) Where the trusts of a charity are at the commencement of this Act wholly or partly comprised in an enactment specified in the Fifth Schedule to this Act, or in an instrument having effect under such an enactment, the operation of those trusts shall not be affected by the repeal of that enactment by this Act.

Amendment. [1]Subsection repealed: Education Act 1973, s 1(4), Sch 2, Pt 1.

PART V

SUPPLEMENTARY

40. Miscellaneous provisions as to orders of Commissioners or Minister

(1) Any order made by the Commissioners under this Act may include such incidental or supplementary provisions as the Commissioners think expedient for

carrying into effect the objects of the order, and where the Commissioners exercise any jurisdiction to make such an order on an application or reference to them, they may insert any such provisions in the order notwithstanding that the application or reference does not propose their insertion.

(2) Where the Commissioners make an order under this Act, then (without prejudice to the requirements of this Act where the order is subject to appeal) they may themselves give such public notice as they think fit of the making or contents of the order, or may require it to be given by any person on whose application the order is made or by any charity affected by the order.

(3) The Commissioners at any time within twelve months after they have made an order under this Act, if they are satisfied that the order was made by mistake or on misrepresentation or otherwise than in conformity with this Act, may with or without any application or reference to them discharge the order in whole or in part, and subject or not to any savings or other transitional provisions.

(4) Except for the purposes of subsection (3) above or of an appeal under this Act, an order made by the Commissioners under this Act shall be deemed to have been duly and formally made and not be called in question on the ground only of irregularity or informality, but (subject to any further order) have effect according to its tenor.

(5) This section shall apply to orders made under any Act amended by this Act, if made by virtue of that amendment, as it applies to orders made under this Act.

[40A. Service of orders and directions under this Act

(1) This section applies to any order or direction made or given by the Commissioners under this Act.

(2) An order or direction to which this section applies may be served on a person (other than a body corporate) –
  (a) by delivering it to that person;
  (b) by leaving it at his last known address in the United Kingdom; or
  (c) by sending it by post to him at that address.

(3) An order or direction to which this section applies may be served on a body corporate by delivering it or sending it by post –
  (a) to the registered or principal office of the body in the United Kingdom, or
  (b) if it has no such office in the United Kingdom, to any place in the United Kingdom where it carries on business or conducts its activities (as the case may be).

(4) Any such order or direction may also be served on a person (including a body corporate) by sending it by post to that person at an address notified by that person to the Commissioners for the purposes of this subsection.

(5) In this section any reference to the Commissioners includes, in relation to a direction given under section 6(3) of this Act, a reference to any person conducting an inquiry under that section.][1]

Amendment. [1]Section inserted: Charities Act 1992, s 47, Sch 13, para 15.

41. Enforcement of orders of Commissioners or Minister

A person guilty of disobedience –
   (a) to an order of the Commissioners under subsection (3) of section six or under section seven of this Act, or to a precept under that subsection; or[1]
   [(a) to an order of the Commissioners under section 7(1) of this Act; or][1]
   (b) to an order of the Commissioners under section eighteen or twenty of this Act requiring a transfer of property or payment to be called for or made; or
   (c) to an order of the Commissioners requiring a default under this Act to be made good;
may on the application of the Commissioners to the High Court be dealt with as for disobedience to an order of the High Court.

Amendment. [1]Words substituted: Charities Act 1992, s 47, Sch 3, para 16.

42. Appeals from Commissioners or Minister

(1) Provision shall be made by rules of court for regulating appeals to the High Court under this Act against orders or decisions of the Commissioners.

(2) On such an appeal the Attorney General shall be entitled to appear and be heard, and such other persons as the rules allow or as the court may direct.

(3) . . .[1]

Amendment. [1]Words repealed: Administration of Justice Act 1977, s 32(4), Sch 5, Pt 1.

43. Regulations

[(1) Save as otherwise provided by this Act, any power to make regulations which is conferred by this Act shall be exercisable by the Secretary of State.][1]

(2) Regulations may be made for prescribing anything which is required or authorised by this Act to be prescribed.

[(2A) Any regulations under this Act may make –
   (a) different provision for different cases;
   (b) such supplemental, incidental, consequential or transitional provision or savings as the person or persons making them considers or consider appropriate.][2]

(3) Any power of the Treasury [or the Secretary of State][1] to make regulations under this Act shall be exercisable by statutory instrument, which shall be subject to annulment in pursuance of a resolution of either House of Parliament.

Amendments. [1]Words substituted: Education Act 1973, s 1(3), Sch 1, para 1(1), (7). [2]Words inserted: Charities Act 1992, s 47, Sch 3, para 17.

44. Expenses

(1) There shall be defrayed out of monies provided by Parliament –
   (a) the remuneration and allowances payable under this Act to the Commissioners and to their officers and servants; . . .[1] *and*

(b) any administrative expenses incurred for the purposes of this Act by the Secretary of State, . . .[2] or the Commissioners.

(2) Any fees received . . .[2] by the Commissioners under this Act shall be paid into the Exchequer.[4]

(3),[2] (4) . . .[3]

Amendments. [1]Words repealed: Superannuation Act 1972, s 29(4), Sch 8. [2]Words repealed: Education Act 1973, s 1(4), (5), Sch 2, Pt I, Pt III. [3]Subsection repealed: Local Government Act 1972, s 272(1), Sch 30. [4]Section repealed: Charities Act 1992, s 78(2), Sch 7.

---

45. Construction of references to a 'charity' or to particular classes of charity

(1) In this Act, except in so far as the context otherwise requires, –

'charity' means any institution, corporate or not, which is established for charitable purposes and is subject to the control of the High Court in the exercise of the court's jurisdiction with respect to charities;

'ecclesiastical charity' has the same meaning as in the Local Government Act 1894;

'exempt charity' means (subject to subsection (9) of section twenty-two of this Act) a charity comprised in the Second Schedule to this Act;

'local charity' means, in relation to any area, a charity established for purposes which are by their nature or by the trusts of the charity directed wholly or mainly to the benefit of that area or of part of it;

'parochial charity' means, in relation to any parish, a charity the benefits of which are, or the separate distribution of the benefits of which is, confined to inhabitants of the parish, or of a single ancient ecclesiastical parish which included that parish or part of it, or of an area consisting of that parish with not more than four neighbouring parishes.

(2) The expression 'charity' is not in this Act applicable –

    (a) to any ecclesiastical corporation (that is to say, any corporation in the Church of England, whether sole or aggregate, which is established for spiritual purposes) in respect of the corporate property of the corporation, except to a corporation aggregate having some purposes which are not ecclesiastical in respect of its corporate property held for those purposes; or

    [(aa) to any Diocesan Board of Finance within the meaning of the Endowments and Glebe Measure 1976 for any diocese in respect of the diocesan glebe land of that diocese within the meaning of that Measure; or][1]

    (b) to any trust of property for purposes for which the property has been consecrated.

(3) *Subject to subsection (9) of section twenty-two of this Act,*[2] A charity shall be deemed for the purposes of this Act to have a permanent endowment unless all property held for the purposes of the charity may be expended for those purposes without distinction between capital and income, and in this Act 'permanent endowment' means in relation to any charity, property held subject to a restriction on its being *so expended*[2] [expended for the purposes of the charity.][2]

(4) References in this Act to a charity *not having income from property to a specified amount shall be construed by reference to the gross revenues of the charity, but without*[2] [whose

income from all sources does not in aggregate amount to more than a specified amount shall be construed –

 (i) by reference to the gross revenues of the charity, or

 (ii) if the Commissioners so determine, by reference to the amount which they estimate to be the likely amount of those revenues,

but without (in either case)]² bringing into account anything for the yearly value of land occupied by the charity apart from the pecuniary income (if any) received from that land; and any question as to the application of any such reference to a charity shall be determined by the Commissioners, whose decision shall be final.

(5) The Commissioners may direct that for all or any of the purposes of this Act an institution established for any special purposes of or in connection with a charity (being charitable purposes) shall be treated as forming part of that charity or as forming a distinct charity.

(6) Any reference in this Act to a charity which is excepted by order or regulations shall be construed as referring to a charity which is for the time being permanently or temporarily excepted by order of the Commissioners, or is of a description permanently or temporarily excepted by regulations, and which complies with any conditions of the exception; and any order or regulation made for this purpose may limit any exception so that a charity may be excepted in respect of some matters and not in respect of others.

Amendments. ¹Words inserted: Endowments and Glebe Measure 1976, s 44. ²Words substituted or repealed: Charities Act 1992, s 47, Sch 3, para 18, s 78(2), Sch 7.

46. Other definitions

In this Act, except in so far as the context otherwise requires, –

. . .¹

[(1)]³ 'charitable purposes' means purposes which are exclusively charitable according to the law of England and Wales;

'charity trustees' means the persons having the general control and management of the administration of a charity;

'the Commissioners' means the Charity Commissioners for England and Wales;

['company' means a company formed and registered under the Companies Act 1985, or to which the provisions of that Act apply as they apply to such a company;]²

'the county of London' means the administrative county of London;

'the court' means the High Court and, within the limits of its jurisdiction, any other court in England or Wales having a jurisdiction in respect of charities concurrent (within any limit of area or amount) with that of the High Court, and includes any judge or officer of the court exercising the jurisdiction of the court;

'institution' includes any trust or undertaking;

'permanent endowment' shall, *subject to subsection (9) of section twenty-two of this Act,*³ be construed in accordance with subsection (3) of the last foregoing section;

'trusts', in relation to a charity, means the provisions establishing it as a charity and regulating its purposes and administration, whether those provisions take effect by way of trust or not, and in relation to other institutions has a corresponding meaning.

[(2) In this Act, except in so far as the context otherwise requires, 'document' includes information recorded in any form, and, in relation to information recorded otherwise than in legible form –

(a) any reference to its production shall be construed as a reference to the furnishing of a copy of it in legible form, and

(b) any reference to the furnishing of a copy of, or extract from, it shall accordingly be construed as a reference to the furnishing of a copy of, or extract from, it in legible form.]³

Amendments. ¹Words repealed: Courts Act 1971, s 56(4), Sch 11, Pt II. ²Words inserted: Companies Act 1989, s 111(2). ³Words inserted or repealed: Charities Act 1992, s 47, Sch 3, para 19, s 78(2), Sch 7.

47. . . .¹

Amendment. ¹Section repealed: Northern Ireland Constitution Act 1973, s 41(1), Sch 6, Pt I.

48. Consequential amendments, general repeal and transitional provisions

(1) The enactments mentioned in the first column of the Sixth Schedule to this Act shall be amended as provided in the second column of that Schedule.

(2) . . .¹

(3) The Commissioners may take the like action under this Act in consequence of any application or enquiry under the Charitable Trusts Acts 1853 to 1939, as if the application or enquiry had been made for the corresponding purpose under this Act: and subsections (3) to (5) of section twenty-five of this Act shall extend (with any necessary adaptations) to documents enrolled by the Commissioners or deposited with them under those Acts.

(4) The repeal by this Act of the Charitable Trusts Acts 1853 to 1939 shall not invalidate any scheme, order, certificate or other document issued under or for the purposes of those Acts, so far as the document is capable after the commencement of this Act of having effect either for its original purpose or for any corresponding purpose of this Act; but any such documents shall continue to have effect for any such purpose (except in so far as they are modified or superseded under the powers of this Act), and shall in the case of an order be appealable, enforceable and liable to be discharged as if this Act had not been passed; and any such document, and any document under the seal of the official trustees of charitable funds, may be proved as if this Act had not been passed.

(5) The repeal by this Act of any enactment which authorises the taking of legal proceedings, or regulates any legal proceedings, shall not affect the operation of that enactment in relation to proceedings begun before the commencement of this Act, nor shall section twenty-eight of this Act apply to any proceeding so begun.

(6) The official custodian for charities shall be treated as the successor for all purposes both of the official trustee of charity lands and of the official trustees of charitable funds, as if the functions of the said trustee or trustees had been functions of the official custodian, and as if any such trustee or trustees had been, and had discharged his or their functions as, holder of the office of the official custodian; and accordingly (but

without prejudice to the generality of the foregoing provision, and subject to any express amendment or repeal made by this Act) as from the commencement of this Act –

    (a) all property vested in the said trustee or trustees shall vest in the official custodian, and shall be held by him as if vested in him under section sixteen of this Act for the purposes for which it was held by the said trustee or trustees; and

    (b) any Act, scheme, deed or other document referring or relating to the said trustee or trustees shall, in so far as the context permits, have effect as if the official custodian had been mentioned instead.

(7) The specific provisions of this Act as to the effect of any repeal shall not be taken to exclude the general provisions contained in section thirty-eight of the Interpretation Act 1889 except in so far as those general provisions are inconsistent with specific provisions in this Act.

Amendment. [1]Words repealed: Education Act 1973, s 1(4), Sch 2, Pt I.

49. Short title, extent and commencement

(1) This Act may be cited as the Charities Act 1960.

(2) This Act shall extend –
    (a), (b) . . .[1]
    (c) to Northern Ireland in so far as it relates to the amendment of Royal Charters;
but, subject to that, this Act shall not extend to Scotland or Northern Ireland.

(3) . . .[2]

Amendments. [1]Words repealed: Statute Law (Repeals) Act 1978, s 1, Sch 1, Pt II. [2]Words repealed: Education Act 1973, s 1(4), Sch 2, Pt 1.

SCHEDULES
FIRST SCHEDULE

Section 1

CONSTITUTION, ETC, OF CHARITY COMMISSIONERS

1. (1) There shall be a Chief Charity Commissioner, and two other Commissioners.

(2) Two at least of the Commissioners shall be barristers or solicitors.

(3) *Subject to sub-paragraph (6) below,*[2] The Chief Commissioner and the other Commissioners shall be appointed by the Secretary of State, and shall be deemed for all purposes to be employed in the civil service of the Crown.

(4) There may be paid to each of the Commissioners such salary and allowances as the Secretary of State may with the approval of the Treasury determine.

(5) If at any time it appears to the Secretary of State that there should be more than three Commissioners, he may with the approval of the Treasury appoint not more than two additional Commissioners.

(6) . . .[1]

2. (1) The Chief Commissioner may, with the approval of the Treasury as to number and conditions of service, appoint such assistant Commissioners and other officers and such *servants*[2] [employees][2] as he thinks necessary for the proper discharge of the functions of the Commissioners and of the official custodian for charities.

(2) There may be paid to officers and *servants*[2] [employees][2] so appointed such salaries or remuneration as the Treasury may determine.

(3) . . .[1]

3. (1) The Commissioners may use an official seal for the authentication of documents, and their seal shall be officially and judicially noticed.

(2) The Documentary Evidence Act 1868, as amended by the Documentary Evidence Act 1882, shall have effect as if in the Schedule to the Act of 1868 the Commissioners were included in the first column and any commissioner or assistant commissioner and any officer authorised to act on behalf of the Commissioners were mentioned in the second column.

(3) The Commissioners shall have power to regulate their own procedure and, subject to any such regulations and to any directions of the Chief Commissioner, any one Commissioner or any assistant Commissioner may act for and in the name of the Commissioners.

(4) Where the Commissioners act as a board, *two shall be a quorum; and*[2] [then –
  (a) if not more than four Commissioners hold office for the time being, the quorum shall be two Commissioners (of whom at least one must be a person having a qualification such as is mentioned in paragraph 1(2) above); and
  (b) if five Commissioners so hold office, the quorum shall be three Commissioners (of whom at least one must be a person having such a qualification);
and][2] in the case of an equality of votes the Chief Commissioner or in his absence the Commissioner presiding shall have a second or casting vote.

(5) The Commissioners shall have power to act notwithstanding any vacancy in their number.

[(6) It is hereby declared that the power of a Commissioner or assistant Commissioner to act for and in the name of the Commissioners in accordance with sub-paragraph (3) above may, in particular, be exercised in relation to functions of the Commissioners under sections 6, 20, 20A and 30 of this Act.][2]

4. Legal proceedings may be instituted by or against the Commissioners by the name of the Charity Commissioners for England and Wales, and shall not abate or be affected by any change in the persons who are the Commissioners.

Amendments. [1]Words repealed: Education Act 1973, s 1(4), Sch 2, Pt I. [2]Words inserted, substituted or repealed: Charities Act 1992, s 47, Sch 3, paras 20, 21, s 78(2), Sch 7.

SECOND SCHEDULE

Sections 4, 45

EXEMPT CHARITIES

The following institutions, so far as they are charities, are exempt charities within the meaning of this Act, that is to say –

(a) any institution which, if this Act had not been passed, would be exempted from the powers and jurisdiction under the Charitable Trusts Acts 1853 to 1939 of the Commissioners *or Minister of Education* (apart from any power of the Commissioners *or Minister* to apply those Acts in whole or in part to charities otherwise exempt) by the terms of any enactment not contained in those Acts other than section nine of the Places of Worship Registration Act 1855;

(b) the universities of Oxford, Cambridge, London and Durham, the colleges and halls in the universities of Oxford, Cambridge and Durham and the colleges of Winchester and Eton;

(c) any university, university college, or institution connected with a university or university college, which Her Majesty declares by Order in Council to be an exempt charity for the purposes of this Act;

[(ca) the Board of Trustees of the Victoria and Albert Museum;

(cb) the Board of Trustees of the Science Museum;

(cc) The Board of Trustees of the Armouries;

(cd) the Board of Trustees of the Royal Botanic Gardens, Kew;]¹

(d) the British Museum;

[(da) the National Gallery Trustees;

(db) the Tate Gallery Trustees;

(dc) the National Portrait Gallery;

(dd) the Wallace Collection Trustees;]⁵

(e) any institution which is administered by or on behalf of an institution included above and is established for the general purposes of, or for any special purpose of or in connection with, the last-mentioned institution;

(f) the Church Commissioners and any institution which is administered by them;

(g) any registered society within the meaning of the Industrial and Provident Societies Act 1893 and any registered society or branch within the meaning of the Friendly Societies Act 1896;

[(h) the Board of Governors of the Museum of London;]²

[(i) the British Library Board;]³

[(j) the Board of Trustees of the National Museums and Galleries on Merseyside.]⁴

Amendments. ¹Words inserted: National Heritage Act 1983, s 40(1), Sch 5, para 4. ²Words inserted: Museum of London Act 1965, s 11. ³Words inserted: British Library Act 1972, s 4(2). ⁴Words inserted: Local Government Reorganisation (Miscellaneous Provision) (No 4) Order 1986, SI 1986/452, art 5(1). ⁵Words inserted: Charities Act 1992, s 47, Sch 3, para 22.

THIRD SCHEDULE

Section 13

ENLARGEMENT OF AREAS OF LOCAL CHARITIES

Existing area	Permissible enlargement
1. [Greater London][1]	Any area comprising [Greater London][1].
2. Any area in [Greater London][1] and not in, or partly in, the city of London.	(i) Any area in [Greater London][1] not in, or partly in, the city of London;
	(ii) the area of [Greater London][1] exclusive of the city of London;
	(iii) any area comprising the area of [Greater London][1] exclusive of the city of London;
	(iv) any area partly in [Greater London][1] and partly in any adjacent parish or parishes (civil or ecclesiastical), and not partly in the city of London.
3. A [district][2]	Any area comprising the [district][2].
4. Any area in a [district][2]	(i) Any area in the [district][2];
	(ii) the [district][2];
	(iii) any area comprising the [district][2];
	(iv) any area partly in the [district][2] and partly in any adjacent [district][2].
5. A parish (civil or ecclesiastical), or two or more parishes, or an area in a parish, or partly in each of two or more parishes.	Any area not extending beyond the parish or parishes comprising or adjacent to the area in column 1.

Amendments. [1]Words substituted: London Government Act 1963, s 81(9)(c). [2]Words substituted: Local Government Act 1972, s 210(9)(f), (10).

FOURTH SCHEDULE

Section 15

COURT'S JURISDICTION OVER CERTAIN CHARITIES GOVERNED BY OR UNDER STATUTE

1. The court may by virtue of subsection (3) of section fifteen of this Act exercise its jurisdiction with respect to charities –

(a) in relation to charities established or regulated by any provision of the Seamen's Fund Winding-up Act 1851 which is repealed by this Act;

(b) in relation to charities established or regulated by schemes under the Endowed Schools Acts 1869 to 1948, or section seventy-five of the Elementary Education Act 1870, [or by schemes given effect under section 2 of the Education Act 1973][1];

(c) in relation to allotments regulated by sections three to nine of the Poor Allotments Management Act 1873;

(d) in relation to fuel allotments, that is to say, land which, by any enactment relating to inclosure or any instrument having effect under such an enactment, is vested in trustees upon trust that the land or the rents and profits of the land shall be used for the purpose of providing poor persons with fuel;

(e) in relation to charities established or regulated by any provision of the Municipal Corporations Act 1883 which is repealed by this Act, or by any scheme having effect under any such provision;

(f) in relation to charities regulated by schemes under the London Government Act 1899;

(g) in relation to charities established or regulated by orders or regulations under section two of the Regimental Charitable Funds Act 1935;

(h) in relation to charities regulated by section thirty-seven of this Act, or by any such order as is mentioned in that section.

2. Notwithstanding anything in section nineteen of the Commons Act 1876 a scheme for the administration of a fuel allotment (within the meaning of the foregoing paragraph) may provide –

(a) for the sale or letting of the allotment or any part thereof, for the discharge of the land sold or let from any restrictions as to the use thereof imposed by or under any enactment relating to inclosure and for the application of the sums payable to the trustees of the allotment in respect of the sale or lease; or

(b) for the exchange of the allotment or any part thereof for other land, for the discharge as aforesaid of the land given in exchange by the said trustees, and for the application of any money payable to the said trustees for equality of exchange; or

(c) for the use of the allotment or any part thereof for any purposes specified in the scheme.

Amendment. [1]Words inserted: Education Act 1973, s 2(7), (9).

★★★★

CHARITABLE TRUSTEES
INCORPORATION ACT 1872

(1872 c 24)

1. Upon application of trustees of any charity, Commissioners may grant certificate of registration as a corporate body

. . .[1] *It shall be lawful for the trustees or trustee for the time being of any charity for religious, educational, literary, scientific, or public charitable purposes, to apply, in manner herein-after mentioned, to the Charity Commissioners for a certificate of registration of the trustees of any such charity as a corporate body; and if the Commissioners, having regard to the extent, nature, and objects and other circumstances of the charity, shall consider such incorporation expedient, they may grant such certificate accordingly, subject to such conditions or directions as they shall think fit to insert in their certificate relating to the qualifications and number of the trustees, their tenure or avoidance of office, and the mode of appointing new trustees, and the custody and use of the common seal; and the trustees of such charity shall thereupon become a body corporate by the name described in the certificate, and shall have perpetual succession and a common seal, of which the device shall be approved by the Commissioners, and power to sue and be sued in their corporate name, and to hold and acquire, . . .[2] and by instruments under their common seal to convey, assign, and demise, any present or future property, real or personal, belonging to, or held for the benefit of, such charity, in such and the like manner, and subject to such restrictions and provisions, as such trustees might, without such incorporation, hold or acquire, convey, assign, or demise the same for the purposes of such charity . . .[1]*

[1. Incorporation of trustees of a charity

(1) Where –
  (a) the trustees of a charity, in accordance with section 3 of this Act, apply to the Commissioners for a certificate of incorporation of the trustees as a body corporate, and
  (b) the Commissioners consider that the incorporation of the trustees would be in the interests of the charity,
the Commissioners may grant such a certificate, subject to such conditions or directions as they think fit to insert in it.

(2) The Commissioners shall not, however, grant such a certificate in a case where the charity appears to them to be required to be registered in the register kept by them under section 4 of the Charities Act 1960 but is not so registered.

(3) On the grant of such a certificate –
  (a) the trustees of the charity shall become a body corporate by such name as is specified in the certificate; and

(b) (without prejudice to the operation of section 5 of this Act) any relevant rights or liabilities of those trustees shall become rights or liabilities of that body.

(4) After their incorporation the trustees –
  (a) may sue and be sued in their corporate name; and
  (b) shall have the same powers, and be subject to the same restrictions and limitations, as respects the holding, acquisition and disposal of property for or in connection with the purposes of the charity as they had or were subject to while unincorporated;
and any relevant legal proceedings that might have been continued or commenced by or against the trustees may be continued or commenced by or against them in their corporate name.

(5) A body incorporated under this section need not have a common seal.

(6) In this section –
'relevant rights or liabilities' means rights or liabilities in connection with any property vesting in the body in question under section 2 of this Act; and
'relevant legal proceedings' means legal proceedings in connection with any such property.][3]

Amendments. [1]Words repealed: Statute Law Revision (No 2) Act 1893. [2]Words repealed: Charities Act 1960, s 48(2), Sch 7, Pt II. [3]Section substituted: Charities Act 1992, s 48, Sch 4, para 1.

2. Estate to vest in body corporate

The certificate of incorporation shall vest in such body corporate all real and personal estate, of what nature or tenure soever, belonging to or held by any person or persons in trust for such charity, and thereupon any person or persons in whose name or names any stocks, funds, or securities shall be standing in trust for the charity, shall transfer the same into the name of such body corporate, [except that the foregoing provisions shall not apply to property vested in the official custodian for charities].[1] *and all covenants and conditions relating to any such real estate enforceable by or against the trustees thereof before their incorporation shall be enforceable to the same extent and by the same means by or against them after their incorporation*[2] . . .[1]

Amendments. [1]Words substituted or repealed: Charities Act 1960, s 48(1), Sch 6, s 48(2), Sch 7, Pt I. [2]Words repealed: Charities Act 1992, s 48, Sch 4, para 2, s 78(2), Sch 7.

3. Particulars respecting application

Every application to the Commissioners for a certificate under this Act shall be in writing, signed by the person or persons making the same, and shall contain the several particulars specified in the schedule hereto, or such of them as shall be applicable to the case. The said Commissioners may require such declaration or other evidence in verification of the statements and particulars in the application, and such other particulars, information, and evidence, if any, as they may think necessary or proper.[1]

[3. Applications for incorporation

(1) Every application to the Commissioners for a certificate of incorporation under this Act shall –
   (a) be in writing and signed by the trustees of the charity concerned; and
   (b) be accompanied by such documents or information as the Commissioners may require for the purpose of the application.

(2) The Commissioners may require –
   (a) any statement contained in any such application, or
   (b) any document or information supplied under subsection (1)(b) above,
to be verified in such manner as they may specify.][1]

Amendment. [1]Section substituted: Charities Act 1992, s 48, Sch 4, para 3.

4. Nomination of trustees, and filling up vacancies

Before a certificate of incorporation shall be granted, trustees of the charity shall have been effectually appointed to the satisfaction of the Commissioners; and where a certificate of incorporation shall have been granted vacancies in the number of the trustees of such charity shall from time to time be filled up so far as shall be required by the constitution or settlement of the charity, or by any such conditions or directions as aforesaid, by such legal means as would have been available for the appointment of new trustees of the charity if no certificate of incorporation had been granted, or otherwise as shall be required by such conditions or directions as aforesaid; *and the appointment of every new trustee shall be certified by or by the direction of the trustees to the Commissioners, either upon the completion of such appointment or when the next return of the yearly income and expenditure of the charity shall or ought to be made to the Commissioners under the general law, with which the certificate of such appointment shall be sent; and within one month after the expiration of each period of five years after the grant of a certificate of incorporation, or whenever required by the Commissioners, a return shall be made to the said Commissioners by the then trustees of the names of the trustees at the expiration of each such period with their residences and additions.*[1]

Amendment. [1]Words repealed: Charities Act 1992, s 48, Sch 4, para 4, s 78(2), Sch 7.

5. Liability of trustees and others, notwithstanding incorporation

After a certificate of incorporation has been granted under the provisions of this Act all trustees of the charity, notwithstanding their incorporation, shall be chargeable for such property as shall come into their hands, and shall be answerable and accountable for their own acts, receipts, neglects, and defaults, and for the due administration of the charity and its property, in the same manner and to the same extent as if no such incorporation had been effected; *and nothing herein contained shall diminish or impair any control or authority exerciseable by the Commissioners over the trustees who shall be so incorporated, but they shall remain subject jointly and separately to such control and authority as if they were not incorporated.*[1]

Amendment. [1]Words repealed: Charities Act 1992, s 48, Sch 4, para 5, s 78(2), Sch 7.

6. Certificate to be evidence of compliance with requisitions

A certificate of incorporation so granted shall be conclusive evidence that all the preliminary requisitions herein contained and required in respect of such incorporation have been complied with, and the date of incorporation mentioned in such certificate shall be deemed to be the date at which incorporation has taken place.

[6A. Power of Commissioners to amend certificate of incorporation

(1) The Commissioners may amend a certificate of incorporation either on the application of the incorporated body to which it relates or of their own motion.

(2) Before making any such amendment of their own motion, the Commissioners shall by notice in writing –
  (a) inform the trustees of the relevant charity of their proposals, and
  (b) invite those trustees to make representations to them within a time specified in the notice, being not less than one month from the date of the notice.

(3) The Commissioners shall take into consideration any representations made by those trustees within the time so specified, and may then (without further notice) proceed with their proposals either without modification or with such modifications as appear to them to be desirable.

(4) The Commissioners may amend a certificate of incorporation either –
  (a) by making an order specifying the amendment; or
  (b) by issuing a new certificate of incorporation taking account of the amendment.]¹

Amendment. ¹Section inserted: Charities Act 1992, s 48, Sch 4, para 6.

7. Commissioners to keep record of application for certificates etc and charge fees for inspection

The said Commissioners shall keep a record of all such applications for and certificates of incorporation, and shall preserve all documents sent to them under the provisions of this Act; and any person may inspect such documents, under the direction of the Commissioners, and any person may require a copy or extract of any such document to be certified under the hand of the secretary or chief clerk of the said Commissioners; *and there shall be paid for such certified copy or extract a fee; to be fixed by the Commissioners, not exceeding [2p]¹ for each folio of such copy or extract.*²

Amendments. ¹Word substituted: Decimal Currency Act 1969, s 10(1). ²Words repealed: Charities Act 1992, s 48, Sch 4, para 7, s 78(2), Sch 7.

8. Enforcement of orders and directions of Commissioners

All conditions and directions inserted in any certificate of incorporation shall be binding upon and performed or observed by the trustees as trusts of the charity, and *shall also be enforceable by the same means or in the same manner as any orders made by the Commissioners under their ordinary jurisdiction may now be enforced.*¹ [section 41 of the Charities Act 1960 (enforcement of orders of Commissioners) shall apply to any trustee who fails to perform or observe any such condition or direction as it applies to a person guilty of disobedience to any such order of the Commissioners as is mentioned in that section.]¹

Amendment. ¹Words substituted: Charities Act 1992, s 48, Sch 4, para 8.

9. . . .¹

Amendment. ¹Section repealed: Finance Act 1949, s 52(10), Sch 11, Pt V.

10. Gifts to charity before incorporation to have same effect afterwards

After the incorporation of the trustees of any charity pursuant to this Act every donation, gift, and disposition of property, real or personal, theretofore lawfully made (but not having actually taken effect), or thereafter lawfully made by deed, will, or otherwise to or in favour of such charity, or the trustees thereof, or otherwise for the purposes thereof, shall take effect as if the same had been made to or in favour of the incorporated body or otherwise for the like purposes.

11. . . .¹

Amendment. ¹Section repealed: Corporate Bodies' Contracts Act 1960, s 4(2), Schedule.

12. Payments on transfers in reliance on corporate seal protected

*Any company or person who shall make or permit to be made any transfer or payment bona fide, in reliance on any instruments to which the common seal of any body corporate created under this Act is affixed, shall be indemnified and protected in respect of such transfer or payment, notwithstanding any defect or circumstance affecting the execution of the instrument.*¹

[12. Execution of documents by incorporated body

(1) This section has effect as respects the execution of documents by an incorporated body.

(2) If an incorporated body has a common seal, a document may be executed by the body by the affixing of its common seal.

(3) Whether or not it has a common seal, a document may be executed by an incorporated body either –
   (a) by being signed by a majority of the trustees of the relevant charity and expressed (in whatever form of words) to be executed by the body; or
   (b) by being executed in pursuance of an authority given under subsection (4) below.

(4) For the purposes of subsection (3)(b) above the trustees of the relevant charity in the case of an incorporated body may, subject to the trusts of the charity, confer on any two or more of their number –
   (a) a general authority, or
   (b) an authority limited in such manner as the trustees think fit,
to execute in the name and on behalf of the body documents for giving effect to transactions to which the body is a party.

(5) An authority under subsection (4) above –

(a) shall suffice for any document if it is given in writing or by resolution of a meeting of the trustees of the relevant charity, notwithstanding the want of any formality that would be required in giving an authority apart from that subsection;

(b) may be given so as to make the powers conferred exercisable by any of the trustees, or may be restricted to named persons or in any other way;

(c) subject to any such restriction, and until it is revoked, shall, notwithstanding any change in the trustees of the relevant charity, have effect as a continuing authority given by the trustees from time to time of the charity and exercisable by such trustees.

(6) In any authority under subsection (4) above to execute a document in the name and on behalf of an incorporated body there shall, unless the contrary intention appears, be implied authority also to execute it for the body in the name and on behalf of the official custodian for charities or of any other person, in any case in which the trustees could do so.

(7) A document duly executed by an incorporated body which makes it clear on its face that it is intended by the person or persons making it to be a deed has effect, upon delivery, as a deed; and it shall be presumed, unless a contrary intention is proved, to be delivered upon its being so executed.

(8) In favour of a purchaser a document shall be deemed to have been duly executed by such a body if it purports to be signed –

(a) by a majority of the trustees of the relevant charity, or

(b) by such of the trustees of the relevant charity as are authorised by the trustees of that charity to execute it in the name and on behalf of the body,

and, where the document makes it clear on its face that it is intended by the person or persons making it to be a deed, it shall be deemed to have been delivered upon its being executed.

For this purpose 'purchaser' means a purchaser in good faith for valuable consideration and includes a lessee, mortgagee or other person who for valuable consideration acquires an interest in property.

12A. Power of Commissioners to dissolve incorporated body

(1) Where the Commissioners are satisfied –

(a) that an incorporated body has no assets or does not operate, or

(b) that the relevant charity in the case of an incorporated body has ceased to exist, or

(c) that the institution previously constituting, or treated by them as constituting, any such charity has ceased to be, or (as the case may be) was not at the time of the body's incorporation, a charity, or

(d) that the purposes of the relevant charity in the case of an incorporated body have been achieved so far as is possible or are in practice incapable of being achieved,

they may of their own motion make an order dissolving the body as from such date as is specified in the order.

(2) Where the Commissioners are satisfied, on the application of the trustees of the relevant charity in the case of an incorporated body, that it would be in the interests of

the charity for that body to be dissolved, the Commissioners may make an order dissolving the body as from such date as is specified in the order.

(3) Subject to subsection (4) below, an order made under this section with respect to an incorporated body shall have the effect of vesting in the trustees of the relevant charity, in trust for that charity, all property for the time being vested –
    (a) in the body, or
    (b) in any other person (apart from the official custodian for charities),
in trust for that charity.

(4) If the Commissioners so direct in the order –
    (a) all or any specified part of that property shall, instead of vesting in the trustees of the relevant charity, vest –
        (i) in a specified person as trustee for, or nominee of, that charity, or
        (ii) in such persons (other than the trustees of the relevant charity) as may be specified;
    (b) any specified investments, or any specified class or description of investments, held by any person in trust for the relevant charity shall be transferred –
        (i) to the trustees of that charity, or
        (ii) to any such person or persons as is or are mentioned in paragraph (a)(i) or (ii) above;
and for this purpose 'specified' means specified by the Commissioners in the order.

(5) Where an order to which this subsection applies is made with respect to an incorporated body –
    (a) any rights or liabilities of the body shall become rights or liabilities of the trustees of the relevant charity; and
    (b) any legal proceedings that might have been continued or commenced by or against the body may be continued or commenced by or against those trustees.

(6) Subsection (5) above applies to any order under this section by virtue of which –
    (a) any property vested as mentioned in subsection (3) above is vested –
        (i) in the trustees of the relevant charity, or
        (ii) in any person as trustee for, or nominee of, that charity; or
    (b) any investments held by any person in trust for the relevant charity are required to be transferred –
        (i) to the trustees of that charity, or
        (ii) to any person as trustee for, or nominee of, that charity.

(7) Any order made by the Commissioners under this section may be varied or revoked by a further order so made.][1]

Amendments. [1]Sections substituted and inserted: Charities Act 1992, s 48, Sch 4, para 9.

13. . . .[1]

Amendment. [1]Section repealed: Mortmain and Charitable Uses Act 1888, s 13, Schedule.

14. Definition of terms 'public charitable purposes', 'trustees'

The words 'public charitable purposes' shall mean all such charitable purposes as come within the meaning, purview, or interpretation of the statute of the forty-third year of Queen

Elizabeth, chapter four, or as to which, or the administration of the revenues or property applicable to which, the Court of Chancery has or may exercise jurisdiction; and the word 'trustees' shall include the governors, managers, or other persons having the conduct or management of any charity.[1]

[14. Interpretation

In this Act –
'charity' has the same meaning as in the Charities Act 1960;
'the Commissioners' means the Charity Commissioners;
'incorporated body' means a body incorporated under section 1 of this Act;
'the relevant charity', in relation to an incorporated body, means the charity the
    trustees of which have been incorporated as that body;
'the trustees', in relation to a charity, means the charity trustees within the meaning of
    the Charities Act 1960.][1]

Amendment. [1]Section substituted: Charities Act 1992, s 48, Sch 4, para 10.

15. Short title

This Act may be cited for all purposes as 'The Charitable Trustees Incorporation Act 1872.'

SCHEDULE

Section 3

The objects of the charity and the rules and regulations of the same, together with the date of and parties to every deed, will, or other instrument, if any, creating, constituting, or regulating the same.

A statement and short description of the property, real and personal, which at the date of the application is possessed by or belonging to or held on behalf of such charity.

The names, residences, and additions of the trustees of such charity.

The proposed title of the corporation, of which title the words 'Trustees' or 'Governors' . . .[1] *shall form part.*

The proposed device of the common seal, which shall in all cases bear the name of incorporation.

The regulations for the custody and use of the common seal.[2]

Amendments. [1]Words repealed: Charities Act 1960, s 48(1), (2), Sch 6, Sch 7, Pt I. [2]Schedule repealed: Charities Act 1992, s 48, Sch 4, para 11, s 78(2), Sch 7.

INDEX

References are to paragraph numbers